Models of Achievement
Reflections of Eminent Women in Psychology

MODELS
OF
ACHIEVEMENT

Reflections of Eminent Women
in Psychology

Edited by
AGNES N. O'CONNELL
and
NANCY FELIPE RUSSO

New York   Columbia University Press   *1983*

Library of Congress Cataloging in Publication Data
Main entry under title:

Models of achievement.

Bibliography: p.
1. Women psychologists—United States—Biography.
2. Psychology—United States—History—20th century.
3. Sex discrimination in psychology—United States.
I. O'Connell, Agnes N.   II. Russo, Nancy Felipe,
1943–   .   III. Title.
BF109.A1M6   1983   150'.88042   82-23583
ISBN 0-231-05312-6
ISBN 0-231-05313-4 (pbk.)

Columbia University Press
New York *and* Guildford, Surrey

Clothbound editions of Columbia University Press books are Smyth-sewn and printed
on permanent and durable acid-free paper.

CONTENTS

125405

IV PERSPECTIVES ON PATTERNS OF ACHIEVEMENT
Synthesis: Profiles and Patterns of Achievement
AGNES N. O'CONNELL

FOREWORD

Although I have been teaching the psychology of women for 12 years at both the graduate and undergraduate levels, and pride myself as one who maintains a healthy and active interest in psychology's rich history, I am still disheartened to learn of the large number of women psychologists whose contributions to psychology have either been minimized or have gone unrecognized. Why haven't students of psychology heard of them before? Where have their accomplishments been hidden? Who is responsible for suppressing this information?

At the same time that I can muster up some quiet rage at the blatant sexism that has existed within psychology, other feelings are stirring. When I read about women psychologists, as I did in *Models of Achievement: Reflections of Eminent Women in Psychology*, I feel pride in discovering some of my roots. Learning about the lives and contributions of women psychologists has given me a better and more complete understanding of my profession's past, which I believe has helped make me a better professional today.

Models of Achievement calls into question "scholarly" writings on the history of psychology which indicate that men were the "prime movers." Like many others who read the same books and listened to the same lectures, I simply thought that psychology's history was comprised of the accomplishments of men because men were the ones who were given credit. Women, I once thought, played only a minor role in psychology's history. It is now becoming recognized that this perception of history is in error, and responsible psychologists are seeking ways to correct the historical record in their lectures as well as in their textbooks.

For this reason alone, *Models of Achievement: Reflections of Eminent Women in Psychology* is a useful and welcome addition to the psychological literature. This book provides us with the autobiographical accounts of seventeen prominent women psychologists who have all played a significant role in the theories and research which have formed the basis of twentieth-century psychological thinking.

These accounts attest to the varied contributions women have made in numerous areas of psychology. *Models of Achievement* helps set straight a rather crooked historical record—but a correction of this sex-biased record is only one of the benefits readers will derive from reading this book.

These stories also help us to appreciate the progress of women in psychology. I remember being interviewed for my first full-time academic position, now nearly two decades ago, when I was asked the occupation of my husband. At the time, I thought the purpose of the question was to assess my likelihood of staying with the job by ascertaining whether my husband was likely to move out of the area. Consequently, I stressed how established he was and how well he was doing. It turned out that this was the wrong tactic. The reason for the question was to judge how much I should be paid—the better off my husband, the lower my rank and salary! It took years of hard work (and the gains of the women's movement) to compensate for that initial disadvantage. Today, thanks to Title IX and Civil Rights legislation, such blatant discrimination is illegal. Such behavior is also prohibited by the revised Ethics Code of the American Psychological Association.

But after reading these stories, the reader also has a better appreciation of how much still has to be done for women in psychology to achieve an equal status with their male counterparts. Despite the difference in the backgrounds and details of the lives of these eminent women, there is a striking similarity in the obstacles they faced because of their gender. Women and men readers will be surprised and humbled to learn that many of the same professional barriers women confront today have been around—in full force— for a long, long time. It makes us wonder exactly how far we have actually come and exactly how much we have gained as women during this century of psychology.

Women's contributions have been and still tend to be invisible compared to similar accomplishments by men. They have been denied credit for works that have easily won men recognition. Their first names continue to be reduced to initials, their last names given second or third place to the names of male co-authors—if their names are even mentioned. The fact is, women's accomplishments and contributions continue to be obscured and trivialized, and, as a result, neither these accomplished psychologists nor the students of psychology—half of whom are women—are able to reap fully the benefits of these women's successes.

Models of Achievement lets us share these women's successes and struggles. It also makes visible a group of active, creative researchers and theorists who deserve public recognition. Thereby, *Models of Achievement* allows women to become more aware of themselves and their past while at the same time it encourages men to reconsider the narrow roles in which women have been traditionally cast.

Throughout my years of teaching I have noticed how positively students respond to information about the lives of people with whom they can identify. Male students, especially, have had repeated and numerous opportunities to use these achievers—from Allport to Zajonc—as role models. Women students have not been so lucky. Until recently, a paucity of scholarly information on women psychologists has meant that women have very few female role models to follow. With this collection, however, female students can see their own hopes and aspirations realized in the lives of other women. Moreover, female readers can take advantage of the effects of having role models of the same sex the way that male students always have. Indeed, female and male students alike will surely find many different aspects of these productive women's lives with which they can identify.

While I am delighted that *Models of Achievement* highlights the accomplishments of women who probably would remain undervalued if this book did not exist, it is also my hope that someday women's accomplishments in and contributions to psychology will be integrated with those of men. It will be interesting to see whether women or men constitute the majority when only achievement and not gender is the major criterion for recognition. Until that time, however, it is critically important to continue to highlight and illuminate women's accomplishments so that one can understand psychology's history and see that it is a discipline built upon the collected accomplishments of women and men—sometimes separately and sometimes together, sometimes harmoniously and sometimes not.

Models of Achievement is a valuable book which provides readers with a deeper understanding of the forces and pressures affecting the lives and productivity of women. The awareness generated from such accounts should help broaden readers' appreciation for the experience of women. Further, these autobiographical sketches give us a unique and rich way of examining psychology, and, indeed, we benefit a great deal from the personal information and insight that is usually absent from objective historical records. I know the pleasure I derived from reading this book, and I am sure others will experience similar effects. It will serve as an important supplement to courses in introductory psychology, history of psychology, psychology of women, and women's studies. It will also serve as a source of inspiration and strategy for individual women readers of all disciplines who may be working in male-dominated settings and thereby lack direct access to female colleagues.

The co-authors of this book, Agnes N. O'Connell and Nancy Felipe Russo, are no strangers to achievement and success themselves. They are two of the more recognized researchers and commentators in psychology today. They have published widely in the psychological literature and have provided many students and peers with support and insight.

This highly successful collaboration is the result of their combination of expertise and interests. I am grateful to the editors and to the prominent contributors for providing readers with the forum and the information which makes the lives and contributions of eminent women in psychology available to us all.

Florence L. Denmark

Florence L. Denmark, Professor of Psychology at Hunter College and the Graduate School of the City University of New York, is a former president of the American Psychological Association.

PREFACE

The idea for compiling stories of eminent women in psychology came from
two convergent sources: the first, the publication of "The History of Psychology Revisited; Or, Up with Our Foremothers" (Bernstein and Russo
1974); the second, a series of workshops at regional and national conventions in 1976–77 chaired by Agnes N. O'Connell as head of the Task Force
on Women Doing Research—APA Division 35. The outcomes of these
workshops underscored the need to preserve the contributions of women to
the field of psychology and the need to provide role models for the accul-
turation of women into nontraditional occupational roles. The Task Force
on Women Doing Research translated the findings of these workshops into
a report on "Gender-Specific Barriers to Research in Psychology" (O'Connell et al. 1978) and recommended that the stories of eminent women in
psychology be published to partially fulfill the needs delineated.

The first realization of this recommendation was made possible when
Georgia Babladelis, then editor of the *Psychology of Women Quarterly*, invited us to serve as guest editors for a special issue of that journal.[1] The
special issue, *Eminent Women in Psychology: Models of Achievement*, which
contained the biographies of seven distinguished women contributors to the
field, was published in 1980.

Committed to the goal of bringing information about the lives of women
in psychology to as many of our colleagues and students as possible, we
began to organize symposia devoted to reflections of eminent women in the
discipline. We were assisted in this effort by the suggestions of Elizabeth
Goodman, who had organized similar sessions. The first of our symposia
was held at the annual convention of the American Psychological Association in 1979. The response to this symposium was so overwhelmingly positive that we continued to organize symposia for the annual conventions of
the Southeastern Psychological Association, 1980, the Eastern Psychological
Association, 1980, and the American Psychological Association, 1980 and
1981. In each instance, the positive response confirmed our belief in the

1. We are indebted to Annette Brodsky for her suggestion that we be invited to edit a special
issue of the *Psychology of Women Quarterly*.

need for a book that would enable more comprehensive versions of these inspiring stories to reach a larger audience.

In addition to providing a sense of history and purpose and serving as a source of inspiration to students and faculty, the reflections, we believe, will widen people's conceptions regarding options for women and how to exercise them. These stories are a step toward providing needed role models and increasing the visibility of distinguished women.

This book is appropriate as supplementary reading in courses in psychology, particularly courses in introductory psychology, social psychology, personality, history of psychology, sex roles, and psychology of women. The book would also be appropriate for women's studies courses in departments of women's studies, sociology, education, and history. We are also hoping that it will be a useful gift for aspiring young psychologists and for women who may be feeling alone or isolated in their profession. Whether this book is used as a supplementary text or as "extracurricular" bedside reading, the description of the creative, productive, and professionally rewarding interactions among colleagues of both sexes found in these stories should serve to inspire both male and female readers.

These reflections have generated an enthusiastic response from countless individuals. Florence Denmark, who herself is an inspirational role model for women who wish to use their skills on behalf of other women, has been an important source of encouragement and support. We are particularly grateful to her for her Foreword. We thank Ludy T. Benjamin, John Janeway Conger, Dorothy Eichorn, Laurel Furumoto, Mary Roth Walsh, Logan Wright, and the countless others who offered their support at various stages of this endeavor. Virginia Staudt Sexton was an invaluable mentor in our search for the right publisher and Vicki Raeburn in her former role as associate executive editor at Columbia University Press nurtured us during the initial stages of the project. Thanks also go to Susan Koscielniak, associate executive editor, and Lisa Moore, editorial assistant, at Columbia University Press for their assistance in the final stages of the publishing process.

A special acknowledgment goes to the wonderful women contributors to the volume who revised and expanded their stories with patience and cooperation. We also appreciate the efforts of Mary Jane Zaucha who assisted in the content analysis of the autobiographies and of Jane Winston, Leni Ward, and Margaret Day who played crucial roles in gathering materials and typing the manuscript.

Agnes N. O'Connell   *Nancy Felipe Russo*
Montclair State College   American Psychological Association

REFERENCES

Bernstein, M. D. and N. F. Russo. 1974. The history of psychology revisited: Or, up with our foremothers. *American Psychologist*, 29:130–34.

O'Connell, A. N. et al. 1978. Gender-specific barriers to research in psychology. Report of the Task Force on Women Doing Research—APA Division 35. *JSAS Selected Documents in Psychology*, MS. 1753, 1–10.

O'Connell, A. N. and N. F. Russo. 1980. *Eminent Women in Psychology: Models of Achievement*. New York: Human Sciences Press. Special issue of *Psychology of Women Quarterly* 5:1.

❧ ONE ❧
General Introduction

MODELS OF ACHIEVEMENT: REFLECTIONS OF EMINENT WOMEN IN PSYCHOLOGY

AGNES N. O'CONNELL   NANCY FELIPE RUSSO

We look to history for many things: for guidance, for inspiration, for trends that help us understand the present and predict the future, for links that help establish self-identity. Historical role models of achievement can yield a new dimension of meaning and significance to the efforts of contemporary women who seek new identities and wider options in their lives.

One purpose of this book is to historically preserve the contributions of women to the field of psychology. The growth of psychology in America has occurred in the last eighty years. The women in this volume were pioneers, part of that growth. The stories of their lives, told in their own words, provide firsthand information about activities and contributions that have been neglected in the history books (Russo and O'Connell 1980). It is hoped that this book will be used by teachers—the gatekeepers of knowledge in the field—to communicate a more complete and a more accurate picture of the evolution of psychology.

A second purpose of the book is to help redress the lack of female role models and the concomitant isolation of women professionals who often feel they are competing alone against insurmountable odds (O'Connell et al. 1978). Recognition of the influence of a same-sex role model has been prominent in the lives of women successful in politics (Kirkpatrick 1974), poetry (Dickinson 1894), the academic world (Almquist and Angrist 1975; Goldstein 1979; Mead 1972) and psychoanalysis (Deutsch 1973). There is also a significant association between career aspirations and reading about notable women (Walum 1974). Whether the role model exists in vivo or in biography, for a young woman to see the realization of her own aspirations "realized and concretized" in the lives of other women "can be a crucial support at those moments of strain when she might otherwise decide that the integration is too difficult and abandon the effort" (Douvan 1974).

The lives of these distinguished role models can serve as a source of insight into how to sort options and develop survival strategies. Their separate and cumulative stories expand our vision of the possible. We hope that reading about the lives of these women will help both male and female teachers, counselors, therapists, and researchers gain a better understanding of the female experience and of the barriers faced by professional women.

Each of the women in this volume has created her own individual definition of fulfillment but this book is more than the sum of its parts. The autonomy and adaptability of these remarkable individuals yield a picture of women's diversity. As we look more closely at these lives, we find that they represent a variety of subdisciplines in psychology and a variety of life-styles. They were married and they were single. They became mothers and grandmothers; some were without children by choice—others wanted children but were unable to have them. Their experiences span a depression and two world wars. Whatever their circumstances, and whether their careers were primary or secondary to their life goals, they were women who were in charge of their lives, flexible, able to make changes in their surroundings as well as able to take advantage of the opportunities that were presented to them.

As women and men adapt to the challenges of the next decades, they will find a blend of reality and reassurance in the lives of these women. But full appreciation of their remarkable strength, talent, and resiliency requires an understanding of the barriers to education and employment they had to overcome. Their stories are a powerful reminder that the societal context can limit one's options and opportunities and cannot be ignored. But they also remind us of what can be achieved even in a society of limited opportunity.

While we mourn for the countless numbers of talented women who are lost to psychology due to prejudice and discrimination, we are inspired by the women who were able to use their limited opportunities to irrefutably establish women as accepted contributors to the discipline. Their legacy of excellence is a foundation for future efforts to widen opportunities in the field.

The remaining years of the twentieth century will be a time of transition and change. We stand at a critical juncture in the history of our country and in the history of psychology. All of the talent, wisdom, dedication, and energy we can muster is needed to ensure a future of excellence, progress, and opportunity. The lessons provided by the lives of these remarkable women are a foundation for that goal.

To emphasize the lessons to be learned from the lives of these women, this book encompasses three levels of analysis. The first level, the universal, is presented by Nancy Felipe Russo in the chapter on the social and historical context of the times. The second level, the group, is presented by Agnes N. O'Connell in the chapter on the similarities and differences among these eminent women. The third level, the individual, is presented by the distinguished women themselves in their autobiographies.

We hope that the lessons provided by the lives of these extraordinary women will be learned wisely and well by both women and men.

REFERENCES

Almquist, E. M. and S. S. Angrist. 1975. *Careers and Contingencies*. Amherst: University of Massachusetts Press.

Deutsch, H. 1973. *Confrontations with Myself*. New York: Norton.

Dickinson, E. 1894. *Letters*. M. L. Todd, ed. New York: Norton.

Douvan, E. 1974. The role of models in women's professional development. *Psychology of Women Quarterly*, 1:5–20.

Goldstein, E. 1979. Effect of same-sex and cross-sex role models on the subsequent academic productivity of scholars. *American Psychologist*, 34(5):407–10.

Kirkpatrick, J. 1974. *Political Woman*. New York: Basic Books.

Mead, M. 1972. *Blackberry Winter: My Earlier Years*. New York: Morrow.

O'Connell, A. N. et al. 1978. Gender-specific barriers to research in psychology. Report of the Task Force on Women Doing Research—APA Division 35. *JSAS Selected Documents in Psychology*, MS. 1753, 1–10.

Russo, N. F. and A. N. O'Connell. 1980. Models from our past: Psychology's foremothers. *Psychology of Women Quarterly*, 5(1):11–54.

Walum, L. 1974. Personal communication. Cited in E. Douvan, The role of models in women's professional development. *Psychology of Women Quarterly* (1976)1:5–20.

∾ TWO ∾

Historical Perspectives

PSYCHOLOGY'S FOREMOTHERS:
THEIR ACHIEVEMENTS IN CONTEXT

NANCY FELIPE RUSSO

Psychology in the United States began its growth at the end of the nine-teenth century, a time of great economic and social change in America. It was a time when the theory of women's innate moral superiority had be-come a truism of American life, and women became called upon to use their superior qualities to reform society (Hymowitz and Weissman 1978). Attending to the needs of the "young, helpless and distressed" (Terman and Miles 1936) was considered a reflection of women's "biological destiny." Thousands of women devoted themselves to such diverse issues as child labor, prohibition of alcoholic beverages, condition of prisons, tax reform, public sewers, free libraries, pure drinking water, ending prostitution, pro-tecting historical landmarks, and peace (Hymowitz and Weissman 1978). It was also a time in America when women demanded equal political rights and better conditions of employment. But these goals became justified as a means to enable women to more effectively reform society. Women's rights were particularly linked with child welfare (Sears 1975).

It was a time when luminaries of psychology such as G. Stanley Hall, the founder of the American Psychological Association, proclaimed that the woman who eschewed marriage in favor of job concentration selfishly vio-lated her biological ethic—to the detriment of her mammary function, among other evils (Ehrenreich and English 1978).

Stephanie Shields (1975a) has developed a classic summary of the ster-eotypes and prejudices pervading psychology at the turn of the century that should be required reading for all persons who aspire to work in the disci-pline. By understanding how research in psychology has been used to create and maintain barriers to women's achievements, we can use our expertise to begin to eliminate those barriers for contemporary and future women.

Leta Stetter Hollingworth stands out as a role model *par excellence* in this regard. Her pioneering work on the psychology of women at a time when psychology was being used to justify women's disadvantaged status makes her a very special foremother (Benjamin 1975).

Leta Hollingworth demanded that psychology apply scientific rigor in investigating social issues. She proceeded to refute the myths of the time through empirical research (Shields 1975b). She realized the importance of the social context for women's achievements and the need to debunk myths in professional and public spheres alike. An active speaker on behalf of women's issues, she became known as the "scientific pillar" of the women's movement (Benjamin 1975).

The growth of psychology also coincided with a time of vigorous expansion for universities in America. Government science was small, and industrial laboratories nonexistent (Clifford 1973). Becoming professionalized meant the erection of a degree barrier that would exclude laypersons from the scientific enterprise. As the universities expanded, formal graduate training in the sciences became widespread enough to assist in the exclusion process. Psychology had the highest percentage of doctorates of all the sciences (92.3 percent), "which perhaps reflects the fact that it, more than any other science, grew up with the American university" (Rossiter 1974). At that time, 84.6 percent of psychologists were employed in academic institutions, making psychology, along with mathematics, the most "academic of the sciences."

By the beginning of the twentieth century, psychology had numerous offshoots that departed from the traditional mold: educational psychology, animal psychology, and the study of mental development and individual differences (Heidbreder 1933). Women were to be found in all areas of the discipline, but it was in these newly developing areas that the majority of women established their careers. They used alternative employment settings as an opportunity to develop innovations in concepts and methods that came to have impact on all of psychology, many of them rising to positions of unquestioned distinction (Bernstein and Russo 1974; Russo and O'Connell 1980).

The Academic Context

Since psychology has been an academic enterprise, the status of women in academe has had a powerful impact on women's ability to fulfill their scientific potential in psychology. It took independence and a strong will to overcome the social, educational, and employment barriers facing women.

The educational barrier in and of itself was formidable. Although Oberlin and Mt. Holyoke had opened their doors to women before the Civil War, it took the founding of the Eastern women's colleges in the 1870s and 1880s and the expansion of the land-grant universities to make an undergraduate college education available to more than a handful of women. Subsequent progress was slow. By 1900, less than one-fifth of all educational degrees went to women (Mandle 1981).

Resistance to coeducation in graduate school proved to be an additional barrier. By 1900, only 6 percent of the doctorates (or equivalent) went to women (Mandle 1981). Even the most talented women were not exempt from the institutional discrimination of our educational systems. Mary Whiton Calkins, who later became the first woman president of the American Psychological Association, was denied a degree for her work at Harvard (Furumoto 1980). The fact that the distinguished William James judged her his brightest student was not persuasive to the Harvard trustees. That institution was not ready for coeducation.

Margaret Floy Washburn had to leave Columbia University for Cornell because there were no fellowships for even the brightest women. Undaunted, she became the first woman Ph.D. in psychology and the second woman to become president of the American Psychological Association. Her landmark work, *The Animal Mind* (Washburn 1908), was a precursor of and impetus to behaviorism (Goodman 1980).

At times the barriers were concrete—for example, Katharine Banham was the first women to obtain a doctorate from the University of Montreal, a Catholic institution. To fulfill her study requirement, she had to go to the Dominican monastery for tutoring by Père Forêt, dean of the Faculty of Philosophy and a Dominican priest. She received her instruction in the only place she could be alone with her professor in the monastery—the confessional! Nonetheless, she obtained her degree "with distinction" (Banham 1980).

Some women organized against such barriers. Ellen Richards, the first woman to receive a bachelor's degree from the Massachusetts Institute of Technology and founder of the field of home economics, established the Association of Collegiate Alumnae, which later became the American Association of University Women (AAUW). That organization worked diligently to obtain fellowship funds for women (Rossiter 1974). Lois Meek Stolz, distinguished pioneer of the progressive education and child development movements, went to AAUW in the thirties to direct their project to disseminate information about child development to AAUW branches.

Such women built a foundation of opportunity for young women today.

But that hard-won foundation—which includes access to education and employment—must not be taken for granted. Legislative efforts to undermine Title IX, which prohibits sex discrimination in education, also serve to remind us that the future of contemporary women can all too easily come to mirror the experience of women in the past.

Despite barriers, women of excellence pursued their careers. By 1920, sixty-two women in America held Ph.D.s in psychology. Fifteen of them had received their degrees from the University of Chicago (Rossiter 1974). From the time it was founded in 1892, that university had accepted men and women on an equal basis in both graduate and undergraduate programs. Cornell and Columbia followed in contributing women Ph.D.s in psychology with figures of ten and nine, respectively (Rossiter 1974).

During this period, Harvard University stands out as an institution particularly resistant to equality for women. Discrepancies between the ideals of excellence in education and the discriminatory practices at Harvard were not limited to psychology, but the stories of the women in this volume who spent time at Harvard help us to understand the legacy of sex discrimination of that institution.

Once women overcame the educational hurdles and obtained their degrees, they faced barriers to employment in the major university settings. Anti-nepotism rules were particularly hard on the large number of married couples in psychology. Again, even the most distinguished women were not exempt. In 1976 a study by the American Association of University Women found that one out of every four institutions still have anti-nepotism policies. Such policies are more likely to be found in large, coeducational and public institutions where larger numbers of psychologists are likely to be employed (Howard 1978).

Although anti-nepotism policies can effect the careers of both spouses, their brunt typically falls upon the woman. Ironically, data comparing pairs who work in the same institution with pairs who are employed in different institutions argue against such policies. Working together appears to be associated with higher productivity (Bryson et al 1976).

Although they failed to be warmly received in the halls of male-dominated academe, women found employment elsewhere. Women's colleges became an alternative to the leading male-oriented institutions. They provided one of the few places where women could pursue scientific careers.

Guidance centers, clinics, schools, educational systems, hospitals, and custodial centers were also institutions that employed women psychologists. By 1940 women psychologists held 51 percent of the positions in these settings although they constituted only 30 percent of all psychologists. By 1944 the figure increased to 60 percent, although the proportion of women over-all in psychology was unchanged (Bryan and Boring 1946).

Minority Women

Some of these women faced additional barriers created by ethnic and racial discrimination. Gerda Lerner (1981) has described how after the Civil War, of the 9,000 teachers in 4,300 freedmen schools, 45 percent were women. The stories of courage and accomplishments of black women who provided leadership in establishing schools for the freedman are myriad. Among the leaders are Charlotte Hawkins Brown, who raised money to establish the Palmer Memorial Institute in 1902 by singing in Massachusetts summer resort hotels. In 1904 Mary McLeod Bethune began the school that today is Bethune-Cookman College on a garbage dump. She earned money to support her students by baking and selling pies to railroad workers (Lerner 1981).

Information about the nature and extent of the contributions of black women to society is scarce. Obtaining adequate historical information about minority women psychologists will take an extensive effort. Robert V. Guthrie (1976) has begun this difficult task with regard to our early black foremothers. In 1863 Mary Jane Patterson at Oberlin College joined John Brown Russworm at Oberlin and Edward Jones at Amherst (Massachusetts) in becoming the first blacks in the United States to receive college degrees. It was not until seventy years later, in 1933, that a black woman, Inez Prosser, would receive a doctorate in educational psychology from the University of Cincinnati (Guthrie 1976).

Guthrie (1976) has described the context of the time and how the urgent need for teachers, preachers, and trade workers had a profound impact on the development of curricula in the black colleges that became established after the Civil War. While white institutions sought to create the discipline in the image of the "hard" sciences, practical concerns forced black colleges to limit psychology to its applied aspects. Psychology in these schools became associated with education departments. As late as 1940 an undergraduate major in the field was offered in only four schools.

Thirty-two doctorates in psychology (Ph.D.) and educational psychology (Ed.D.) went to blacks in the years between 1920 and 1950; eight of these degrees (four Ed.D.s, four Ph.D.s) were obtained by black women. In 1934, Ruth Howard (Beckman), whose autobiography is in this volume, became the first black woman to receive a Ph.D. in psychology.

Perhaps the most famous black married couple in psychology is Kenneth and Mamie Phipps Clark. Clark's autobiography in this volume describes their joint professional efforts which have had such a profound impact on social policy. Their co-authored research cited in *Brown vs. the Board of Education* was instrumental in the United States' Supreme Court ruling to desegregate the nation's classrooms.

In discussing ethnic and racial discrimination, the pervasive discrimination against Jews that taints the history of the United States, particularly in the decade of the thirties, must also be mentioned. The autobiographies of Mary Henle and Eugenia Hanfmann remind us that bias and discrimination come in many guises.

From 1920–1974, 48 percent of the Ph.D.s in developmental and gerontological psychology went to women. Thirty-two percent of Ph.D.s in school psychology went to women. These figures are in contrast to 6 percent in industrial; 14 percent in psychometrics; 15 percent in comparative; 18 percent in experimental; 20 percent in physiological; and 23 percent in social psychology. For the fields of clinical, counseling and guidance, and general psychology, the figure is the same, 24 percent; for educational psychology, it is 25 percent (Harmon 1978). This legacy of segregation is reflected in today's statistics. Although approximately one in four Ph.D.s in psychology in 1980 is held by a woman, psychology's subfields still vary widely in their proportion of women and men (Russo et al., 1981).

How did so many scientifically trained women become concentrated in applied settings? Answering that question requires looking beyond the lives of individuals. It requires understanding the evolution of conceptions about women's proper roles and the evolution of institutional structures that reflect and reinforce those conceptions. Institutional structures perpetuate sex segregation in contemporary psychology just as they create separate worlds of work for women and men in the larger society.

THE EVOLUTION OF PSYCHOLOGY

Psychology has evolved as both a science and as an applied profession. The tension between these two facets of the discipline that has been with us since psychology's beginnings has received much attention. The contribution of sex-role stereotyping and sex discrimination to the creation of subfields in psychology has only begun to receive discussion.

The forces that produce the sex segregation of psychology's subfields are complex and reflect the effects of forces in the larger social context. The historical opportunities for women's employment in women's colleges, state colleges, schools, and guidance clinics are important factors. Such opportunities reflect the progressive reform and child development movements at the turn of the nineteenth century that interacted with the stereotypes about women at the time and created employment settings hospitable to women. Another force was war, which stimulated interest in child development during the first three decades of the twentieth century and masculinized psychology thereafter.

Women in Progressive Reform and Child Guidance Movements

Women played numerous roles in the reform movements that multiplied in the nineteenth century. The movement to reform conditions for the mentally ill was no exception. Indeed, the person described as "the most effective advocate of humanitarian reform in American mental institutions during the nineteenth century" was Dorothea Lynde Dix (Goldenson 1970).

The effectiveness of this remarkable woman's efforts to reform the deplorable treatment of the mentally ill makes her a powerful model for all persons who wish to use their skills to affect society (Tiffany 1890, Marshall 1937, Viney and Zorich 1982). More than 32 mental hospitals, 15 schools for the feebleminded, a school for the blind, and numerous training facilities for nurses were built or enlarged as a result of her efforts (Viney and Zorich 1982).

A model for the eighties can also be found in the leadership and vision of Jane Addams, who founded the first settlement house in the United States in the slums of Chicago (Crovitz and Buford 1978). The significance of Hull House goes beyond its intent to help the poor.

In the latter half of the nineteenth century, a mysterious "epidemic" of "invalidism" swept middle- and upper-middle class women in both England and the United States. Diagnostic labels for the malady included "neurasthenia," "nervous prostration," "dyspepsia," and "hysteria." Poor women, however, were not affected. Feminist saw a link between the vacuous role expectations for women in the upper classes and the "female invalidism" that such women suffered (Ehrenreich and English 1978). Hull House was established in response to Addams' recognition that educating young girls without providing meaningful work for them creates suffering and despair. Addams herself underwent bouts of "nervous prostration" until she became inspired to create Hull House, which she described as "a place for invalid girls to go and help the poor" (Hymowitz and Weissman 1978). The field of social work was born.

In 1909 the Juvenile Psychopathic Institute, the first child guidance clinic, was established under the direction of psychiatrist William Healy (Reisman 1976). Augusta Bronner, who had trained at Teachers College at Columbia University, under Thorndike, joined the institute staff in 1913. As early as 1916 she argued that test-taking attitudes could affect test scores. Bronner advanced the concept of special reading disabilities in children of average intelligence, stimulating the development of performance tests, including one by William Healy and psychologist Grace Fernald. She and William Healy subsequently organized the Judge Baker Foundation, which made diagnostic evaluations for the law court (Reisman 1976).

Child guidance clinics multiplied in the twenties. In 1924 child guidance clinicians founded the American Orthopsychiatric Association; and in 1931 Augusta Bronner was elected to its presidency (Reisman 1976).

It was considered appropriate for women to be involved in child guidance, which was thought to prevent juvenile delinquency. Thus, when the popular concern with prevention of juvenile delinquency stimulated the development of ground-breaking bridges between psychology and the legal system, women were involved (Senn 1975).

Women's Work: Mental Tests, Child Development, and Progressive Education

The universal draft of World War I required all American males to take the new mental tests and receive physical examinations. Their poor showing resulted in a boom of funding for the development of tests, education, and child welfare research.

MENTAL TESTS

The turn of the nineteenth century had begun an era of burgeoning study of individual differences. James McKeen Cattell, who founded the third psychological laboratory at the University of Pennsylvania, introduced the term "Mental Tests and Measurements" in 1890 (Cattell 1890).

Cattell established the psychological laboratory at Columbia, America's largest university, in 1891. As Boring (1950) has pointed out, during his tenure at that institution Cattell undoubtedly influenced more students in psychology than any other of his contemporaries. Cattell is significant here because—in the words of his student Margaret Floy Washburn—as a "life-long champion of freedom and equality of opportunity, it would never have occurred to him to reject a woman student on account of her sex" (Sexton 1974).

The area of mental tests includes both tests of intelligence and techniques to diagnose psychiatric problems. Women became prominent in both approaches. Further, their concentration in the fields of child development and child guidance is reflected in their contribution to the development of tests with children (Russo and O'Connell 1980).

Mental tests became increasingly used as research tools. In the debate over nature vs. nurture, which had continued in the thirties, the nurture viewpoint gained ascendence after Beth Wellman reported that nursery school attendance conferred a mean increase of five I.Q. points. Wellman was one of the first to point out that deprived environments could result in marked I.Q. losses, while enrichment could produce gains (Wellman 1932a, 1932b).

As the field of clinical psychology evolved, clinicians increasingly viewed the testing function as restrictive and even distasteful. There was a tendency for psychologists to be relegated to "second-string jobs" in clinics and bureaus, with physicians at the head of the organization. Along with inferior responsibilities went lower salaries (Reisman 1976). In 1947 Alice Bryan and E. G. Boring underscored the difference between "men's work" and "women's work" in psychology: the men being the researchers and writers; the women the practitioners. By 1944, 60 percent of the positions in guidance centers, clinics, schools, educational systems, hospitals, and custodial centers were held by women. In contrast, 74 percent of the positions in universities and colleges were held by men. The devaluation of women's work was reflected in the salary differential between the sexes, with fully employed women earning about 20–40 percent less than men (Bryan and Boring 1947).

PROGRESSIVE EDUCATION AND CHILD DEVELOPMENT

With the turn of the century came a change in attitudes toward children and a "professional approach to child care." The role of mother became viewed as "a scientific vocation that required intelligence and training" (Filene 1975). While this view of motherhood reinforced women's ties to home, it also provided a "legitimate" sphere for women in the world of work. The first three decades of the twentieth century became a heyday for the child guidance and progressive education movements, which provided a place for women to apply their talents in a way congruent with society's conceptions of women's interests and abilities. Women shaped these movements through their own efforts and through their influence on prominent men.

Numerous women were involved in the early psychoanalytic circle that had an impact on the development of clinical and child psychology. Early greats such as Frieda Fromm-Reichmann, Karen Horney, Melanie Klein, and Claire Thompson challenged the givens of the Freudian psychoanalytic scheme that so contributed to the myths held about women at the time (Russo and O'Connell 1980). For a biography of Karen Horney, see O'Connell 1980.

Other eminent figures include Susan Isaacs, who was a co-founder of the British Psychoanalytic Society. Studies of children based on psychoanalytic perceptions of Anna Freud, Melanie Klein, and Susan Isaacs are considered to have been particularly important in stimulating child development researchers to go beyond the question of how to the question of why (Senn 1975). There was also Charlotte Buhler, who was one of the first to begin to look at age and class variables in research on children and is regarded as the first "humanistic psychologist" (Krippner 1977).

Morton Senn (1975) has provided a marvelous account of the child development movement in the United States. Although there are other historical treatments of the field (e.g., Anderson 1956, Sears 1975), his is the only one that gives visibility to women (Anderson even goes so far as to title a separate section "Men").

In the 1920s economist Lawrence K. Frank, along with Beardsley Ruml, played a key role in shaping opportunities for women in psychology. Frank developed a vision of comprehensive programs of child development research organized in conjunction with universities having elementary and secondary laboratory schools. This vision was implemented through management of the Laura Spelman Rockefeller Memorial. By the financial crash of 1929, the memorial had spent over $7 million (in 1920 dollars!) to finance institutes for child study that provided supportive environment settings for women to work in the area of child development.

It might be argued that the institutes took pressure off the universities to change their sexist ways. In addition, they contributed to the separation of the worlds of work for men and women, a trend already sufficiently fostered by the rapidly growing "female" science of home economics. At that time there was some tension between the women who chose to pursue careers in male-dominated "scientific" fields and those who pursued the more "feminine" applied fields of child development and education. Nonetheless, the institutes created a supportive environment and source of employment for women that provided access to stimulating colleagues and research facilities. The list of women associated with them reads like a *Who's Who* of psychology foremothers (Russo and O'Connell 1980).

Men's Work: War

World War I stimulated the "feminine" fields of child development and education, creating employment opportunities for women. World War II had the reverse effect. Of 1,006 psychologists entering the armed forces, only 33 were women (Marquis 1944b).

One of these unusual women was Mildred Mitchell, who achieved the rank of lieutenant (jg) in the Bureau of Naval Personnel during her war service at the United States Naval Hospital in Bethesda. Of the 30 psychologists doing hospital work in the Navy, Mitchell was the only woman. Her autobiography is included in this volume.

In 1943, the army established a course in advanced personnel psychology in the Army Specialized Training Program (Marquis 1944a). In addition to such training experiences, the military provided a hospitable research environment. Many of the nation's leading psychologists became involved in such things as devising methods for the selection and training of personnel, human factors research, and civilian morale studies. This wartime experience stimulated the fields of psychometrics and social psychology and created social networks among researchers that shaped the postwar development of psychology.

The American Psychological Association (APA) played an active role in organizing psychologists during the war, but its initial efforts reflected the interests of the male-dominated subfields. During the 1939 APA convention, the APA authorized the creation of an Emergency Committee in Psychology, without representation of women psychologists. A New York group of women psychologists organized what became the National Council of Women Psychologists (NCWP) "to promote and develop emergency services that women psychologists could render their communities as larger numbers of their male colleagues were drawn into military services" (Finison and Furumoto 1978).

This is not to say that women were not involved in every facet of psychology's wartime effort. There have been a number of summaries of the research and service of women psychologists during the war years (Finison and Furumoto 1978, Murphy 1943, Portenier n.d.). Several of these focus on problems of civilian morale, relocation, refugees, children, and families in wartime. In her autobiography in this volume, Eugenia Hanfmann communicates the excitement as well as the frustration of being a psychologist in the war effort.

After the war the NCWP voted to change its name and purpose. In 1947 the International Council of Women Psychologists was born, with Gertrude Hildreth as president. Its purpose became to "further international understanding by promoting intercultural relations to practical applications of psychology" (Portenier n.d.). Males were admitted to the organization. In 1960 the group was renamed the International Council of Psychologists (Portenier n.d.) and continues with that title today.

After the war the country began to adjust to the return of its men. The war had created new and highly desirable positions in business and industry. In 1944 Donald Marquis provided an analysis of postwar reemployment prospects in psychology in the *Psychological Bulletin*. Psychologists contemplating careers at the time received the following message:

Business and industry offer fields with almost unlimited possibilities for development. . . . The Veterans Administration has a need for 200–400 trained vocational counselors. . . . These *men and women* will work in association with newly established college centers in the examination and vocational counseling of disabled veterans. . . .

It is fortunate that the expansible fields in psychology are just the fields for which experience in military psychology is most valuable. Business and industry will want *men* with backgrounds in testing, classification and personnel work; the Veterans Administration and similar agencies will want *men* with military experience in testing and clinical psychology. (Marquis 1944b) [Italics mine]

Given the military's stimulation of training and personnel psychology and the expectation that opportunities in business and industry were open to *men*, it is not surprising that industrial and personnel psychology has remained the subfield of psychology with the highest proportion of that sex, even into the eighties.

The needs of the male-oriented employment settings shaped the knowledge base of psychology, even in those cases where women psychologists participated. There were 16 million veterans of World War II and 4 million veterans of previous wars. The Veterans Administration (VA) claimed that it alone needed 4,700 clinical psychologists and vocational counselors. The states asked for 2,100 vocational advisers. There were 1,500 positions in vocational guidance waiting to be filled, but there were 1,000 vocational counselors in the entire United States. The VA and the United States Public Health Service cooperated to create funds for clinical training to meet the demand. In 1946 the National Institute of Mental Health began its program of training grants. Standards were a concern, and the VA required the doctorate for clinicians seeking employment in its installations. By doing so, it was attempting to raise professional standards in psychology. However, it shut out qualified M.A. clinicians and influenced the type of clinician trained—one experienced in working with hospitalized male adults. Experience in working with outpatients and women and children was neglected (Reisman 1976). The regressive fifties began.

LESSONS OF THE PAST: FOUNDATION FOR THE FUTURE

History is a continuum. The choice of when to begin and when to end a historical discussion is arbitrary. The forces that set the context for the courses and directions of the careers for women in this volume primarily occur in the first half of the century, and that time span has been the focus here. The conditions of the last thirty years are well portrayed in the words of the women themselves. The question for all of us is what can be learned from the lives and times of these women?

Our first lesson is perhaps the knowledge that barriers can be overcome with motivation, enthusiasm, and creativity. Barriers can become challenges. We can go a long way on a little opportunity. Despite limited opportunity, these women irrefutably established members of their sex as accepted contributors to psychology. Their excellence provides a solid foundation for our own efforts.

A second lesson is appreciation for the role of the broader social context in determining the evolution of psychology and in shaping the contribution of women to the discipline. The more we study the history of psychology, the more we see the power of societal norms and institutions to influence the career paths of individuals. We have seen how social forces such as war and the progressive education and child development movements have shaped the evolution of psychology. We have seen how the traditional devaluation of women's work has been counterbalanced by other forces and how the demand for knowledge produced in the fields of child development and counseling and guidance engendered funding for those fields.

The position of women psychologists in the eighties has many similarities to that of our early foremothers. The women's movement of the sixties and seventies has regained some of the opportunities that were lost after World War II. Women have once again organized on behalf of women in psychology (Russo 1980). Led by women, both women and men are working to eliminate sex bias in psychology and related fields and to legitimize the study of women's experience (cf. Carmen, Russo, and Miller 1981, Sherman and Denmark 1978, Sobel and Russo 1981b).

This is a new "women's work" in psychology, but there is a difference. Both female and male psychologists are applying their knowledge and expertise to understanding the detrimental effects of women's unequal status on their mental health, well-being, and achievement. There is an increased awareness of the significance of the social context in determining opportunity in psychology and an increased recognition of the ethical obligation to ameliorate women's disadvantaged status through affecting social change (Sobel and Russo 1981a).

Continued progress in the coming decade will require strength, patience, and steadfastness on the part of all women in American society. Like our foremothers, we may experience frustrations and setbacks, but from our foremothers we have learned that setbacks are not defeat. It is not an issue of *if* we will achieve our goals of full participation of women in psychology and in society—it is a question of *when* we will achieve those goals. The energies of today's women will provide a legacy of opportunity and excellence for future generations of psychologists. Contemporary women can take pride in their contributions to that legacy.

REFERENCES

Anderson, J. E. 1956. Child development: An historical perspective. *Child Development*, 27(2):181–96.

Banham, K. M. 1980. Personal communication.

Benjamin, L. T., Jr. 1975. The pioneering work of Leta Hollingworth in the psychology of women. *Nebraska History*, 56(4):493–505.

Bernstein, M. D. and N. F. Russo. 1974. The history of psychology revisited: Or, up with our foremothers. *American Psychologist*, 29:130–34.

Boring, E. G. 1950. *A History of Experimental Psychology*. New York: Appleton-Century-Crofts.

Bryan, A. I. and E. G. Boring. 1946. Women in American psychology: Statistics from the OPP questionnaire. *American Psychologist*, 1:71–79.

Bryan, A. I. and E. G. Boring. 1947. Women in American psychology: Factors affecting their professional careers. *American Psychologist*, 2:3–20.

Bryson, R. B., J. B. Bryson, M. H. Licht, and B. G. Licht. 1976. The professional pair: Husband and wife psychologists. *American Psychologist*, 31(1):10–16.

Carmen, E. H., N. F. Russo, and J. B. Miller. 1981. Inequality and women's mental health: An overview. *American Journal of Psychiatry*, 1,319–30.

Cattell, J. 1890. Mental tests and measurements. *Mind*, 15:373.

Clifford, G. J. 1973. The psychologist as professional man of science. In M. Henle, J. Jaynes, and J. J. Sullivan, eds., *Historical Conceptions of Psychology*. New York: Springer Publishing.

Crovitz, E. and E. Buford. 1978. *Courage Knows no Sex*. North Quincy, Mass.: Christopher Publishing House.

Ehrenreich, B. and D. English. 1978. *For Her Own Good*. New York: Anchor Press.

Filene, R. 1975. *Him/her/self*. New York: Harcourt Brace Jovanovich.

Finison, L. and L. Furumoto. 1978. *An historical perspective on psychology, social action and women's rights*. Presented at the Annual Meeting of the American Psychological Association, Toronto, in August.

Furumoto, L. 1980. Mary Whiton Calkins (1863–1930). *Psychology of Women Quarterly*, 5(1):55–68.

Goldensen, R. M. 1970. *The Encyclopedia of Human Behavior: Psychology, Psychiatry, and Mental Health*. 2 vols. Garden City, N.Y.: Doubleday.

Goodman, E. 1980. Margaret F. Washburn (1871–1939): First woman Ph.D. in psychology. *Psychology of Women Quarterly*, 5(1):69–80.

Guthrie, R. V. 1976. *Even the Rat was White*. New York: Harper & Row.

Harmon, L. R. 1978. *A Century of Doctorates: Data Analyses of Growth and Change*. Washington, D.C.: National Academy of Sciences.

Heidbreder, E. 1933. *Seven Psychologies*. New York: D. Appleton-Century.

Howard, S. 1978. *But We Will Persist. A Comparative Research Report on the Status of Women in Academe*. Washington, D.C.: American Association of University Women.

Hymowitz, C. and M. Weissman. 1978. *A History of Women in America*. New York: Bantam Books.

Krippner, S. 1977. Humanistic psychology: Its history and contributions. *Journal of the American Society of Psychosomatic Dentistry and Medicine*, 24(1):15–20.

Lerner, G. 1981. *Teaching Women's History*. Washington, D.C.: American Historical Association.

Mandle, J. D. 1981. *Women and Social Change in America*. Princeton, N.J.: Princeton Book.

Marquis, D. G. 1944a. The mobilization of psychologists for war service. *Psychological Bulletin*, 41:469–73.

—— 1944b. Post-war reemployment prospects in psychology. *Psychological Bulletin*, 41:653–63.

Marshall, H. E. 1937. *Dorothea Dix, a Forgotten Samaritan*. Chapel Hill: University of North Carolina Press.

Murphy, G. 1943. Service of women psychologists to the war: Foreword. *Journal of Consulting Psychology*, 7:249–51.

O'Connell, A. N. 1980. Karen Horney: Theorist in psychoanalytic and feminine psychology. *Psychology of Women Quarterly*, 5(1):81–93.

Portenier, L. G., ed. n.d. *The International Council of Psychologists, Inc.* Altadena, California: International Council of Psychologists.

Reisman, J. 1976. *A History of Clinical Psychology*. New York: Irvington Publishers.

Rossiter, M. W. 1974. Women scientists in America before 1920. *American Scientist* (May–June), 62:312–23.

Russo, N. F. 1983. *Careers for Women in Psychology: Strategies for Success*. Washington, D.C.: American Psychological Association.

Russo, N. F. and A. N. O'Connell. 1980. Models from our past: Psychology's foremothers. *Psychology of Women Quarterly*, 5(1):11–54.

Russo, N. F., E. Olmedo, J. Stapp, and R. Fulcher. 1981. Women and minorities in psychology. *American Psychologist*, 36(11):1315–63.

Sears, R. R. 1975. *Your Ancients Revisited: A History of Child Development*. Chicago: University of Chicago Press.

Senn, M. L. 1975. Insights on the child development movement in the United States. *Monographs of the Society for Research in Child Development*, 40 (3–4, Serial No. 16):1–106.

Sexton, V. S. 1974. Women in American psychology: An overview. *Journal of International Understanding* (Spring), 9(10):66–77.

Sherman, J. and F. Denmark, eds. 1978. *The Psychology of Women: Future Directions in Research*. New York: Psychological Dimensions.

Shields, S. A. 1975a. Functionalism, Darwinism, and the psychology of women. *American Psychologist* (July), 30:739–54.

—— 1975b. Ms. Pilgrim's progress, the contribution of Leta Stetter Hollingworth to the psychology of women. *American Psychologist* (August), 30:852–57.

Sobel, S. B. and N. F. Russo. 1918a. Equality, public policy, and mental health. *Professional Psychology*, 12:180–89.

Sobel, S. B. and N. F. Russo, eds. 1981b. Sex roles, equality, and mental health. *Professional Psychology*, Whole No. 1.

Terman, L. M. and C. C. Miles. 1936. *Sex and Personality*. New Haven: Yale University Press.

Tiffany, F. 1890. *Life of Dorothea Lynde Dix*. Boston: Houghton Mifflin.

Viney, W. and S. Zorich. 1982. Contributions to the history of psychology: XXIX. Dorothea Dix and the history of psychology. *Psychological Reports*, 50:212–18.

Washburn, M. F. 1908. *The Animal Mind*. New York: Macmillan.

Wellman, B. L. 1932a. Some new bases for interpretation of the I.Q. *Journal of Genetic Psychology*, 41:116.

—— 1932b. The effects of preschool attendance upon the I.Q. *Journal of Experimental Education*, 1:48.

THREE

Personal Perspectives: Autobiographical Sketches

KATHARINE M. BANHAM

It must have been about the year of the great earthquake in the San Francisco Bay area, when I first became acquainted with psychology, or rather, some of its subject matter. It was during a geography lesson at the Sheffield High School for girls in England. The teacher, Miss Porter, had given us slips of paper on which to write the names of the capes and bays of England, in order, going clockwise round the coast. I had finished my list before the other pupils and turned the paper to see what was on the other side. For economy's sake, old examination papers were torn in half and used for scrap writing paper at the school. What I read on the back of the slip was something about the association of ideas by similarity and by contiguity. This intrigued me. I was not sure what contiguity meant, but I determined to find out. I decided, there and then, that when I grew up I was going to learn more about that.

My next acquaintance with psychology came three years later. A university lecturer from London came to visit our school in Sheffield. She wanted small groups of children, of different age levels, to do some psychological tests that had been published in France and translated into English. I was selected as one of the children in my age group to do the tests. I regarded this as quite an honor. Although I did not know it at the time, the lecturer, Miss Katherine Johnston, was one of the assistants working with Professor Cyril Burt on the standardization of the 1908 version of the Binet-Simon Tests of Intelligence for use with English children.

Miss Johnston was such a gracious person. She gave me a smiling welcome as I entered the classroom at Sheffield University, where the tests were being conducted. She asked a few questions and listened attentively to what I had to say. In short, she treated me like a grown-up, making friendly conversation, rather than expecting me just to sit still and listen to what she had to say. On my way home, I thought how much I would like to become a university lecturer myself, and do the sort of things Miss Johnston was doing.

Three or four years later, I really did have an opportunity to study the subject matter of psychology. It was my last year in the sixth form at Shef-field High School. I was taking only three subjects for the Oxford and Cam-bridge Higher Certificate, required for entrance to either university. This allowed me time to enroll as a special student in a course on psychology for students in the Froebel kindergarten teacher-training program. This was a two-year program for older girls at our school. Texts for the introductory psychology course were: *An Introduction to Social Psychology* by William McDougall (1908), and *Psychology in the Schoolroom* by Dexter and Garlick (c. 1898). The latter was systematic, simple, and easy to read, albeit rather dogmatic in style. I liked it and found it understandable. When I took up residence in the United States years later, I looked in college libraries for the text, to see how it compared with more recent ones, but I never found it.

The Froebel students had a special library, housed in the fifth-form class-room. I was not allowed to borrow the books, but I could read them in the room after school hours. Among these books I discovered the two-volume work *The Principles of Psychology* by William James (1890). I found that fascinating. Day after day, I stayed in the classroom late in the afternoon, reading until it was too dark to see the fine print. The vast realm of the mind, as opened up before me in William James' beautiful language, be-came more than ever a topic of absorbing interest to me. I was quite certain by this time that the subject I wanted to study in college was psychology.

My science mistress, Miss Brook, advised me to take up chemistry or physics at the university. I had done well in these subjects at school. She was disappointed when I said that I wanted to study psychology. She had little notion of what that was, herself. She said "and when you have studied it, what are you going to do with it? There are few teaching positions in psychology in universities and none in schools." I did not say so, but I felt convinced that the subject was so important that there would soon be many more openings for psychologists in teacher-training colleges and universities.

Selecting a university was my next problem. My father was an army offi-cer during the First World War and could not afford the fees needed for me to go to Cambridge, my first choice. He had been at the Perse School there himself, and his father (my grandfather) was a graduate of Sidney-Sussex College in Cambridge. Fees at Oxford or London would be as high as those at Cambridge, and these were the only universities I knew that offered courses in psychology. The father of one of my schoolmates, Mr. Quine, was a government school inspector (supervisor). I thought he might have infor-mation about British universities, courses offered, and cost of tuition, so I went to seek his advice. He told me that Owen's College, recently renamed the Victoria University of Manchester, offered courses in psychology. Fees would be less expensive there than in the older established universities. He advised me to write for a prospectus. I did so, and learned that students might enroll for a B.A. or B.Sc. in psychology, depending on whether other basic subjects were taken among the arts or the sciences. Fees and cost of residence in hall were not prohibitive. Upon Mr. Quine's further recommendation, I applied for, and was granted, an educational bursary by the National Board of Education. This would pay for university tuition. That left only the cost of room and meals in hall for my father to pay. He agreed to do that.

In the autumn of 1916 I went to take up residence in Ashburne Hall for women and register for courses at the University of Manchester. As science had been my strong subject in high school, I decided to enroll in a B.Sc. course of studies. My selection of courses included chemistry, botany, and zoology. I knew that physics might be more appropriate, but I liked the idea of studying botany. I had not had botany in high school. I was delighted with my choice. During my first year as a "fresher," part of the requirement in botany was to go on hikes in Cheshire or the Derbyshire hills at weekends. These were health-giving and exhilarating, besides being interesting and informative.

I was the first student to register for an honors degree in psychology at Manchester, and the course program was still in the planning stage. Some lectures were to be taken in the Faculty of Arts, some in the Faculty of Science, and some in the School of Medicine. Psychology was not offered until the second, or sophomore year. My first course in psychology was with Professor Samuel Alexander of the Department of Philosophy. He used as a text *Manual of Psychology* by G. F. Stout (1899). His lectures contained almost as much philosophical thought as psychology, and were intensely interesting. I would like to have had more of them. The following year, I took a laboratory course in experimental psychology with Thomas H. Pear. He was an enthusiastic and stimulating young lecturer, a graduate of the University of London. He used as his text *An Introduction to Experimental Psychology* by Charles S. Myers (1911). This was very similar to Edward Titchener's (1910) *A Text Book of Psychology* used in American universities about that time.

In my final year, I came down with the "Spanish flu," and had it worse than anyone else in the hall. My temperature soared so high that the housekeeper sat up all one night, bathing me with cold water to try to bring my temperature down. That illness left me very weak. Also, it kept me from my studies for two or three weeks. On Mr. Pear's recommendation, I gave up the notion of working toward an honors degree in psychology. Instead, I changed my registration to that for an ordinary B.Sc. degree in psychology and physiology. The courses in neuroanatomy and physiology given by Dean Elliot-Smith of the School of Medicine, had been most enjoyable, and I had done well in the term tests. Anthropology was one of the dean's hobbies. He digressed, every now and then, to tell of some of his experiences in his travels to Egypt and across the Pacific Ocean.

Professor William Stirling taught general physiology to medical students. He was a tall, dignified man, who always wore a long, black frockcoat to lectures. He had a cross-over cravat tie around his stiff collar, a gold watch-chain across his waistcoat (vest), and a black ribbon attached to the monocle held in his right eye. Upon entering the lecture hall, he addressed the students, saying "Good morning ladies and gentlemen." He allowed no late-comers to class. The porter, on his orders, locked the lecture-room door ten minutes after the bell rang for classes to begin. There was, however, an emergency exit through the laboratory behind the lecturer's desk. I remember only one student daring to come in late that way. The professor looked astonished as the student walked round from behind him. For a moment, there was dead silence in the room. Then some of the students began to titter. Professor Stirling quickly called the class to order and the lecture proceeded. The only two women in the class of nearly a hundred were Miss Edith Attenborough and myself, both studying for a B.Sc. in psychology and physiology. Professor Stirling said one day in class that he did not know why we wanted to take his course, we were not students of medicine, but we were welcome to stay.

In spite of his formal manner Professor Stirling was a brilliant lecturer. He was a scholar of the old school, with a wide range of interests and knowledge. He quoted poetry in his lectures, and sometimes they sounded more like after-dinner speeches then class-room lectures. After I had passed the physiology examinations for degree credit, I audited the course a second year, for the sheer joy of hearing it all over again.

During my time as an undergraduate at Manchester the course programs for degrees in psychology became fully established. In the year of my graduation, 1919, psychology was made a separate discipline or department. Thomas H. Pear was promoted to a professorship and appointed head of the new department.

Following my graduation, with a B.Sc. in psychology and physiology, I spent another year in Manchester, taking the teacher-training course for a diploma in education. Then came the day of reckoning. It was time for me to begin earning my living. Psychology was not a subject that could be taught in elementary or high schools. Either a master's or a doctoral degree was requisite for a university teaching position. I was in need of further graduate study. My father had returned to his medical practice in Sheffield at the end of World War I. He kindly offered to pay my expenses for a year of graduate study at Cambridge, although I had now reached legal adulthood and was no longer a minor. I was delighted and selected Girton, the older of the two colleges for women in Cambridge, for my year of residence. That year was the height of bliss for me. I stayed all through "the term in the long" (summer vacation) and left only at the end of August.

My first tutor and thesis supervisor was Dr. Charles S. Myers, who had been instrumental in setting up the psychological laboratory on Downing Street, Cambridge. His latest project, begun just before my residence in Cambridge, was that of establishing the Institute of Industrial Psychology in London. This occupied much of his time, and Dr. Frederick C. Bartlett took over the supervision of my experimental work in his absence. Besides taking lecture courses given by my tutors, I studied abnormal psychology with Dr. J. F. Engledue Prideaux and attended lectures by C. Lloyd Morgan, Charles Sherrington from Oxford, W. H. R. Rivers, the ethnologist, and Edgar D. Adrian the physiologist. All of these men were deep thinkers and inspired students to think for themselves.

I shared a research room with Mr. Whately Smith, who was studying the effect of emotion on memory and the claims of mediums to telepathy of thought. He introduced me to the Society for Psychical Research. After hearing Sir Gerald Fielding describe some scientific investigations of poltergeist activities, I joined the Society. I wanted to continue inquiry into these extraordinary phenomena. My own experimental studies were on the subject of mental conflict, its effect on memory, conscious experiences and emotional reactions. Mr. Whately Smith and I took turns in the use of a new electrical apparatus for the measurement of emotion. It was a simple Wheatstone Bridge arrangement, devised by Dr. Waller in Germany. Whately Smith had constructed it from wires and wet batteries borrowed from the Cavendish Laboratory. We operated it ourselves, and it worked surprisingly well.

Among my student colleagues were Robert H. Thouless and Mary M. Sturt. She was the daughter of Henry Sturt, philosopher at Oxford, and had been studying with William McDougall before he left for the United States. Mary and I joined the "Moral Science Society," known jokingly by students as the "Moral Stinks Society." It was a student organization, primarily for those reading philosophy for a Moral Science tripos (honors degree). We met for discussion of fundamental topics in the college rooms of Professor

George E. Moore. He was small of stature, with a round face, and was very dynamic. He would kneel on the seat of his padded, wicker armchair, peer over its high back at us, and talk so excitedly that his hair became dishevelled. He looked something like "Dennis the Menace" in Hank Ketcham's present-day cartoons.

Before the end of the year, I presented my little thesis, in handwriting as legible as I could make it, for my tutors to read. They were satisfied that it fulfilled the requirement of an M.Sc. degree. But I was unable to submit it to the university authorities for a degree, as only men might do that at Cambridge. Women were admitted to all classes, and they could sit for examinations, but they were not granted university degrees. At Oxford University, women were admitted to full membership of the university, and were granted degrees, in 1920. A convocation was called in Cambridge, in 1921, to consider the granting of degrees to women, but this was denied. It was not until 1948 that women were admitted to full membership of the university in Cambridge.

I felt that I had reached as far as I could go with my studies of psychology in England and I must look toward possibilities abroad. I met Professor Alfred Clarence Redfield, an American who was staying with some elderly cousins of mine in Cambridge. He was on leave of absence from Harvard University. I asked him whether he knew of any research fellowships available to foreigners in American universities. He suggested that I write to the psychology departments of several colleges and universities in the United States, including Bryn Mawr Seminary for Ladies and the University of Toronto in Canada. I had never heard of a university at Toronto, but I followed the professor's suggestion. I wrote to Bryn Mawr, and to Professor George S. Brett, Head of the Department of Philosophy at Toronto.

To my surprise and delight, in about two weeks time, I received a cable from Professor Brett saying that they had no research fellowships but there was a lectureship vacancy in psychology for which I might apply. It carried a salary of $1,200.00 a year. Would I cable my decision by return? I thought quickly. A lectureship was really the goal for which I wanted a research fellowship and further study to prepare me. I cabled back applying for the position and sent by mail my credentials, testimonials from my tutors and from Miss Jex-Blake, Mistress of Girton College. Two more weeks passed and there came another cablegram from Professor Brett offering me the lectureship. I cabled back my acceptance. The following day I received a letter from Bryn Mawr offering me one of their three international fellowships. Regrettably, I had to decline this. It was an honor I should have liked to accept. When Maud Matthews, one of the girls at the Sheffield High School, had been awarded a Bryn Mawr fellowship, the whole school was given a day's holiday in recognition of the honor.

My father took me to Liverpool and saw me on to the Canadian Pacific S. S. Melita, to take me to Canada. As I stood on the deck and watched him disappear through the gate on the quay the whole world seemed to whiz round in circles and disappear with him through the gate. It took twelve days to cross the ocean and sail up the beautiful St. Lawrence river. The maple leaves were turning red on the eighteenth of September 1921. The Montmerency falls were a white cascade tumbling over the high cliffs and, nearer to Montreal, little white wooden churches with tall, narrow spires dotted the landscape. I had arrived in the new world, and saw it was good.

Edward Bott met me at the railway station in Toronto, and he and his wife Helen helped me to find a furnished room for my residence. Later I was taken to see Professor Brett, who welcomed me warmly and told me what my duties would be. After I had started my first teaching courses in experimental psychology and in social psychology in the School of Social Work, I asked Professor Brett if I might register for an M.A. degree in psychology. He asked me why I wanted to do that. He thought it unnecessary. My bachelor's degree from Manchester and subsequent graduate work in Cambridge were, in his opinion, the equivalent of a master's degree at Toronto. I said, "but an M.A. looks better on paper." He smiled and let me work for an M.A. along with my teaching. I did a little more experimental work and made some additions to the thesis I had written in Cambridge, and offered this as part of the requirement for an M.A. degree. It was found to be acceptable and I was awarded the M.A. degree in 1923.

From Toronto I went to Montreal, where I was appointed research psychologist for the Canadian National Committee for Mental Hygiene, to work with Professor J. Winfred Bridges on the problem of juvenile delinquency. A year later, when the McGill University Nursery School was opened for child study, I was requested to carry on psychological research there. It was at this nursery school, and at two foundling hospitals in Montreal, that I made studies forming the basis of my book, *The Social and Emotional Development of the Preschool Child* (1931). I taught developmental psychology to medical students specializing in pediatrics and was promoted in 1929 to the position of assistant professor of abnormal psychology in the McGill School of Medicine. This was a unique occurrence. I marvel still that it ever happened. I was only the second woman to be appointed to a faculty position in the School of Medicine. The first was Dr. Maud Abbot, associate professor of medicine, and a noted heart specialist. We were good friends, and walked beside each other in academic robes on Degree Day, or Commencement.

I became very conscious of my need for a doctorate to make any further progress, either in academic psychology or the growing field of applied psychology. I felt, however, that I could not, in all fairness, try for a degree at McGill and put my friends and colleagues in the embarrassing position of having to pass or fail me upon examination. To solve this problem I applied for admission as a doctoral candidate at the University of Montreal. This was a French Canadian university, and all lectures were delivered in French. My knowledge of the language was only at a high-school level. But my French Canadian friends kindly offered to help me with the French language. I was accepted as a candidate for a D. Phil. degree in psychology. Part of my study requirement was a tutorial course on Thomasian philosophy with Père Forêt, Dean of the Faculty of Philosophy. He was a genial person, with a kindly smile. He had patience with my halting French and encouraged me in my work. I had to go to the Dominican monastery for my tutorials, as Père Forêt was a priest of that order. He wore a white habit and open sandals on his bare feet, even in the cold Canadian winter.

It was very unusual at that time for a woman to be admitted to a monastery, and I was made conscious of this fact throughout my tutorial series. The first day, when I pulled the heavy chain that rang the doorbell, a solemn-looking face appeared at the narrow window in the door. Then the door was opened a crack and I was asked my business, in French. I told the doorkeeper that I had an appointment with Père Forêt. He admitted me and told me, abruptly, to go to the right. I walked down a long hall and met Père Forêt, who came to greet me with a welcoming smile. He conducted me to a confessional box and bade me sit at the side of it. He sat inside, and we conversed through an open window between us. The same procedure was repeated on subsequent occasions.

My work at McGill University had been reduced to part-time in the early 1930s, so I spent the spring of 1931 in France, studying at the Alliance Française and with Professors Piéron and Wallon at the Sorbonne. Professor Wallon took me to Perray Vaucluse, to see the institution for mentally deficient children, where Alfred Binet and Théodore Simon had studied learning abilities and had devised their scales of intelligence. Dr. Théodore Simon was still working there. He welcomed me cordially, showed me round the austere premises, and invited me to use his scale for testing one of the children. I accepted the invitation, and was gratified to find that the child understood what I said with an English accent.

In July 1934, I submitted my thesis, "The Emotional Development of the

Preschool Child," for the doctoral degree. The oral examination was held in a large lecture hall. All teaching staff and members of the university convocation were invited to attend a doctoral examination. There were representatives present from the arts, the sciences, philosophy, and medicine at my examination. The benches in the tiered lecture room were nearly three-quarters full of learned men, wearing academic robes or monastic habits. The provost of the university and the deans sat in the front row. The whole examination was conducted in French. Anyone might ask me questions. There were some from the monastic philosophers that certainly put me to the test.

At the end of the required time, the provost and other dignitaries left the room to discuss the merit of my performance. I stood facing the convocation of men, some of whom were chatting together. The period of waiting may have been only about ten minutes, but it seemed like an eternity to me. Eventually the side door opened and Père Forêt came forward with a smile on his face, leading the others. He bowed to me saying, "Madame, j'ai l'honneur de vous présenter le docorat en philosophie, avec distinction." Then he held out his hand and shook mine. That was one of the most ecstatic moments of my life. Next morning, French-Canadian newspapers had large headlines: "Une Jeune Fille Soutient une Thèse." This, apparently, had never happened before. I was the first woman to obtain a D. Phil. at the University of Montreal.

That degree has served a good purpose for me ever since. Two years later I was invited to take a position as psychologist and director of psychological services in the schools of the city of Leicester, England. This was a temporary position during the absence of Dr. Raymond B. Cattell, who was on leave to work with the British Eugenics Board. I accepted it and went to England, presumably just for a year. At the end of that time Raymond Cattell was invited to New York to work with Professor Edward Thorndike. He relinquished his position in England, and I was asked to stay on. The Second World War broke out in 1939, and civilian travel across the Atlantic was severely restricted until its end in 1945.

It was not until late in 1942 that a passage became available for me, on a troop ship carrying soldiers on leave, or those wounded in battle. I took this opportunity to return to Montreal. On my arrival, I learned that there were no vacancies in the psychology department at McGill University, and no positions for psychologists in the school systems. I did, however, manage to obtain a part-time position as clinical psychologist at the Montreal Institute for Mental Hygiene, at a salary of $90.00 a month. When an assistant psychiatrist left, my position was made full-time at a salary of $125.00 a month. It was difficult to live on that small income in the city of Montreal.

Word must have got around that I had returned from England, for I received an invitation from Dr. Robert R. Sears to fill a position at the State University of Iowa that had been vacated by Dr. Harold Skeels. He was serving in the U.S. Air Force. The duties sounded to be most attractive, and the salary of $2,600.00 a year was a considerable improvement over mine in Montreal. I accepted the offer, and for the following two years I was director of psychological services for the Iowa Board of Control and research associate at the State University. Part of my work involved traveling across the state to visit homes where infants had been placed for adoption. I evaluated their progress in mental development and in adjustment. This was a wonderful introduction to the American life-style in rural areas.

While in Iowa I attended a special meeting of the American Psychological Association at Evanston, Illinois. I was then a member of the Standards Committee. Dr. Florence Goodenough told me about the work of the International Council of Women Psychologists and their concern for the problems of women and children during wartime. She urged me to join, and I did so. For several years I served on the Membership Committee and on the Board of Directors of the Council. I was elected president in 1954, but had to resign before I could take office because of my mother's illness.

When Dr. Skeels returned to Iowa City in 1945, I went to Trenton, New Jersey, to occupy a new position as psychologist for the New Jersey State Board of Children's Guardians. Dr. Yepsen, in the New Jersey Department of Institutions and Agencies, told me that a male psychologist had been sought, but as none was available with suitable qualifications and experience I was offered the position. My duties were similar to those in Iowa, supervising psychological services in institutions for delinquent or mentally deficient children and examining infants for adoption placement.

I had scarcely been in New Jersey a year, when one of my superiors in the State Department, Dr. Quinter Holsopple, invited me to meet Dr. Donald K. Adams, a professor of psychology at Duke University. He was looking for a clinical psychologist to help start a clinical training program in the psychology department at Duke. I was interested to hear this. I had reached middle age, and it was appropriate for me to think in terms of helping to train younger psychologists.

Dr. Adams invited me to visit him and his wife, Naomi, in Durham, North Carolina. I went there in June 1946 and was shown the beautiful Gothic buildings on the university campus, the winding red-clay roads through the wooded countryside, and I was introduced to several deans and members of the University faculty. They greeted me in a friendly manner and made me feel that this was a setting in which I could work happily. I enjoyed my work in New Jersey and was not unhappy there. But I felt that university life would offer more scope for the future.

Dean Wannamaker offered me a position as associate professor of psychology, with duties requiring part-time teaching, and part clinical work, research, and writing. I accepted this, and went to take up residence in Durham in September 1946. Dr. Wally Reichenberg-Hackett came shortly after, as visiting lecturer for the year. We were the first two women faculty members in the Department of Psychology. I was the first to be granted tenure and Dr. Reichenberg-Hackett was promoted to a full professorship before her retirement in 1965.

Starting the clinical training program, along with Dr. Donald Adams, Louis D. Cohen, and Dr. Reichenberg-Hackett was a challenge to all of us. It brought me new experiences and much personal satisfaction. But, in the course of time, I was required to do more teaching of introductory psychology to undergraduates and less clinical work and research supervision in the graduate program. A vacancy occurred for a senior psychologist in the North Carolina State Board of Public Welfare, Division of Psychological Services. I applied for this, and was accepted to the position of Acting Director of the Division of Psychological Services. Duties involved traveling to county welfare departments across the state, consulting with superintendents and social workers concerning psychological problems of children, testing their intelligence levels, and evaluating infants for adoption placement. I enjoyed the work and found the whole experience uplifting and morale-boosting. The orderliness of the state government work, under the leadership of Commissioner Ellen Winston, I found very congenial, and the clinical work made me feel useful. I was doing something with psychology, not just talking about it. The only part of the experience that I found tiring, and somewhat of a strain, was the long hours of automobile driving from county to county and back to Raleigh. I knew, as I grew older, that this task would become harder rather than easier. So, after a trial year, I returned to Duke University. Coming in contact with social and psychological problems in the wider community had given me fresh ideas for research and public service.

Following my retirement from teaching at Duke University in 1967, I did psychological evaluations of infants in a rehabilitation project at the North Carolina Cerebral Palsy Hospital. It was directed for a three-year period by Miss Edna M. Blumenthal, a physical therapist. This highlighted the need for more effective instruments for measuring different aspects of mental ability in young children, social, emotional, and motor development. To fill some of this need, I devised two or three simple rating scales.

Looking back on the years, I do not think that the fact, in itself, of being a woman has interfered with my progress as a psychologist. If I lost out in any competitive situation, there were always other factors that had to be taken into consideration. I have often done "chore jobs" in connection with my professional work, but that was probably because I was willing to do them. I could have been less cooperative and said "no" when asked, if I had chosen to do so. But it was a personal satisfaction to me to feel that my services were wanted. I think that a woman psychologist can make important contributions to the science and practice of psychology, partly because of the fact that she is a woman, with biological and cultural assets in her favor, her viability, and her concern regarding family affairs.

REFERENCES

Banham, K. M. *See* Representative Publications.

Dexter, T. F. G. and A. H. Garlick. 1898. *Psychology in the Schoolroom.* London and New York: Longmans Green.

James, W. 1890. *The Principles of Psychology.* Vols. 1 and 2. New York: Holt.

McDougall, W. 1908. *An Introduction to Social Psychology.* London: Methuen.

Myers, C. S. 1911. *An Introduction to Experimental Psychology.* Cambridge, England: Cambridge University Press.

Stout, G. F. 1899. *Manual of Psychology.* London: H. K. Lewis.

Titchener, E. B. 1910. *A Text Book of Psychology.* New York: Macmillan.

Representative Publications by Katharine M. Banham

1925.   Some observations on contrariness or "negativism." *Mental Hygiene*, 9:521–28.

1926a. A form of psycho-genic tiredness. *Mental Hygiene*, 10:90–101.

1926b. With J. W. Bridges. A psychological study of juvenile delinquency by group methods. *Genetic Psychology Monographs*, 1:(5)410–506.

1927a. Factors contributing to juvenile delinquency. *Journal of Criminal Law and Criminology*, 17:531–80.

1927b. Critical notes on mental tests for children of pre-school age. *Pedagogical Seminary*, 34:38–44.

1927c. The occupational interests of three-year-old children. *Pedagogical Seminary*, 34:415–523.

1928.   A pre-school character rating chart. *The Psychological Clinic*, 17:61–72.

1929.   The occupational interests and attention of four-year-old children. *Pedagogical Seminary*, 36:551–70.

1930.   A genetic theory of the emotions. *Journal of Genetic Psychology*, 37:514–27.

1931.   *The Social and Emotional Development of the Preschool Child*. London: Kegan Paul.

1932a. Emotional development in early infancy. *Child Development*, 3:324–41.

1932b. Age and emotion. *The McGill News*, 14:36–38.

1933.   A study of social development in early infancy. *Child Development*, 4:36–49.

1934a. Measuring emotionality in infants. *Child Development*, 5:36–40.

1934b. L'age et les émotions. *L'Union Médicale du Canada*, 63:878–82.

1934c. Le type émotionnel chez le jeune enfant. *L'Année Psychologique*, XXXVe, 1:158–66.

1935.   Le développement des émotions chez le jeune enfant. Monograph published as a series of seven articles. *L'Union Médicale du Can-*

ada, 64:15–19, 130–39, 374–84, 491–502, 745–54, 862–76, 1219–29.

1936a.   Le développement des émotions chez le jeune enfant. *Journal de Psychologie XXXIIIe*, 1–2:40–87.

1936b.   The development of the primary drives in infancy. *Child Development*, 7:40–58.

1937.   The education of retarded and difficult children in the Leicester Schools. Ed., Leicester Education Committee. Leicester, England.

1940.   A social behavior scale for elementary school children. *British Journal of Educational Psychology*, 10:224–26.

1944.   Rehabilitating problem children. Iowa State Board of Control.

1950.   The development of affectionate behavior in infancy. *Journal of Genetic Psychology*, 76:283–89.

1951.   Senescence and the emotions: A genetic theory. *Journal of Genetic Psychology*, 78:175–83.

1952.   Obstinate children are adaptable. *Mental Hygiene*, 36:84–89.

1955.   Recreation for older people. *North Carolina Public Welfare News*, 17:6–7.

1956.   Estimating social incompetence in adults. *Mental Hygiene*, 40:427–37.

1958a.   With Edna M. Blumenthal. A cerebral palsied infant under treatment. *Physical Therapy Review*, 38:323–26.

1958b.   Maturity level for reading readiness. *Educational Psychology Measurement*, 18:371–75.

1967.   *Fifty Years On—Remunerated work and Hobbies for Mature Women*. Durham, N.C.: Altruss Club.

1972a.   Activity level of retarded cerebral palsied children. *Exceptional Children* (April), pp. 641–43.

1972b.   Progress in mental development of retarded cerebral palsied infants. *Exceptional Children* (November), p. 240.

1973.   Social and emotional adjustment of retarded cerebral palsied infants. *Exceptional Children* (October), p. 107.

1976.   Progress in motor development of retarded cerebral palsied infants. *Rehabilitation Literature*. Vol. 37.

1978.   Measuring functional motor rehabilitation of cerebral palsied infants and young children. *Rehabilitation Literature*. Vol. 39.

TESTS

1950. School readiness inventory. Educational Test Bureau, Minneapolis.

1952. Social competence inventory for adults. Family Life Publications, Durham, N.C.

1959. Maturity level for school entrance and reading readiness. Educational Test Bureau and American Guidance Service, Minneapolis.

1963. Quick screening scale of mental development. Psychometric Affiliates, Chicago.

1965. Ring and peg tests of behavior development. Psychometric Affiliates, Chicago. Revised 1975.

1968. Social competence inventory for older persons. Family Life Publications, Durham, N.C.

MYRTLE B. MCGRAW

At the outset let it be said that both the place and the timing of my borning exercised considerable impact through the years both upon my education and the selection of my career.

The place of my aborning was on the outskirts of Birmingham, Alabama. The time, August 1, 1899, was during the predawn of the nineteenth century. My grandparents were of the Civil War generation. The war had left turmoil, destruction, and confusion in its wake. The challenge confronting the first post-Civil War generation, the generation to which my parents belonged was how to pick up the pieces and bring some order out of the chaos. Despite a lack of formal education many at the time achieved workable efficiency and independence. It was not altogether uncommon to find persons of success and distinction in that post-Civil War generation who could not read or write. Still, many members of the second-post-Civil War generation, including myself, became motivated toward formal education.

Here, for the sake of clarity, may I ask the reader, especially the young reader of today, to think of two aspects of education: First of all, there are the organized, institutionalized systems of training for particular purposes or objectives, such as schools, colleges, and universities. It is this type of education we generally think of when we use the word education. Second, there is that broad, informal system of education that derives merely from meeting the demands of living and providing for the necessities and certain extras when we learn not from an authorized teacher but through a process of osmosis through communication within and between the generations.

EDUCATION

Having been born in the southland at a time when it had not yet recovered sufficiently from the war to have enough public schools, my basic education was rather haphazard. Perhaps a few sentences of explanation is justifiable before trying to explain my choice of psychology as an area of specialization.

I entered the public school first grade at about the age of six. The first three years were a complete bore. What I learned then was the art of day-dreaming, wondering what it would be like when I really grew up. I managed to finish the sixth grade and then I became what would in these days be called a "drop-out," i.e., I didn't complete the eight grades that were at the time considered a formal education.

Having noticed that some young women were being employed as secretaries in business offices, I registered for a course in typing and shorthand in a local school for business training. After finishing that course I was employed in a small law office where I worked for more than two years. Because of my interest in reading, the lawyer suggested that I should further my formal education and he arranged for me to be admitted to Snead Seminary, a Methodist boarding school, where I could work in the office of the headmistress to cover expenses. Thereupon, I was launched upon the pursuit of secondary and higher education, which extended for many years.

During my sophomore year there I received a copy of a magazine called *The Independent* (long since defunct), which contained an article about John Dewey entitled "The Teacher of Teachers." John Dewey was at the time a professor at Columbia University in New York City. I wrote him a fan letter. I assume he was so puzzled that a young teenage girl in the mountains of Alabama had even heard of him that he answered. We corresponded for well over a year until he left for a sojourn of several years to China.

There were others—many others—who, through suggestions, recommendations, introductions, and otherwise, helped me in my pursuit of higher education. The necessity of combining job-earning opportunity together with course study were factors to be always taken into account. In any event, after graduating from Snead Seminary I went to Ohio and the following fall was registered at Ohio Wesleyan University, with the promise of part-time work in the office of the Department of Education as a typist. In that office overhearing the discussions between professors and their students provided a valuable addition to the formal education that was taking place in my course work. At the end of my four years there I left with an A.B. degree in hand and dreams again focused on Columbia University.

In 1923 I registered at Teachers College, Columbia University, but still without a clear idea of a career. Influenced by the counsel of devoted friends, Teachers College alumni, I declared for a major in religious education. Within a few weeks I was aware that I had made the wrong choice. In the spring a solution came. A man arrived recruiting graduate students to teach in a United States "government school" in Puerto Rico.

In 1925 I returned to Columbia University with the firm decision to make psychology my major subject. It was then that the twenties were becoming known, in academic circles, as the "Era of the Child." The Rockefeller Foundation was providing funding to research institutes for the study of children at many different universities throughout the land. Once again circumstances and the ever-pressing job demand influenced ultimately the particular aspect of psychology in which I would find my career. The Institute of Child Development at Teachers College was just being established under the direction of Dr. Helen Woolley, who had come to Teachers College from the Merrill-Palmer Institute. I was hired by Dr. Bess Cunningham, the director of research (who had been an instructor in child psychology at Teachers College), as "research assistant." This was a glorious title, but my main function was to corral infants and young children as experimental subjects for the regular research staffers. It was a full-time job, but I was allowed to register for courses at available hours. I worked there for two years and learned a lot.

During this time I met Larry K. Frank, secretary general of the General Education Board of the Rockefeller Foundation. In 1927, Frank offered me a Laura Spelman Rockefeller fellowship so that I could finish the required course work without the diversion of holding a full-time job. Having completed the course requirements for the Ph.D. during that year but still needing to do research for the thesis, I accepted in September 1927 a teaching job in the psychology department at Florida State College for Women. The position provided me with teaching experience and the possibility to conduct my thesis research. I accomplished both objectives, but was still confronted with the necessity of analyzing the data and writing the thesis manuscript.

At that time the two "theoretical schools" of psychology most talked about were Behaviorism and Freudianism. Since my exposure to clinical psychology had been limited I sought and was appointed to a position as a "psychology intern" at the Institute for Child Guidance, under the direction of Dr. Lawson Lowrey and Dr. David Levy. The tasks of the psychology interns included administering numerous standardized tests to the patients, report writing, and attending case conferences. The work load was heavy, nonetheless I did manage, during that year, to get my thesis manuscript written and submitted to my Graduate Committee at Columbia. So the time has come to call a halt on further discussion of my long pursuit for general, formal education and preparation for a career in psychology.

CAREER

During 1929 the nation was thrown into a state of shock by the sudden Wall Street monetary crash. Obviously neither I nor my non-existent financial reserves could be directly affected by that appalling event. But as the weeks and months passed by I began to realize that even secondary staff positions would not be easily available in the clinical and experimental areas. So I decided to hit the job-hunting trail. For several years I had been awestruck by the mountain of brick at West 168th Street, New York City, which housed a cluster of medical departments and institutes known as the Columbia-Presbyterian Medical Center. I found my way to the office of Dr. Adolph Elwyn, (with whom I had previously taken a course in neuroanatomy) located in Physicians and Surgeons, the training school for medical students. He suggested that I go to see Dr. Frederic Tilney, Director of the Neurological Institute, who was known to have a number of different investigations going on under his supervision.

By appointment I arrived for the interview with Tilney. It was fairly lengthy and consisted mostly of probing on his part. As I started to leave he reminded me that I had not been hired and said he would phone me. After three or more weeks of waiting by the telephone, the anxiety overcame me, so I phoned his secretary. Her immediate response was that Dr. Tilney wanted to see me, and she set up an appointment. The second interview was brief. Tilney explained that he planned to extend his animal studies, on the correlation of the nervous system and behavior, to the human level and he needed someone to provide him with protocol for infant behavior development beginning with the newborn. Then he added that I was hired and should report for duty September 1, 1930. Thus was initiated the beginning of the most exciting, challenging, and informative twelve years of my professional career. (Note: Later I was told that such strategies were part of Tilney's technique for appraising personnel candidates.)

The thirties were the decade of the Great Depression. There was a sense of uncertainity even among secondary personnel in academic institutions. In any event I had a job assignment for a year—how much longer no one could tell. Dr. Tilney was the only person with supervisory authority over the proposed project. For days, even weeks, he couldn't be reached by phone or otherwise—he was too busy. At long last I received a message that I should meet him in the office of Dr. Benjamin Watson, Director of Obstetrics and Gynecology. He explained to Dr. Watson what it was he wanted me to do which would involve Dr. Watson's department. Then he skillfully let me know that from there on out I was on my own. Clearly he did not want to have one of his underlings to get to be dependent and running to him continuously.

The problem of setting up an operating arrangement for the longitudinal study of infants was colossal, especially since it involved setting up managerial and diplomatic arrangements in such a way as to overcome regulations and constraints of several different departments of the medical center.

Initially an attending physician at the Neurological Institute was appointed administrative director of the general project. That appointment was essential for us to even get started on the organization of a laboratory and experimental procedures. He had easy access to Dr. Tilney and other members of the medical profession throughout the Center. Since he had no personal plans for participating in the actual research he could probably pick up and report more frank opinions from them than I could obtain by direct interview, also he could report and sign for our anticipated needs. One day he came to tell me that Dr. Tilney had arranged with Dr. Herbert Wilcox, director of Babies Hospital, for floor space to set up the laboratory in Babies Hospital. A great leap on the way to organization. So we began to concentrate on other hurdles to be overcome—laboratory personnel, facilities, and the transportation of infants from nursery and home for sequential observations.

But the man who gave the needed boost in this direction was L. K. Frank who had dropped in one day to see how things were going. He told me that he would provide for two interns to work with us for a year, during which time we should consolidate our study plans and draw up a written application to the General Education Board for long-term funding. Both promises materialized.

Once, while talking to Dr. Tilney about how I could possibly find a way to record the spontaneous vocalizations of the growing infant, he suggested that I go see Mr. Kelley, manager of the Bell Telephone Laboratory, and ask his advice. When I went on that first occasion I had hardly spoken to Mr. Kelley five minutes until he had me sitting around a table with about eight men. He announced, "These are engineers, tell them your problem." The proposals were many, the discussion lengthy, and not much of which I could understand. Nothing concrete came out of their suggestions because the design of such equipment would be more costly than our slender budget could accomodate. A year or more went by. Notwithstanding the outcome that initial visit to the Bell Laboratory proved to be an event of a lifetime.

Once the research interns, proposed by L. K. Frank, had been selected and were on the staff there was an upsurge in organizational activity. New proposals were made. One was that since Dr. Tilney was concerned with the cellural development of the brain and nervous system and we with overt behavior development why not try to record the brain waves (then called the Berger rhythm, since known as the alpha wave) of infants from the newborn through the preschool years. A good idea. I advised the two interns to go to the Bell Telephone Laboratory to get information as to how it could be done. For weeks on end they went down there practically every day. Then I noticed that they weren't going to the Bell Laboratory anymore. Instead one of the engineers, R. F. Mallina, whom I had met on my first visit, was coming to our place to help the young men assemble the necessary apparatus for the recording of brain waves of infants and prelinguistic children. Naturally, I was gratified and the engineer and I became friends. All the activities reported took place during the early years of the Great Depression. Apparently a depression can bring forth ingenuity, good will, and cooperation between individuals and institutions of diversity.

With the long-term grant from the General Education Board the laboratory thrived throughout the depression years. As soon as functional operation of the laboratory had been achieved it was officially recognized and given the title of "Normal Child Development Study." One of the ranking physicians of Babies Hospital, Dr. Ashley Weech, was appointed director and I became associate director. On the part of some present-day readers there may occur the impression of discrimination against women. Not so. At that time physicians represented a most prestigious profession. Not only the director but younger physicians on the pediatric staff were given responsibility for the physical examinations and health care of all infants who came to the laboratory. These services were volunteered by the Department of Pediatrics. No Ph.D. psychologist could possibly have inspired such comparable confidence on the part of parents to yield their infants as "subjects" of investigation. Furthermore, it freed the investigative staff to explore additional areas of study with infants and young children.

One of the major controversies in psychology at the time was a dichotomy "maturation vs. learning." It occurred to me that if we could provide daily practice in those activities in which the infant had some capability we might determine a time when it would be possible to state when a program of training would be profitable. That prospect necessitated bringing some infants, preferably twins, to the laboratory every day for a period of years. The study was undertaken and was reported in 1935 in *Growth: A Study of Johnny and Jimmy*. Despite the Great Depression the laboratory activities were flourishing; attracting the interest of professionals of diverse disciplines, concerned laymen, journalists, and news reporters. This interest led to some difficulties. In line with the medical ethics of the day publicity was not sought after but rather to be avoided. A young reporter from *Life* magazine was permitted to interview me for an article as long as my name was not used.

At the end of the decade of the thirties there were several episodes which could have been interpreted as reflecting a bias against women in psychology. *Growth: A Study of Johnny and Jimmy* had been published in 1935. Many of the psychological textbooks during the immediately succeeding years never cited that publication in their references. Instead, if they made any reference to our laboratory work, they were more likely to quote some newspaper report of an APA session or of some demonstration of the infants which had been arranged for a select audience in the amphitheater of Babies Hospital. I never interpreted the rejection of the textbook writers as indicating a position against women in psychology. Instead I thought of it as a rejection of my methodology of studying overt behavior development in infants. The only methods available to me were direct observation and filming—a divergence from the requirements of "objectivity, measurement, and quantification" advocated by most professors in my field. Sometimes such remarks as: "She's a nice young woman sentimental about babies, but she's no scientist," floated back to me. I didn't let them upset me too much. After all, my interpretation of process, the interconnection of forces and systems, and the synthesis of multiple forces and systems in neuromotor development had the endorsement of Dewey, Tilney, and Frank.

SUPPORT FACTORS

It would be grossly unfair to leave the reader with just any image built up of Frederic Tilney from my remarks in earlier paragraphs. Tilney might appear tough in his handling of young personnel, but once convinced of a person's qualifications and dedication to the goals he would do everything conceivable to promote the underling's efforts and his self-confidence.

L. K. Frank had a burning ambition, specifically to bring about a synthesis of the biological and the behavioral and social theories or "models" of child development. Once, when he and John Dewey were having lunch together, he mentioned that the General Education Board was contemplating the liquidation of its principal. He would like to propose that they make the donation to Columbia-Presbyterian Medical Center, then our laboratory at Babies Hospital could become a nucleus offering the opportunity for every department to concentrate investigation or experimentation on the same child subjects. I expressed a dim view of the proposal, stating that large amounts of inexhaustible funding did not always promote investigative ingenuity, and that the outcome might be that each department of the Medical Center might spend its energy struggling to see who would get the largest piece of the pie. Perhaps I was fearful that our laboratory, which was going along so well, would be swallowed up in the transformation. Both Dewey and Tilney endorsed my speaking out forthrightly, despite what they might have thought of my fund-raising aptitudes.

John Dewey's influence over my personal, intellectual, and career development was so extensive, intensive, and profound that it is absurd to mention it in a couple of sentences in a manuscript. Some years ago a man came to interview me about Dewey. We made a tape of the interview which was headed for the Dewey Archives. (Note: I can't recall the name of the interviewer or the location of the archives. Reference books probably have them listed.)

There were many other persons and episodes which were "support factors" in my education and career development. In fact too many to enumerate. One man mentioned above deserved discussion. At first it was difficult to decide whether it should fall under Support Factors, or the following category, "Personal and Professional Adjustments." Finally I selected the latter.

PERSONAL AND PROFESSIONAL ADJUSTMENTS

In 1936 Rudolph Mallina and I were married. I did not want a church wedding, and just to have a clerk at the license bureau seemed inappropriate for the event. After inquiry I learned that in New York State a law was enacted just after the First World War providing for marriage by contract. At that time only one previous couple had been married under the contract law. It was the answer. A lawyer drew up the contract for us. The ceremony took place in the home of John Dewey, his son, and daughter-in-law. All the persons mentioned above were invited and many others. Theodora Abel (the psychologist and a lifelong friend) and Arthur E. Burns (an economist friend) served as witnesses to the contract and John Dewey made a moving talk on the meaning of marriage. Rudi and I verbally expressed our vows. It was a joyous occasion, with both a magnificent dinner and stimulating conversation.

In 1937 our daughter was born. The following year, 1938, we moved to a house in the suburbs (the same one I am living in now). New decisions were confronting us. However, there are occasions when events with which one is not directly connected can make decisions for one.

During the last quarter of the thirties and the beginning of the forties the general atmosphere in this country was becoming ominous and uncertain, worse in Europe. In the laboratory the question prevailed as to whether or not it could continue beyond the terminal date of the General Education Board grant. Staff members were looking for, or one by one leaving for, other occupations. I was busy compiling a manuscript which Columbia University Press had agreed to publish dealing with the subject of neuro-muscular maturation of the human infant. In general, funding foundations seemed less enthusiastic about supporting funds for academic investigations of infant development; other subjects were more pressing. Dr. Ashley Weech, the director, and other pediatric physicians, of course, were still around because they belonged to the department of pediatrics. For months I had been pondering the conflict of pursuing a career and doing justice by my family as suburban wife and mother. Then in 1941 the sudden attack by the Japanese on Pearl Harbor: our nation was at war. That determined my decision. I stayed on until early 1942 to attend to the preservation of records and the dismantling of laboratory facilities. The thirties had been a glorious decade when the babies had been my teacher. Now I should use what I learned to take care of my own. The decision was made.

Diverse occupational opportunities for women have been advancing at an amazing rate during this century. It has been brought about by the rapid changes in social reorganization, as well as functional and institutional changes brought about by scientific and technological production. The women's movement enhanced it. There is every prospect that these trends will continue into the next century. It behooves not only psychologists but professional women of all disciplines to begin thinking now about redesigning institutions and training personnel to provide for the psychological and physiological development of future generations of infants and young children.

As professionals we must learn to read the signals of change in our society. The life span is being extended into the nineties and one hundreds. The question is: how can women contribute to the reorganization of society so that members of every generation, including the young and the old, are productive, interrelated, and at the same time functional—from the beginning and throughout a life span.

A word to young readers. The report of my growing up in the earlier decades does not necessarily provide guidelines for you today because our society has changed incredibly since that time. Furthermore, it is continuously changing. Items written a few decades ago may be completely out-of-date by the time your generation comes along. Don't be fearful of questioning. Face criticism as well as praise: perhaps the most disturbing reaction to one's performance or thinking is to be considered by others as too naive to justify evaluative criticism.

Representative Publications by
Myrtle B. McGraw

1935. *Growth: A Study of Johnny and Jimmy.* New York: Appleton-Century. Rpt. New York: Arno Press, 1975.

1939. Swimming behavior of the human infant. *Journal of Pediatrics,* 15:485–490.

1939b. Later development of children specially trained during infancy: Johnny and Jimmy at school age. *Child Development* (March), 10(1):1–19.

1940. Neural maturation as exemplified in achievement of bladder control. *Journal of Pediatrics,* 16:580–590.

1943. Let babies be our teachers. In *The March of Medicine.* New York: Columbia University Press.

1945. *Neuro-Muscular Maturation of the Human Infant.* New York: Columbia University Press. Rpt. New York: Hafner, 1963.

1946. Maturation of behavior. In L. Carmichael, *Manual of Child Psychology.* 1st ed. only. New York: Wiley.

RUTH W. HOWARD

I was born in our nation's capital, Washington, D.C., the youngest of eight siblings. My father was a Protestant clergyman. Before marriage my mother was a teacher in a one-room rural school. After marriage her life was devoted to homemaking and child rearing. I was born at the beginning of the century when the family's youngest were "seen and not heard." I followed that pattern. But I used my eyes and sometimes my ears. As soon as I could read I attempted to read everything in sight. Much of it I could not comprehend.

The home was full of books and periodicals. Some were of a general nature; others were related to a profession. My father had theological periodicals; my physician brother had medical literature. My schoolteacher sisters had educational magazines, some of which related to the specific fields of music, nature study, or literature, according to the subject each taught. The daily paper was banned when I asked the meaning of "ransom," which I could pronounce but not understand. My elders recognized that the word was used in a kidnapping story which they thought was not good for me to read.

Fortunately I was given books suitable for my reading age and interest. Among my first books, the ones I remember best were from a series, "Our Cousins": *My Indian Cousins, Our German Cousins*, etc., which were stories of children in different lands. I identified with their countries and ways of life. The existence of the children to whom I was introduced in a book became even more real to me when I drove by foreign embassies in Washington.

Reading took precedence over playing with dolls. My siblings were too old to be my playmates, and there were no children in the neighborhood.

At age six I made my first trip to the public library unaccompanied by an adult. Proudly I held my very own library card in my hand. I announced to the librarian that I wished to take out a book entitled A *Short History of England*. I did not know whether it was a child's book, but I did know that its title was similar to some books in our bookcases at home. Suppressing a smile, the librarian went to the library stacks and took out a book with a title comparable to the one for which I asked. And I went home pleased that I could use my library card by myself.

I enjoyed books and reading so much, my first vocational choice was to be a librarian. During a summer vacation while I was in college I had the opportunity to experience being a librarian. I spent the vacation with a sister who lived in Harrisburg, the capital of Pennsylvania. I served as a volunteer intern at the state library, where I was assigned to the catalogue division. This experience was helpful in my later use of libraries.

Although I still loved books and reading, enthusiasm for a librarian's vocation faded during my last year at Howard University. It was displaced by my interest in people, especially those persons termed "disadvantaged," who could not cope with problems of poverty, limited education, and lack of skills.

Again my family influenced me. My clergyman father had an office at the church, but a number of people came to the home to consult him. Some were social workers; some were persons with problems seeking advice. I did not know exactly why they came, but I sensed that it concerned someone in trouble. This focus on people with various problems made me want to work to alleviate their problems. I decided that social work was the best approach. So I applied to the National Urban League for a fellowship. In September 1920, I enrolled in the social work division of Simmons College, Boston. Simmons had a broad curriculum encompassing different aspects and techniques of social work. In addition to the regular staff there were lecturers, consultants, and seminar leaders from universities, government, and social agencies in greater Boston.

For some classmates field work meant a great social adjustment, because this was their first contact with different ethnic groups and the underprivileged. For me, this was not a cultural shock because I am a Negro, and I had experienced contact with the socially deprived.

Studying social work at Simmons offered many opportunities for broadening my experiences and testing my attitudes and concepts. This was my first school experience away from hometown Washington where government was the chief occupation and interest.

Also at Simmons I was introduced to a new concept of the role of women at work. Today this sounds naive, but in the first quarter of the century the pattern was different. Then women in the executive and legislative parts of the government were unusual. Those working at the "white collar" levels were teachers or clerks. Below them were domestic workers. On the Simmons staff was Dr. Lucille Eaves, who may be called one of my mentors. In Boston she directed an agency where "women in industry" was promoted.

The Urban League scholarship included a summer session related to social research. This was done under the guidance of Dr. Charles Johnson, sociologist of the National Urban League office. The locale of my assignment was a small Long Island community. I observed the physical makeup of the area, types of people seen on the streets, and their activities. I saw young males, not attending summer school or working. When I was in view they concentrated on me, a young woman stranger whose purpose in being there was a mystery to them. Attempts to engage an individual or a group in conversation were largely unproductive. This community study revealed a need for community planning for young people during the summer in educational, recreational, and counseling programs.

EXPERIENCE AS A SOCIAL WORKER

When I completed my year of social work training I went to Cleveland, Ohio, for my first social work position. It was at the Cleveland Urban League where I counseled persons who had a variety of problems. Also I coordinated activities and created programs for community groups.

For me this position involved a new dimension of human relationships. As a case worker and counselor I focused on one person or one family group for the solution of a problem. Work with a community group involved a composite of attitudes and objectives which were to be welded together for a common goal. Neighbors may share a common concern, but they could have widely different perceptions of the problem's solution. Here I had an education in social psychology.

After leaving the Cleveland Urban League I accepted a position with the city's Child Welfare Agency. I dealt with children living with their own inadequate families or in foster homes. My work territory included different ethnic neighborhoods. I had conferences with school personnel, medical and child guidance clinics. The staff in many of these agencies didn't know about and, more important didn't understand or sympathize with cultural groups other than their own. This was markedly true about Negroes for whom they had firmly fixed preconceived ideas. They did not bother to learn about the social milieu of these people. They did not explore the abilities, attitudes, frustrations, and ambitions of the children and their guardians. Since the staff did not know about the cultural climate in which their clients lived and how it influenced their behavior, their clients' visits to the mental health clinic were of little value.

One person, the chief psychologist of the Board of Education, showed awareness of how the total environment influenced the child's feelings, attitudes, and behavior. Talks with this woman crystallized for me a growing realization that I wanted to learn the dynamics of how a person thinks, feels, and behaves. That meant the study of psychology.

Then followed the questions: Where would I study psychology? How would I support the years of study? I reviewed the financial aid I had previously received—the scholarship at Howard University and the Urban League fellowship at Simmons College.

Why not try my luck again? So, one Saturday afternoon when I was visiting my sister in New York I went to the Rockefeller Foundation. There I had a pleasant conversation with an official and related to him my specific purposes for studying psychology. In a few weeks I received a letter from the foundation awarding me a Laura Spelman Rockefeller Fellowship. In September 1929 I enrolled at Columbia University.

STUDY AND RESEARCH FOR THE DOCTORATE

The year I studied in New York I lived at International House. Because of a heavy school schedule including travel about the city and suburbs I was not free to be involved in many House activities. I did establish some meaningful relationships.

My experiences at International House included relationships with a White Russian, a South American, a white South African, and an East Indian. They were not classroom study, but they belonged in my education portfolio. These contacts widened my understanding of different cultures and their folkways.

During my New York year I had classes at Columbia's School of Education and the New York School of Social Work. At the latter school I had courses in psychology, child development, and a practicum in parent education.

One parent education group was made up of the parents of children attending the Practice School of Teachers College. The second group, which met in a New York suburb, was composed of parents and foster parents from the lower-middle class. These two groups differed culturally in some attitudes and practices in child rearing, but they were alike in wanting to be good parents.

The role of parent educator was new for me. It tested my flexibility in dramatizing the developmental levels of children and the needs of each family group. It was challenging and group response was heartening.

The teaching staff at Columbia was stimulating. For example, Dr. Goodwin Watson lectured and lived social psychology. Evenings at his home were outstanding events. There was opportunity for personal contact with several staff members. One mentor during that year was Dr. Lois Meek Stolz. I recall a conference with her when she discussed the importance of charting steps toward achieving a goal.

The Laura Spelman Rockefeller fellowship permitted me to attend two universities. At the end of the spring session in New York I transferred to the University of Minnesota. There I was registered at the Institute of Child Development, which was founded in 1925. Enrollment in the institute admits students to the programs and facilities of any university department having offerings related to the institute's objectives.

When I enrolled, the student membership was small, divided between doctoral and master candidates. All were women except for one man who remained a short time. The students in the group were from different parts of the United States and had attended many different colleges. We attended some classes together, did some of our fellowship work together, usually lunched together, and walked to and from school together because most of us lived near the university. There was a general camaraderie within the group, but naturally some persons formed closer friendships. After our child development seminar in the early evening, the group went to a nearby place for refreshments and talk.

When a student was scheduled for the oral, the critical examination for qualifying for the Ph.D., fellows gave cheer and encouragement.

Dr. Florence Goodenough was my chief adviser and mentor. She offered suggestions and guidance in a matter-of-fact, but nondictatorial, way that prompted the student to think and arrive at a judgment.

While I was at Minnesota, Dr. Goodenough was validating data on her research, the Draw-a-Man test. This research model was good for the fellows. Another staff member, Dr. Mary Shirley, also was validating data on her research, "The First Two Years: A Study of Twenty-Five Babies." It was stimulating to be close to research which was unique and so appropriate for the study of child development. Dr. Shirley was younger than most of the professors. She was understanding and warm and gave me a great deal of support.

Dr. Edna Heidbreder, with whom I had a course in the history of psychology, was a model college professor.

I did some of my fellowship work in the laboratory of Dr. Edith Boyd, the anatomist. She talked with me about bone growth, but I did no investigative work with her.

The candidate for an advanced degree gives a good deal of thought to the subject of the research to be presented as evidence of capability. As I reviewed the areas of research and my interests related to child development, I decided on a study of nature-nurture. Freeman had done research in this field. Other studies were made of twins. I decided on a study of the development of triplets because they offered three biological possibilities: (1) three single-egg persons; (2) three persons from one egg; (3) two persons from one egg and one person from another egg. Observation could be made, then, of relationships of nature and nurture. The title of the study is "The Developmental History of a Group of Triplets." The report is published in the *Journal of Genetic Psychology* (1947).

This study is based on questionnaire data obtained on 229 sets of triplets and on a more detailed examination of twenty-nine sets with whom personal contact was possible. Anthropometric measurements on the test group were made with the cooperation of the staff at the Institute of Child Development.

When I would leave Minneapolis to see several sets of triplets, nurse Ellen Church would accompany me. My relationship with her was warm. She served in several capacities at the institute. Before joining that staff, she had inaugurated the position of stewardess on commercial airlines.

Working together in trips away from the university permitted two persons, Ellen and me, to evaluate the triplets. I did the psychological; Ellen, the biological. Her warmth and expertise in several areas were helpful and furnished support. Our friendship continued after we left Minneapolis. Both of us moved to the Chicago area. On one trip she gave a seminar for my class with nurse trainees at Provident Hospital.

The staff and scholars in several university departments were generous in affording time for discussing approaches and techniques for studying nature–nurture in triplets. Dr. Miles Tinker, then active in psycho-educational test construction, helped select the types of tests best able to elicit the desired information. The dental professor affiliated with the institute shared his knowledge about early dental development.

On a very warm evening in June 1934, I marched into the University of Minnesota stadium. This was my first trip into this favorite campus spot, but on many balmy Saturday afternoons I had gazed out of my apartment window to see happy college students, alumni, and friends walking to the stadium. They were anticipating another victory for their football team. That was the era when Minnesota was champion of the Big Ten college league. I was not a part of that group because I was busy doing school assignments. On this evening I was joyfully bound for the stadium to attend graduation and receive my diploma for the Ph.D. in psychology.

FOLLOWING GRADUATION

Internship

A few months after leaving Minnesota, I married Dr. Albert Sidney Beckham, a psychologist, and moved to Chicago where he was employed. I had declined an offer for a staff appointment at a teachers college in the District of Columbia. This was appropriate for two reasons. I was marrying and joining my husband. Second, I was accepting an internship at the Illinois Institute of Juvenile Research, an affiliate of the University of Illinois Medical School located in Chicago. An internship in clinical psychology with children was the next step in training as preparation for a professional career in working with children and young people.

There were several other young interns with whom I was associated. Part of the time was spent in evaluation and therapy with clients (or patients, according to the term designated).

Clients included a juvenile who was referred because of a problem and the parent or other family member involved. Contacts were made with the teacher and social agency involved. Also there were conferences with other IJR staff members whose specialty would have input in the client's problem or situation. Following the work-up, an extended staff conference was held including all disciplines represented, psychologist, psychiatrist, social worker, community worker, and recreation specialist.

One sociologist, Saul Alinsky, was then pioneering a technique in youth therapy with street-corner groups which stimulated rehabilitation of neighborhood gangs. Another approach to community self-help was the Chicago Urban League's staff member Frayser Lane's Block Club movement. Neighbors joined together to improve their immediate block, then spread out to the larger community. Both these programs are still active, surviving the deaths of the organizers. IJR (as it is popularly known) had a two-way reach. It might begin with the child and parent referred there because of a problem. Or it could go to the neighborhood to seek resources to help the parent and child.

The IJR building was not the locale for all the internship. I also spent a period of time at a community hospital for training and experience. Another location was at a state school for delinquent girls. These two years of internship gave me experience in dealing realistically with situations, personalities, and problems.

National Youth Administration (NYA)

When I completed my internship, the Great Depression still prevailed. There were few jobs in the private sector. The federal government through state and local bodies administered a program for training youth in work skills which would be marketable in the improved economy. Adults were employed to train and supervise the youth. Remuneration for both youth trainees and adult supervisors was modest but welcomed since other employment was practically non-existent.

I was recruited for a supervisory position with NYA. Criteria for job level assignment were skill and education. My job was entitled "Director of Mental Health and Training Program." It encompassed several job descriptions. I was expected to assess the suitability of the youth's work assignment, the work progress, and the attitudes of youth workers and supervisors. Counseling was necessary when indicated.

I learned that both youth trainees and adult supervisors felt that the NYA wage was a means of at least partial self-support. It was not a dole which could defeat self-worth. The work program for all participants afforded opportunity to learn and practice new skills. Some felt degraded by the change in their life-styles. Others apparently accepted the change with some equanimity. How did individuals react? Did attitudes and behavior change with time? Did resistant persons learn to accept their situations? What could possibly trigger such an improvement? Might a psychologist introduce a technique for changing attitudes and thus create constructive behaviors? Observations of NYA personalities and their responses to environmental conditions were like case studies which might be used by the psychologist in other situations.

Through the years I have had contact with several of the youths who later were well employed and living productive lives. They spoke well of their NYA experience. Any negative attitudes were forgotten. A backward glance at interpersonal relations between youths and supervisors might be helpful. Youths who had negative experiences with teachers or employers before coming to NYA regarded supervisors as "bosses"—an unpleasant connotation. Antiethnic feelings influenced negative attitudes of some supervisors toward trainees. This was their closest contact with young people not in their own ethnic grouping.

For me the NYA experience yielded a number of positive values. My recent internship gave me keys to different agencies, neighborhood cultures, and facilities which were important to a new arrival in the city.

Professional Career as Psychologist

Appointment to the National Youth Administration was my first employment after internship. Following that I was selective of the type of professional psychological experience I wanted. Private practice with my husband, Albert Beckham, was coordinated with other schedules. We had a happy marriage with our profession as one of the bonds. In professional activities, as in marriage relations, we were partners. We named our practice in developmental and clinical psychology the Center for Psychological Service.

My first employment after NYA was in nursing education. This continued my interest in physical health fields. I served for 15 years as psychologist with the Provident Hospital School of Nursing. This hospital was formed in response to the need for a training school for Negro nurses.

When I came to the school all student nurses were young women. Some were emotionally immature. For example, they felt inadequate in giving professional orders to older patients. These students were guided into mature behavior: in the nurse-patient relation, age seniority was not relevant; situational responsibility was the key factor.

During my tenure at Provident male students were admitted. Initially, they were cautious as they entered this female territory, but soon were integrated.

For a number of years I was staff psychologist at Abraham Lincoln Centre. This agency served the needs of a thickly populated community of differing cultural and economic strata. I worked with children, parents, and staff.

CONTINUATION OF EDUCATION

As I dealt with clients in my private practice and at agencies I felt the need for refresher courses. Then I went to the nearby University of Chicago to canvas its curriculum. I was welcomed as a postdoctoral student. I could enroll in classes, practicums, and seminars on a non-fee basis. Over a period of time I enrolled in projective techniques with Dr. Robert Havighurst, client-centered therapy with Dr. Carl Rogers, reading therapy with Dr. Helen Robinson, and play therapy with Virginia Axline, who was then writing about her work.

I published an article based on my experiences in play therapy. The insights I gained in all the classes and contacts with teachers were helpful and stimulating. Probably for me reading problems were the most difficult to assess. I classified those with reading problems as belonging in the classroom with some assistance from the opthalmologist. Much later I realized the role of motivational and emotional involvement. When I probed the emotional I had a handle with which to effect therapy.

I worked with Dr. Robinson, attending lectures and seminars. Then I graduated to the Reading Clinic, tutoring children, first with supervision, and then with review by a staff person. This training experience prepared me for working in reading therapy—that is, helping people gain self-confidence. Later I joined the staff for a time.

PROFESSIONAL RELATIONSHIPS

I soon became involved with professional organizations. These included membership in APA, IPA, Chicago Psychologists, and International Council of Women Psychologists, later reorganized to include men. Other organizations with strong psychological components in which I had an interest included the International Reading Association—I found its *Research Quarterly* very pertinent—and educational groups composed of professionals and parents.

I am a long-time member of the American Association of University Women, to which I once gave a great deal of volunteer time. That organization and APA have common interests. Also in the early days of my Chicago residence I helped organize the National Association of College Women, a Negro-based group. One of its early objectives was to raise the standards of Negro colleges. That organization and APA have a common concern not just to increase the number of psychology courses and the availability of student counseling, but to help colleges meet their students' needs. In this, strides have been made, and these organizations continue to monitor the progress made toward their objectives.

Another women's organization of which I am a long-time member is Women's International League for Peace and Freedom (WILPF). Social psychology is a large part of its program.

I was invited by several civic social agencies to do volunteer service. Affiliation with these agencies gives the psychologist an opportunity to know the facilities in the community and to discreetly interpret to board members and staff the appropriate psychological needs which their programs can meet. The agencies with which I was a long-time volunteer were Young Women's Christian Association and Bartelme Homes. The latter was named for Judge Mary Bartelme, the first woman judge in Chicago's Juvenile Court. She was concerned about the psychological and personality development of girls who came through her court.

Another volunteer organization which I joined was Friends of the Mentally Ill. Some "Friends" were professionals; others were lay people concerned about patients in mental hospitals recovering from serious illnesses. We visited them, corresponded with them when they had no other contacts, and served as First Friend. My "friend" was German-born, a musician who came to the United States with her musician husband; he died after reaching here. She was lucid but very lonely. She wrote me many interesting letters which I plan to use in an article.

My college sorority Delta Sigma Theta's graduate chapter has outreach programs for girls. I think of one activity for which I served as psychological counselor.

PAST, PRESENT, AND FUTURE

I have had a long career in psychology. My first vocational choice, librarian, was based on youthful, even childhood, interests. As I matured I abandoned that. My second choice brought me satisfaction and helped me to understand myself. Then followed the search for a better understanding of the dynamics of human nature. This brought me to psychology.

Assessment of the growth and value of the discipline of psychology in affecting human progress gives us pride. Women psychologists played a substantial role in this. As pioneers, women made many contributions; some worked alone and some collaborated with their husbands or fellow staffers.

Women psychologists continue to influence programs in ways that are not recognized. For example, many marriages are now congenial partnerships in parenting because both parents have experience in psychology.

Men on the boards of management recognize the efficiency of women on the lower rungs of administration and promote their advancement. This is an example of "good salesmanship" by women. Our efficiency and readiness for larger responsibility is a commodity to be sold to whomever is a potential buyer.

Qualified women of so-called minority groups share in this advancement, in the field of psychology as well as other fields. This trend will continue because women psychologists are capable and acquit themselves well when given the chance.

I salute women psychologists as they receive recognition within their field and when they help other women attain their potential.

Representative Publications by Ruth W. Howard

1944. Fantasy and Play Interview. *Character and Personality*, 13:151–65.
1946. Intellectual and personality traits of a group of triplets. *Journal of Psychology*, 21:25–36.
1947. The developmental history of a group of triplets. *Journal of Genetic Psychology*, 70:191–204.
1955. *Faith of the Young Child*. New York: Hearthstone.
1963. Predicting Success in Nurse Training at Provident Hospital. Manuscript.
1965–1968. *Reports for Staff Bulletins*. Abraham Lincoln Centre.
1976. *Two Early Black Psychologists: Beckham and Howard*. A speech reprinted August 12.

ALICE I. BRYAN

My forebears on both sides of the family were Europeans who emigrated either to the English colonies in North America or, many years later, to the United States of America. First of my known lineage to arrive were the English ancestors of my maternal grandmother, who settled in New England. Among them were the Whipples (William Whipple was a signer of the Declaration of Independence) and the Emersons. My grandmother, Isabel Emerson, was born in Haverhill, Massachusetts, about 1850; she was a cousin, several generations removed, of Ralph Waldo Emerson.

Also of English ancestry was my maternal grandfather, Joseph Lawrance, born a few years earlier in London, England. When, at age seventeen, his parents urged him to prepare for entrance to the ministry, a vocation to which he felt no call, he left home to see the world as an apprentice seaman. He "sailed the seven seas" before settling in New York City to work as a cabinetmaker (a trade learned at sea) and to become an American citizen. After marrying Isabel Emerson, he bought a house and workshop in Jersey City Heights, New Jersey, where he established his own business. My mother, Caroline Ayer Lawrance, was born there in 1876; she was the middle child, between two brothers, Edward and Frank.

Both of my paternal grandparents were born in Europe of German parentage. My grandfather, Ewald von Bévern, whose ancestors for generations had lived in Alsace-Lorraine, was born in Berlin, Germany, about 1835. Several years later my grandmother, Cornelia Weigle, was born in Stuttgart in the kingdom of Württemberg (one of four independent, south German states) to a family of well-to-do architects and artists. After they married, my grandparents had four children: Paul, Alice (who died at twenty-one and for whom I was named), Hedwig (called Hetty, who helped me at the start of my career), and Ewald (my father, born in Stuttgart in 1871 during the Franco-German War).

After the defeat of the French army at Sedan in 1870, north and south Germany were unified by Bismark to form the new German Empire, with King William of Prussia to be called the German Emperor. France, by signing the Treaty of Frankfort in 1871, after the surrender of Paris, ceded to Germany nearly all of Alsace and eastern Lorraine. My democratically-minded grandfather, alienated by these events and convinced that the prevalent nationalism and militarism would lead to future wars, resigned from a responsible position with the North German Lloyd Steamship Company to emigrate with his family to the United States. He started a grocery importing business in St. Paul, Minnesota, changed his name legally to Ewald Bever, and became an American citizen.

After his death at age forty-nine, my grandmother, with the aid of family friends in New York, moved her teenaged children to a farm in Boonton, New Jersey, where she supplemented their income by providing lodging and country fare to summer vacationers. Paul and, later, my father found employment in New York (my father with the Citizens Savings Bank, where he stayed until retirement). Hetty, a talented musician, gave singing and piano lessons for several years before enrolling in a business school in New York.

Meanwhile, my mother, Caroline Lawrance, grew up uneventfully in the house where she was born and in time graduated from high school. Her career choices were limited: teaching or secretarial work. She chose to enter the same business school that Hetty Bever had selected; they met and became good friends. Hetty introduced Caroline to her brother Ewald and they dated occasionally. After completing her course my mother became a secretary with a law firm and began "reading law" under the guidance of her employers in preparation for taking the bar examination. In 1897, however, she married Ewald Bever, which meant giving up her job and her ambitions for a professional career. My parents lived in New York until the birth of their first child, Joseph Ewald, in August, 1899, then moved to a three-storied house, enlarged by porches and ample outdoor living space, in the Arlington section of Kearny, New Jersey.

My grandmother Bever was invited to share their home, which was within easy visiting distance from Hetty (living in Montclair, New Jersey, with her husband and two sons) and Paul (in Rutherford, New Jersey, with his wife and, eventually, five children), as well as being near to my mother's relatives. Family ties were strong and these visits were happy occasions, especially on holidays. My grandmother lived with us until her death in 1914; she was adored by everyone for her buoyant, enthusiastic temperament and her warm, loving nature. I was born at noon on September 11, 1902, and christened Alice Isabel in the Episcopal church my mother attended; my father and grandmother were Lutherans. In September 1904 my younger brother, named Ralph Waldo Emerson, arrived to complete our family.

Mine was a happy, healthy, busy childhood. My mother and grandmother were my first teachers and mentors; both loved children and because there was no kindergarten in our public school they created one for us at home. I liked to draw, use crayons and paint, and create designs on paper for rugs and wallpaper. When I was old enough, my mother arranged for me to attend an art class for children every Saturday morning at the studio of Annie and Edith Payne, one a painter and the other an art teacher in our public schools. I was given piano lessons by Aunt Hetty. Occasionally I had opportunities to play a suitable role (such as Ariel in scenes from *The Tempest*) in amateur theatrical productions of the Arlington Players Club, of which my parents were members, and in dramatic programs of the Arlington Woman's Club, of which my mother was an officer. In addition to giving us every possible chance to discover and develop our individual talents, my mother sought constantly to instill in all of her children what she considered cardinal virtues: self-reliance, initiative, perseverance, responsibility, honesty, and self-respect; whatever life work we chose, she wanted us, above all, to become good citizens.

When I reached the age of five and a half, I was permitted by the principal of the public school in our neighborhood to enter first grade on April first, an event I had long been awaiting with eagerness. I had already learned at home to read and write and was promoted in June to second grade. Later I skipped another year when, in company with several other pupils, we were given extra instruction and homework, enabling us to complete the work of the seventh and eighth grades in one year and pass the state examination for entrance to high school.

I entered Kearny High School in September 1914. New Jersey had excellent public schools. Our teachers all held or were working toward graduate degrees and the program of studies I completed provided a sound preparation for college. Although I worked hard enough to graduate near the top of my class, I had time to engage in many extracurricular activities. I served as secretary of my class, was a member of the school's debating team, twice represented my class in the school's annual prize-speaking contest, and in each of my last three years played the leading female role in the school's annually produced, three-act play. I also attended school dances and other social events. During my last year, when the United States had entered World War I, almost all my free time was spent in volunteer work for the Red Cross.

During my last term in high school, I was sent occasionally by the principal to serve as a substitute teacher in a grammar school in town because of the acute teacher shortage. Ever since I can remember, I had wanted to be a teacher. Perhaps I was influenced by my mother's high regard for her first cousin, on the Lawrance side of the family, Elizabeth Josephine Sautter, an instructor in history at the Paterson, N. J. Normal School (now William Paterson College). Certainly Miss Sautter influenced her niece (my second cousin), Amelia Fletcher, who recently retired from a long, successful career as a teacher of history and modern languages, to become an educator. When told by young Amelia that she might, instead, choose nursing, Miss Sautter had replied, "We don't nurse, we teach!"

My first awareness that being a woman might be a disadvantage in practicing one's chosen profession came in June 1918 during an informal talk near the end of my senior year in high school with two of my most admired women teachers who stopped me in the hall one afternoon to inquire about my post-graduation plans. When informed that I wanted to enter a teacher-training college to become a teacher of English literature, they painted a dismal picture for me of the economic and social discrimination encountered by many women teachers in this traditional woman's profession. The United States then had been at war with Germany for more than a year. In unprecedented numbers women were entering the labor force to fill jobs vacated by servicemen, many in occupations formerly barred to them. My two mentors advised me to take advantage of the seemingly unlimited career opportunities now opening to ambitious young women. Start by acquiring some business skills, they advised, that will open doors for you.

The day after graduation I answered a newspaper advertisement and obtained a job as a payroll clerk in a local construction firm. My Aunt Hetty, then living in New York with her second husband, a wealthy manufacturer of sandpaper, talked with me and my parents and with some knowledgeable friends, and then offered to pay my tuition either to attend Barnard College or to enroll in a two-year program of academic and secretarial studies then offered by Columbia University in its Extension Division. I chose the latter option with a view to entering the publishing field as an alternative to teaching English literature. By late September 1918, I had resigned from my job and was commuting to New York five days a week by train and ferryboat, then by subway, to the university.

The following summer I worked as a stenographer and proof reader at the Cosmopolitan Book Corporation, a job I obtained through a letter of introduction written by a friend of my aunt. While completing my second year at Columbia I took elective courses in editorial and publicity work. In June 1920, again with the help of my aunt, who knew the treasurer of the company, I obtained a position in the editorial department of the American

Book Company, then located in Washington Square, where I assisted in the preparation of a series of public school readers. One day that fall when I saw students returning to their classes at New York University, I was saddened by the realization that my own school days now were over. Suddenly the thought occurred to me: "But, you can take evening courses!" I did, at Columbia and New York universities.

During these teenage years I went out on dates with half a dozen young men. In two instances I formed lasting friendships. In a course on magazine article writing at Columbia, I met Paul Gallico, whose books later brought him fame and fortune. He took me to lunch, out to dinner and dancing, and to my first night club, prize fight, and trotting races. He wrote me many amusing letters and our friendship continued throughout his life. Marc Edmund Jones, whom I met at a Christian Endeavor Society dinner in Arlington, became an ordained Protestant minister, earned a doctor's degree at Teachers College, Columbia, and wrote books on occult philosophy and astrology. He invited me to join a study group that met in his New York apartment and later in a bookshop called the North Node. Through Marc I made some other interesting friends. I learned how to meditate, cast a horoscope, use the tarot cards. I read books on theosophy, mysticism, alchemy, and the eastern religions, and became interested in the field of psychical research, now known as parapsychology.

Upon the suggestion of an older woman friend, who arranged an interview for me, I applied for and obtained a position in January 1921 as an instructor in advertising with the Extension Division of the United Y.M.C.A. Schools, where she was similarly employed. Begun as a postwar activity, this division offered correspondence courses in a variety of fields to war veterans returning to civilian life. The department heads were men, but women had a chance for employment as instructors under their supervision.

In addition to assisting in the preparation of catalogues, booklets, posters, and other advertising material for use by the school, the instructors in advertising guided their students by correspondence through a series of thirty lessons consisting of readings and exercises or experiments based on a textbook and accompanied by additional references for further reading. The author of the course and the textbook was Harry L. Hollingworth, a psychologist with whom, much later, I took several psychology courses at Barnard College, Columbia. The course, together with the text, was published under the title of *The Psychology of Advertising and Selling* (1923) by Columbia University, where it was used by its own Home Study Division of University Extension. While working through the reading assignments for our course, a lesson or two ahead of my first students, I found this text immensely interesting. It served as my introduction to the general field of psychology, in which I then began to read other material.

By August 1923 the Extension Division of the United Y.M.C.A. Schools had enrolled over forty thousand students. The Y.M.C.A. War Work Council then was disbanded and the Extension Division was instructed to discontinue the enrollment of students, but to continue to serve those already enrolled until they all had completed their courses. In October 1924 the school was moved to Columbia University for the purpose of completing the liquidation through its Home Study Division. All of the remaining instructors were placed on a part-time basis. I stayed on as the sole instructor in advertising until the work was finished in 1929.

Meanwhile, in June 1924, I married a mechanical engineer, twelve years older than I, named Chester Ward Bryan. He was an employee of my aunt's husband, who was introduced to me at a specially arranged dinner party at their home. While continuing my part-time teaching work, I began taking courses in the Columbia University School of General Studies as a candidate for the B.S. degree with a major in psychology. Some of my courses were taken at Barnard College, including four in philosophy. The history of the mind-body problem interested me especially because of its bearing on some controversial issues in psychology; the course in logic proved helpful in learning to construct and evaluate hypotheses. By the time I was awarded the bachelor's degree in 1929, I was certain that I wanted to become a psychologist. I applied for and was accepted for admission as a graduate student in the Columbia department. My husband, who, I had discovered, did not want children and was absorbed in some technical engineering project of his own in his spare time, was pleased that I had found some constructive use for my free time and energy.

About the same time that my work as an instructor in advertising ended in 1929, I was unexpectedly given an opportunity to teach several courses in psychology on a part-time basis at the Child Education Foundation in New York, a privately endowed institution for training teachers of nursery school children. This door was opened for me by a much older woman, Zoe Bateman, the dean of the school, whom I met while we were both attending Professor Robert Woodworth's course in contemporary schools of psychology. She said I would be an excellent example for the young women students (the term "role model" was not yet in vogue). I continued this part-time employment for the next ten years.

In 1930 I received a master's degree in psychology; my thesis was a report of an experimental study on the extent to which changes in blood pressure in young women subjects who were, and who were not, attempting to deceive the investigator were related to their scores on three standardized tests designed to measure temperamental and intellectual traits (1930). I then began work for the doctoral degree. In addition to satisfying the department's course requirements, I spent an extra year taking courses at Teachers College, Columbia, in educational and clinical psychology and in psychological counseling; I also took courses at Columbia University's College of Physicians and Surgeons in neuroanatomy and neurophysiology. I wanted to prepare as broadly and soundly as possible for effective competition in the job market, for it was tacitly agreed among the graduate students that men were the preferred candidates both for university instructorships as well as for most teaching positions at the college level. And I did want to teach.

As a result of some interdepartmental negotiations, joint arrangements were made for me to conduct an experimental research project, appropriate for a doctoral dissertation in psychology, in the laboratory and under the supervision of Dr. Frederick Pike, my professor in the course in neurophysiology I had recently completed at the College of Physicians and Surgeons. I planned to study learning and relearning of specified tasks by dogs before and after they had undergone brain surgery performed by Dr. Pike. Our collaboration had been underway for several months when he learned that his foundation grant had become a casualty of the economic depression of the early thirties; he could no longer afford to feed his animals and they had to be destroyed.

I then began work on another dissertation project in which five-year-old children were the subjects. My advisor was Professor Henry E. Garrett. This study, the "Organization of Memory in Young Children" (1934), was concerned with a problem that Carl Spearman (1927) regarded as fundamental, namely, the nature of the relationship between memory and intelligence. I found verbal ability to be closely related to memory ability at that age, with no significant or reliable sex differences in the functions tested. My Ph.D. degree was granted in 1934 and soon thereafter I was elected to the Columbia University chapter of Sigma Xi, the national honorary scientific society. That year, also, I was granted a final decree of divorce from Chester Bryan. We parted amicably, divided our worldly possessions equitably, and remained friends.

During 1934–35, I held a part-time position teaching psychology at Sarah Lawrence College, for which I had been recommended by the Columbia psychology department. With the aid of a research grant from the American Council on Education in 1934, Henry Garrett, Ruth Perl, and I collaborated on a study of the age factor in mental organization (1935). Ruth Perl and I then made a comparison of women students preparing to enter three different vocational fields (art, music, and teaching) and found variations among the three groups on tests designed to measure intelligence, memory, motor speed, and personality traits (1938). While gathering data for this study in 1935 at the School of Fine and Applied Arts at Pratt Institute, I was invited to have lunch with the director and a few faculty members especially interested in my work.

In answer to their inquiries, I described some of the services a psychologist could perform in a professional school such as theirs. As a result, I was appointed to the faculty to teach courses in psychology in the teacher-training program, to counsel students on individual problems, and to conduct research aimed at the development of tests for art aptitude and achievement. Although I was employed and paid on a part-time basis (three days a week), my teaching load consisted of six different courses, for each of which I had to prepare a course outline, assignments, lectures, and reading lists. I felt compensated for all the extra, unpaid, weekend hours this entailed, however, when given the title of head of the psychology department. Under the sponsorship of the Anthropology and Psychology Division of the American Association for the Advancement of Science, and with the cooperation of the United States Forest Service, I organized a one-semester project at Pratt entitled "Forest conservation through fire prevention" and helped devise a new technique for measuring changes in school children's information and attitudes toward fire prevention before and after seeing a film on the subject. This project was described in an article published in *School and Society* (1939d). With the aid of a small grant from the Carnegie Corporation, I also conducted and published a research study on grades, intelligence, and personality of art school freshmen (1942b).

The year 1936 was an eventful one for me, both personally and professionally. First, my mother died unexpectedly from a heart attack at age fifty-nine; my grief over losing her was heightened the following year by my father's death from cancer. That summer I married Frank Marvin Blasingame, a sculptor and painter whom I had met the previous year. He was about my own age and a native of California who had come to New York to further his professional career, after a divorce from his first wife. He had a small son who lived with us; I loved them both very much.

Then, in September, a third part-time position was added to my schedule of work at Pratt Institute and the Child Education Foundation, when I was appointed consulting psychologist and associate in library service at the School of Library Service, Columbia University. This was a graduate professional school, then offering a second bachelor's degree in library service and an advanced program of courses, plus a thesis, leading to a master's degree. The dean, Dr. Charles C. Williamson, who also was the director of the Columbia University Libraries, was an economist who believed it essential for administrators of large libraries to utilize scientific research methods in the solution of library problems and for library school students to be prepared to plan and conduct such research. He had decided to employ a psychologist for the Columbia school to teach a two-semester course in research methodology to the candidates for the master's degree and, in cooperation with the faculty, to develop a program of objective, comprehensive examinations to be administered to the bachelor's degree candidates upon completion of their course work. Professor Albert Poffenberger of the Columbia psychology department, whom he had consulted, had recommended me for this position on the basis of the work I was doing at Pratt Institute.

When librarians heard of my appointment to the Columbia school, I began to receive invitations from various organizations, libraries, and other library schools to give talks, read papers, and serve as a panel member or discussion leader. In cooperation with a committee of the Association of American Library Schools, I conducted a survey among its institutional members on present policies and future plans with respect to tests and examinations and published the findings under the title of "The testing program in the library school" (1939f). Soon the dean was asked by a group of professional librarians to arrange for an evening course in applied psychology for librarians to be given by me for credit, which he did. Then, acting on a recommendation made by the school's Committee on Instruction, Dr. Williamson asked whether I would be interested in a full-time position on the faculty and would be willing to give up my other two positions. Although the salary he could offer me as an assistant professor, plus an additional stipend for teaching two courses in summer session, meant that I would have to take a cut of more than one fifth of my total earnings, I welcomed the opportunity to concentrate my professional interests and energy as a member of the faculty of a graduate school in my own alma mater. My appointment took effect on July 1, 1939.

In appointing me to this post, Dr. Williamson emphasized that I was being employed as a psychologist and that he expected me to continue to develop as a psychologist, not to become a librarian. He wanted me to serve my own profession, as well as the library profession and the Columbia school. He said he knew from his own experience, both as an economist as well as a library administrator and educator, that serving two professions was not an easy assignment, but he thought I would find it an interesting and rewarding one. He made it clear that, in time, I could expect academic advancement.

In the course of the next thirty-two years I tried to carry out his mandate. His wisdom and vision sustained and motivated me long after his retirement.

In the late 1930s, I was invited to give three papers at meetings of library associations on topics related to the field of bibliotherapy, a term first used during World War I when hospital librarians, especially those working in veterans' hospitals, were utilizing books in cooperation with psychiatrists as an aid in diagnosis and therapy. In one of these papers (1939b) I defined bibliotherapy as the prescription of reading materials that will help to develop emotional maturity and sustain mental health; I proposed that such materials be used not only as an alleviative or curative measure for persons already ill, but as a preventive agent to keep people well.

Forty years later, Rhea Joyce Rubin, editor of *Bibliotherapy Sourcebook* (1978), in the introduction to Part I, commented on my work as follows:

Alice I. Bryan, Consulting Psychologist in the School of Library Service at Columbia University, was the foremost bibliotherapy theoretician of the 1930's. In "The Psychology of the Reader" (reprinted here), published in 1939 and followed by articles in August and October—the last one entitled "Can There Be a Science of Bibliotherapy?"—she answered her own question in the affirmative, stating that the field already had a philosphical justification, a working hypothesis, and a definition, but greatly needed experimental data and scientifically trained workers.

In December 1940, while the United States was in an early stage of mobilization of defense resources against the contingency of entry into World War II, I initiated a project designed to help public libraries strengthen civilian morale in their communities by holding a series of programs utilizing documentary films, group discussions, and exhibits of relevant, available reading materials. The library film forum project, as it was called, was conducted and evaluated by a joint committee of the American Library Association and the American Association for Applied Psychology (of which I was co-chairman) with the cooperation of the American Association for Adult Education and the American Film Center. I directed the research and, with the aid of a grant from the Carnegie Corporation, prepared the final report for publication by the Joint Committee on Film Forums (1944a).

Just before and immediately after Pearl Harbor, I was one of a group of women psychologists who, because women were denied representation on a joint committee to deal with the national emergency, decided to form a new organization called the National Council of Women Psychologists (later, the International Council of Women Psychologists). The preliminary organization meeting was held in November 1940 in my apartment; I was a member of the committee on Constitution and By-laws, a member of the Executive Board, and served terms as vice president and president.

The National Research Council then appointed me to membership on its Emergency Committee in Psychology as a representative of the new women's organization. I also served as a member of the Emergency Committee's subcommittee on Services of Women Psychologists and of its subcommittee on Survey and Planning. Later I was a delegate to and secretary for the Intersociety Constitutional Convention, held by the Emergency Committee, and a member of its Continuation Committee. An interesting and accurate account of the formation and work of the Emergency Committee in Psychology and the formation of the National Council of Women Psychologists is given by Donald Napoli in his doctoral dissertation entitled "The architects of adjustment: The practice and professionalization of American psychology" (1975). He describes the role played by "Alice I. Bryan, the executive secretary of the AAAP [American Association for Applied Psychology] and one of the chief architects of the revised by-laws" of the American Psychological Association, in effecting unification of the science and profession of psychology (pp. 267–270).

It was while we both were serving on the Emergency Committee's subcommittee on survey and planning that Dr. E. G. Boring (then chairman of the psychology department at Harvard University) and I collaborated on three studies that we published under the general title of "Women in American psychology" (1944c, 1946b, and 1947). Boring later wrote a paper on "the woman problem" that was reprinted in his autobiography, *Psychologist at Large* (1961). He implied, in a new foreword to this article, that I had been unwilling because of my "feminist" bias to accept and present as our joint conclusions some "admonitory" generalizations that he thought could be inferred from our data. Instead, we had to "retreat" and present only our factual findings, even if (surprisingly) this did win us a prize.

As Boring himself indicates, there was no disagreement as to the findings of our surveys. Some of the conclusions Boring wanted us to draw, however, especially those of an "admonitory" nature, were in my opinion personal value judgments not warranted by our findings. It was for that reason that I could not consent to their inclusion. I was glad that Boring subsequently published his own paper because it affords an opportunity for any interested reader to compare the views expressed as his "truth" with the findings of our studies. Although we had occasional, amicable disagreements, we remained good friends until his death and I continue to remember Gary Boring with great respect and affection.

While, in 1944, the country was heartened by news of the Allied landing in Normandy, and in 1945 could rejoice at the ending of the war, two events occurred in my life that were very distressing to me. My husband and I had tried for some years to cope with what seemed insoluable problems. He had found it difficult to adjust to life in New York and was unable to achieve the artistic and monetary success he had worked and hoped for. Finally, we agreed to separate and in 1944 were divorced.

Advancement in my academic career then was effectively blocked in 1945 by my second dean, Dr. Carl M. White, who had succeeded Dr. Williamson upon his retirement in 1942. Dr. White, after obtaining a Ph.D. in philosophy, with a minor in psychology, had decided to enter the library field; he had taken a library degree at the Columbia school, then been employed as a library administrator and educator. As noted by Ray Trautman (1954), he had accepted the deanship with the stipulation that he intended gradually to reduce the number of women on the faculty.

When, toward the end of 1945, I asked Dr. White for an increase in salary (having received none since my appointment as an assistant professor in 1939) and inquired about my prospects for a promotion in rank, he replied by pointing out my "inadequacies": I did not have a library degree nor had I worked in a library. He told me that, unlike himself, I "had broken into the library profession through the back door without adequate training or experience." Not only would the fact that I was an "outsider" count against me, but also the fact that I was a woman and that "the university is still very much a man's world." My prospects, he said, were "dim." He professed to be unaware of the terms of my appointment (namely, that I had been employed as a psychologist, not a librarian) and asked me to write a history of that appointment, of my work at the school, and of all my professional activities since my part-time appointment in 1936; I was to include whatever documentation I could provide.

Early in the spring of 1946 I presented Dr. White with a twenty-page report, supplemented by ten pages of exhibits. Fortunately, I was able to obtain letters from Dr. Williamson, Robert Lester (Secretary of the Carnegie Corporation), and some prominent male librarians who knew the circumstances of my appointment and vouched for my knowledge and competence in studying library problems. Also, at my request, a few distinguished male psychologists with whom I had worked wrote Dr. White personal letters regarding my competence and reputation as a psychologist. I listed my publications and professional association appointments in both fields. In a letter acknowledging receipt of my report, he evaded the issue of my status at the school and my request for a salary increase by inquiring, instead, whether I would be willing to engage in studies of library problems that would take me away from the campus for varying periods of time. In a later interview, he said he would try to obtain a grant for me to conduct a study at the New York Public Library. There the matter rested, still unresolved, for the next six years.

Meanwhile, I decided that during my first sabbatical leave, due in the academic year 1948–49 (after my first nine years as an assistant professor), I would work toward a master's degree in library science at the University of Chicago. I was accepted for candidacy and awarded a fellowship, for which I also had applied. I planned to complete my course work in the winter, spring, and summer quarters of 1949, writing my thesis in the area of library personnel. Then, one day in the spring of 1948, Dr. Robert D. Leigh called on me at my office and introduced himself. He was a well-known political scientist of broad experience in teaching, administration and research, who had been appointed by the Social Science Research Council to direct a project called "The Public Library Inquiry," described in detail in Leigh's final report (1950).

This project, initially financed by a $200,000 grant from the Carnegie Corporation, was undertaken in response to a request from the American Library Association for a study that would provide "an appraisal in sociological, cultural, and human terms of the extent to which the librarians are achieving their objectives," and "an assessment of the public library's actual and potential contribution to American society" (p. 3). To insure objectivity and detachment from any official or unofficial library controls, all members of the "Inquiry" staff were to be drawn by the director from social science disciplines or from one of the communications fields. All were to be non-librarians.

Dr. Leigh then said that I had been suggested as the person to conduct a study of personnel and personnel administration for the "Inquiry," that he had talked with a number of librarians and psychologists who knew me and had heard "nothing but good" about me. Then he asked me whether I would be interested in undertaking this assignment. I responded with enthusiasm; my appointment was confirmed shortly afterwards. When I told Dr. White that I had been chosen to conduct the personnel study for this prestigious project, he seemed a bit stunned, then excited, and lost no time informing our faculty and the president of the university.

During the summer and fall of 1948, I planned my study, prepared interview schedules and questionnaires, and visited nearly all of the sixty public libraries in our national sample, collecting data from the library administrators and from more than 3,000 professional and subprofessional librarians. As planned, I was in residence at the University of Chicago for the first three quarters of 1949, attending courses and seminars, taking the comprehensive examinations, preparing a thesis proposal, and writing a first draft of my report for "The Public Library Inquiry." Dr. Leigh, who also was visiting our libraries, stopped by to see me several times. He thought it a bit absurd, as did some of my other professional friends, that I should be taking a library degree in order to feel more secure in my position at the Columbia school, but I found it a stimulating experience and made some lasting friendships. I was awarded my master's degree in 1951. My book, *The Public Librarian*, was published the following year by Columbia University Press (1952). Also in 1952, I received my promotion to an associate professorship.

In the fall of 1949, I returned to the Columbia school and the following year Dr. Leigh accepted an invitation to join the faculty as a visiting professor. Dr. White then asked me to make a study of the doctoral programs in the other graduate, professional schools of Columbia University and to submit alternate proposals and recommendations for establishing a doctoral program in the library school. This study was used as a basis for faculty discussions that eventuated in the adoption of a program of advanced studies leading toward a professional degree of Doctor of Library Service. Then, by separation of the position of dean from that of director of university libraries and making each a full-time assignment, the status and independence of the school were strengthened. In 1954, Dr. White, who had chosen to retain the deanship, resigned from this position. Dr. Leigh then served as acting dean until 1956 when he was appointed dean, a position he held until his retirement in 1959.

Two significant events occurred in my life in 1956. In June, I was promoted to a full professorship, the first woman in the history of the school to be given that rank. Then, in October, I married George Virgil Fuller, a widower and a retired colonel in the United States Air Force Reserve. He owned an ocean-front, summer hotel in Gloucester, Massachusetts, that was destroyed the following fall by an arsonist; I helped him rebuild it as a modern summer inn. He was genuinely interested in and supportive of my work and this marriage was, by far, my happiest. His death from cancer at age sixty-four in October 1960 was a grievous loss. He willed me the inn and I continued to operate it for five summers until it was sold advantageously. In recognition of his interest in my work, I established an annual award in his name for a doctoral student at the Columbia library school.

After the establishment of the doctoral program, I continued to teach the basic course in research methodology (as well as two other courses), followed by an advanced doctoral seminar. I worked in close cooperation with each doctoral candidate's advisor from inception to completion of the student's dissertation. Dean Leigh established a Committee on the Doctorate and appointed me as chairman, a post I continued to hold under his successors, Dean Jack Dalton and Dean Richard Darling. During these years I also served as chairman of the doctoral colloquia and as chairman of all the examining committees appointed by the dean to conduct the oral defense of each candidate's dissertation. Dr. Leigh and I continued to work together harmoniously; I assisted him on various projects described in my sketch of his career in the *Dictionary of American Biography* (1978). It was a privilege to work under his wise and stimulating guidance.

Not only Dean Leigh, but also Deans Dalton and Darling gave me unfailing support and encouragement in my work and I continue to enjoy a warm friendship with both of them and their wives. Under the administrations of these three deans, the climate in the Columbia library school again became and continued to be, hospitable and supportive toward the women members of the faculty. One of my deepest satisfactions has been the appointment to professorial positions of four women (Miriam Braverman, Phyllis Dain, Jane Hannigan, and Susan Thompson) who were my students while earning their doctoral degrees.

In 1971 I retired from active service at the Columbia school, but, as professor emeritus, I still participate in many of its activities and feel close to faculty and students. Soon after my retirement I decided, as my grandfather Lawrance had (albeit at seventy instead of seventeen), that it was time to see the world and I have traveled quite extensively during the past decade. I continue to be blessed with good health, good friends, and a loving family. My three nieces and several of their children have added new branches to the family tree. I am glad that one of my nieces chose teaching as her vocation and is combining a successful professional career with a happy marriage and the rearing of two sons. She is Sally Bever Zwiebach, daughter of my brother Ralph and wife of Dr. Burton Zwiebach, a professor of political science at Queens College. Both she and her husband chose to earn their graduate degrees at Columbia University.

REFERENCES

Boring, Edwin G. 1961. *Psychologist at Large.* New York: Basic Books.
—— 1951. The woman problem. *American Psychologist,* 6:679–82.
Bryan, Alice I. *See* Representative Publications.
Hollingworth, H. L. 1923. *The Psychology of Advertising and Selling.* New York: Columbia University Press.

Leigh, Robert D. 1950. *The Public Library in the United States.* New York: Columbia University Press.

Napoli, Donald Seymer. 1975. The architects of adjustment: The Practice and professionalization of American psychology, 1920–1945. Dissertation, University of California, Davis.

Rubin, Rhea Joyce, ed. 1978. *Bibliotherapy Sourcebook.* Phoenix, Ariz.: Oryx Press.

Spearman, C. 1927. *The Abilities of Man.* New York: Macmillan.

Trautman, R. 1954. *A History of the School of Library Service, Columbia University.* New York: Columbia University Press.

Representative Publications by Alice I. Bryan

1930.   Blood pressure deception changes and their use as an index of personality. Master's thesis, Columbia University.

1934.   Organization of memory in young children. *Archives of Psychology*, No. 162. Dissertation, Columbia University.

1935.   With Henry E. Garrett and Ruth E. Perl. The age factor in mental organization. *Archives of Psychology*, No. 176.

1938.   With Ruth E. Perl. A comparison of women students preparing for three different vocations. *Journal of Applied Psychology*, 22:161–68.

1939a. The art of interviewing. *A.L.A. Bulletin*, 33:480–84.

1939b. Can there be a science of bibliotherapy? *Library Journal*, 64:773–76.

1939c. Personality adjustment through reading. *Library Journal*, 64:573:76.

1939d. A progressive education project on the college level. *School and Society*, 50:694–98.

1939e. The psychology of the reader. *Library Journal*, 64:7–12.

1939f. The testing program in the library school. *Library Quarterly*, 9:32–62.

1940a. With Walter H. Wilke, Bryan-Wilke Scale for Rating Public Speeches. *Psychological Corporation*.

1940b. Personality adjustments and the school librarian. *Proceedings of a Conference on School Library Service*. New York: Columbia University, School of Library Service.

1940c. The personality of the school librarian. *Wilson Library Bulletin*, 15:129–33.

1940d. The reader as a person. *Library Journal*, 65:137–41.

1941a. Library film forums on national defense. *Library Journal*, 66:241–43.

1941b. With Walter H. Wilke. A technique for rating public speeches. *Journal of Consulting Psychology*, 5:80–90.

1942a. With Walter H. Wilke. Audience tendencies in rating public speakers. *Journal of Applied Psychology*, 26:371–81.

1942b. Grades, intelligence, and personality of art school freshmen. *Journal of Educational Psychology*, 33:50–64.

1942c. With Edwin G. Boring, Edgar A. Doll, et al. Psychology as science and profession. *Psychological Bulletin*, 39:761–72.

1942d. Psychological service in the library field. *Journal of Consulting Psychology*, 6:73–77.

1943a. Educating civilians for war and peace through library film forums. *Journal of Consulting Psychology*, 7:280–88.

1943b. Tasks confronting the Intersociety Constitutional Convention. *Bulletin, New York State Association for Applied Psychology*, 6:1–2.

1944a. Library film forums. Joint Committee on Film Forums. Mimeo. New York. November.

1944b. With Albert Poffenberger. Toward unification in psychology. *Journal of Consulting Psychology*, 8:253–57.

1944c. With Edwin G. Boring. Women in American psychology: prolegomenon. *Psychological Bulletin*, 41:447–54.

1945.   Legibility of Library of Congress cards and their reproductions. *College and Research Libraries*, 6:447–64.

1946a. Women in American psychology: factors affecting their careers. *Transactions of the New York Academy of Sciences*, Series 2, 9:19–23.

1946b. With Edwin G. Boring. Women in American psychology: statistics from the OPP questionnaire. *American Psychologist*, 1:71–79.

1947.   With Edwin G. Boring. Women in American psychology: factors affecting their professional careers. *American Psychologist*, 2:3–20.

1948.   The library. In D. H. Fryer and E. R. Henry, eds. *Psychotechnology and Psychological Practice*. New York: Farrar and Rinehart.

1950.   Librarianship. In D. H. Fryer and E. R. Henry, eds., *Handbook of Applied Psychology*. New York: Rinehart.

1951.   Professional and subprofessional public library personnel. Master's thesis, University of Chicago.

1952.   *The Public Librarian*. New York: Columbia University Press.

1978.   Robert Devore Leigh. In Bohdan Wynar, ed., *Dictionary of American Library Biography*. Littleton, Colo.: Libraries Unlimited.

LOIS BARCLAY MURPHY

I was the oldest of five children—two brothers and two sisters—of a father and mother who were both deeply interested in education. There were books on "nature and nurture" along with a large library of philosophy, history, literature, especially poetry, religion, and education. My mother had been a teacher before her marriage and was so inspiring to her students that on the fiftieth anniversary of their sixth-grade year with her, the surviving class-mates had a celebration in honor of their teacher, May Hartley. After his early years as pastor of a church, my father became Secretary of Religious Education for the Methodist Church and from that time on proceeded to a series of editorial and administrative assignments, the last of which was Sec-retary of Religious Education in the Foreign Field, involving travels around the world to missions in Oriental and South American countries. My par-ents had met at the University of Iowa late in the 1890s, where my mother had been especially influenced by two students of William James, Carl Sea-shore and G. W. H. Patrick. My father talked more about his graduate school experience at the University of Chicago, especially John Dewey, and about social leaders such as Jane Addams who developed the famous Hull House in Chicago and Walter Rauschenbush, a great liberal in Christianity. Visitors included liberal leaders in the church like Bishop McConnell and Harry Ward.

Both my parents believed in "instilling high ideals," sharing the culture of the past, and carrying on serious conversation at dinner and at other times and expecting all their children to "make a social contribution." So, I grew up in an unusually intellectual atmosphere compared to the home life of my acquaintances and friends, and I felt that my parents knew more than almost anybody else in Chicago where we lived from the time I was five to twelve years old. My father read poetry and excerpts from classics to us. I remember vividly the resonance and deep feeling in his voice as he read Robert Burns' "A Man's a Man for All That." Themes of the brotherhood of man and democracy as involving equality and respect for all people were not only implied in that poem but also in the interest of my parents in people of varied backgrounds in Chicago.

However, their inconsistency bothered me: they were disturbed because I was picking up "poor English" from some of my friends, children of immigrants whom I enjoyed for their warmth and their interesting food. We moved down to Hyde Park near the University of Chicago where we were no longer exposed to "poor English." While I was upset at losing my friends, there were side benefits in the closeness to Lake Michigan, Jackson Park, and Washington Park with wonderful places to explore. In addition, there was the marvelous Field Museum with fascinating Egyptian exhibits—great tombs with their aura of continuity, mummies, interesting sculptured cats, and fascinating jewelry. There were also special exhibits, such as the development of a chicken embryo in the egg, showing stages from fertilization to the funny little wet creature that was almost ready to peck its way out of the shell. This reinforced my interest in development.

Another contradiction made me somewhat skeptical about the grownups. As a Methodist minister in those early years, my father dutifully adhered to the rules, such as no alcoholic drinks, no dancing, no card-playing, and, worst of all, no fun on Sunday. However, in describing his explorations of Europe just before his marriage, he told how in France, Germany, and Italy it was necessary to drink beer or wine because the water was not good. In my simple-minded childish way, I thought "Is it right or is it not right to use alcoholic drinks?" That did not make sense to me. Such contradictions added to the conviction that *I had to think for myself*—that grownups did not always make sense.

But other formative influences contributed to autonomy and *confidence in my own conclusions*. Since my mother was busy with two little boys born while I was still a preschool child, I was taken for visits to my grandparents on their beautiful farm in east Iowa—my paradise. Grandpa said that I must never go into the pasture where the cattle with their sharp horns might hurt me, but he and grandmother allowed me complete freedom to explore all the rest of the farm. I could climb up the high mountain of sawdust in which blocks of ice were packed during the winter for use during the summer. There, I could hunt for eggs which some of the hens had hidden high up where the grownups could not easily find them. My gifted grandmother was a superb seamstress who made exquisite dresses for me with tiny, elegant stitching that rivalled the dresses from Paris which my mother's best friend—a banker's wife—bought for her little daughter. But grandmother needed me to thread her needles.

Such experiences as this gave me the *feeling that I could do things* that grownups couldn't do. My aunt read Kipling's *Just So Stories* to me and once commented, not disapprovingly, that I had more curiosity than the elephant's child! I was allowed to roam in the orchard and, since there was far more food than the family could use, no one objected when I picked apples, plums, cherries, and threw away any that contained a worm or bad spot, keeping only the perfect ones. This might have contributed to the development of a differentiating orientation.

In addition to the autonomy fostered by my grandparents' permissiveness to explore the extraordinary environment of the farm I learned a good deal by watching. Grandmother let me help while she plucked the chickens which the hired man had killed to be cooked for dinner. I watched while she took out the "innards" of the hens and was fascinated with the sequence of eggs from an egg nearly ready to be laid through smaller and smaller sizes of eggs to the tiniest beginning ones. Of course, the experiences on the farm gave me a deep sense of *growth* in many areas of life—plants, animals, as well as human beings.

When I was about five and six years old, my father took my brother and me out for walks, telling us to keep our eyes open and "remember everything you see, then we'll talk about it when we get back." After a walk of several blocks and our return, we would sit down at the table and he would ask us what we had seen. My brother always remembered more than I did, and this probably stimulated me to try even harder to observe and to remember; certainly, it was good *early training for observation.*

At home, my mother discovered that at the age of five I could put the baby to sleep more easily than the grownups could, so this job was assigned to me—another experience which contributed to my confidence. I enjoyed the succession of babies and enjoyed helping with them so much that, by the age of ten, when I was caring for my baby sister, I was considered "the little mother" in the neighborhood. Babies fascinated me—I was one of David Levy's "baby-buggy peekers" (a term the child psychiatrist invented to refer to girls and women who enjoy babies and children and who habitually stop to enjoy passing babies and their caregivers).

I felt that I understood the children, and, on some of the occasions when one or another of the children was disciplined, I felt the grownups did not understand why the children had done what they did—in fact that grownups do not understand children. This feeling was strong enough so that, at the age of about eight, I decided to run away with my three-year-old brother, feeling that I could take better care of him than the grownups did. I had sense enough to reconsider that idea after getting five or six blocks away and realizing that providing shelter and food and other necessities might be rather hard to manage.

Each of the children was different from the others. My first brother was large, growing rapidly strong, extremely active. The next brother was slow-growing and was all through school the smallest in his class, the shyest and most quiet. But he continued to grow until the age of twenty-two and became a tall, strong, brilliant man. There were other differences that impressed me also among all the different neighbors around, the different places we had lived, and the differences between personalities in my father's family and my mother's family.

When I was seven years old, I read the wonderful story of *Heidi* which I loved and reread many times. The conception of someone who could help another person to get well was very exciting and it probably contributed to my great satisfaction in helping members of the family get well and also in my later work in the Head Start Project as well as in college teaching, helping students to make progress. It may have contributed to my interest in what can bring about change in people and in the role of coping in developing strength.

INTELLECTUAL INFLUENCES IN ADOLESCENCE

In high school, I enjoyed geometry and found it easy to solve problems dealing with space. But most absorbing were the languages: German, French, and Latin, and, at that point, I thought I would be a language teacher. Earlier, I had gone through stages of wanting to be an artist, a dancer, a poet. However, these were abandoned one by one as my mother said, "You should not be an artist unless you're a genius" and an English teacher had written on a long poem "excellent effort," which I interpreted to imply that the result was not as excellent as the effort. At Vassar, there was a wealth of intellectual delights: Latin, French and English poetry, each with inspiring teachers; other courses in literature and history, and also open stacks in the library where I discovered Henry Adams' *Mont-Saint-Michel and Chartres*, a magnificent first edition with incredibly beautiful illustrations of the architecture and stained-glass windows. I stayed up all night to read it—the first time I had been so deliriously ecstatic about a book.

It seemed natural to take psychology, and the chairman of the department, Margaret Floy Washburn, at that time president of the American Psychological Association, taught introductory psychology, social psychology, and abnormal psychology. She was a brilliant lecturer and flexible enough to be free to weave in bits of wisdom and advice, along with well-organized and beautifully-expressed scientific presentations. She urged us to get married and have families, possibly regretting her lonely, unmarried status, distinguished though she was. I sailed through a course in child psychology without doing any work because my experience and reading at home had given me such a head start.

I also had a course in testing, which I quickly put to good use in applying for a volunteer job during the summer after my sophomore year, at the Psychological Laboratory of the Vocation Bureau of the Board of Education in Cincinnati. The following summer it became a paid job and, the first year out of college I was appointed to be assistant to the director, along with doing more testing. Helen Woolley had been the director—but just before I started my work there, she left to develop the Merrill-Palmer Institute in Detroit. Mabel Fernald took her place, another gifted, warm, sensitive psychologist, loved and respected by all of us. There was an emphasis on giving a live, vital picture of a child along with the technical information from the tests—an emphasis which I appreciated and which influenced all my future work in writing about children.

Despite all the psychology at Vassar, I majored in economics—actually not an accurate name for a department which included a variety of courses that would now be listed under the heading of social science. I was tutor for the department and enjoyed helping girls with literary talents but no gift for economic theory to master basics enough to pass exams after they had failed them before. However, a deeper interest was reflected in my senior honors study of the New York Training School for Girls—a reform school in which I saw a vivid illustration of the negative impact of a hostile, punitive environment. Sullen, angry attitudes pervaded the institution. The girls wore dull, gray seersucker uniforms.

I was so curious about it that I asked for an opportunity to spend some time there and was invited to come during spring vacation to take the place of a matron who herself "wanted a vacation." When I arrived I found that she had been gagged and bound by three girls who snatched her keys and escaped but were captured and locked in the guard house. As a substitute matron, I was told to unlock the door of each girl's room in the morning, tell her to attend to her wants—which meant going down to the bathroom— and lock her in after she came back. One by one, I did this for each of the girls. I had been so appalled by the severe restrictions that I thought I could at least smile at each girl as I opened the door. However, the first girl grabbed me around the neck and dragged me down to the floor. I did manage to get up and proceed with the routines, bewildered as to how I could safely introduce a little warmth into the miserable atmosphere. After the girls had "attended to their wants," I was to proceed with them downstairs to the dining room where they would have breakfast without speaking to each other during the meal.

Needless to say, the two weeks there made an interesting report. The head of the economics department, Herbert Mills, had some clout in the State of New York, and it may have been a result of my report that through his influence the current superintendent was discharged and a wonderful woman, Fanny Morse, was brought in as superintendent. She threw away the gray seersucker uniforms, bought beautiful materials for the girls to make their own dresses and set up sewing classes for them to learn how. In addition, she found a nice old farm house on the property where she assigned the girls to scrape off the paint, repaint, make curtains and pillows and other furnishings to make an attractive recreation house. She brought up J. L. Moreno to provide spontaneity training to prepare the girls for effective work on jobs afterward. When I went back a few years after my first experience, I found the atmosphere completely different. Where there had been sullen, withdrawn hostility, there was warmth, alert interest and achievement, joy, an exciting and impressive example of change.

My last year at Vassar, I was advised to take advanced statistics. However, I wanted to take a fascinating course in comparative religion which my roommate had taken the year before and also a wonderful course in the appreciation of music. There wasn't room for statistics. In the comparative religion course, I became especially interested in the religions of India; the Bhagavad Gita made sense to me. Arjuna says "I am the god of the beautiful and the terrible." That seemed to be fair to what I had seen of the universe. The beauty of trees and orchards, flowers, and lakes that I'd grown up with certainly attested to some deep creative force, but also there were destructive storms, tornadoes, and hurricanes. In addition, the Bible didn't quite make sense: the idea of God taking care of every sparrow seemed ridiculous in view of the fact that he was not taking care of my mother who was growing increasingly handicapped by dreadful rheumatoid arthritis. The music course with its vivid presentation of the structure of symphonies and sonatas gave me the feeling that one might write books like that—taking a theme, developing it in different ways, integrating in a coda at the end.

The faculty of the economics department had previously told me that since I was the leading member of the department I would certainly receive a graduate fellowship if I wanted it. But the committee was so distressed at my bypassing the statistics course for music and comparative religion that they decided it was obvious that I "had no professional commitment" and they gave the fellowship to someone else. However, intrigued by awareness of the needs for students to get a perspective on and resolve religious conflicts, I thought that getting further preparation to teach comparative religion would be a useful plan. Union Theological Seminary had scholarships for students who took competitive exams and after reading for the exams, I received the scholarships which took me through Union Seminary to a B.D. (later changed to a Master of Theology). President MacCracken of Vassar, advisor to the interesting new Sarah Lawrence College, recommended me to the President and I joined the faculty in 1928, the year I completed my M.Th.

MARRIAGE AND FAMILY

Although I had found Miss Washburn's lectures very interesting, I had mixed feelings about psychology. She had made certain provocative remarks: she told us not to read Freud, and she mentioned that there were two psychologists by the name of Prince—Morton Prince and Walter Prince and said that "the former was a scientist and the latter was a fool." I decided to explore these *biases* and found Freud's *Group Psychology and the Analysis of the Ego* and *The Ego and Id* which had both been published recently. They made sense to me, and I didn't see what all the fuss was about. I also read publications by both Morton Prince and Walter Prince and felt that Walter Prince's work was just as sound as that of Morton Prince. In the course of this snooping, I had come across a book by F. W. H. Myers, *Human Personality and the Survival of Bodily Death* (1903). Reading this book, I came across his exciting phrase "subliminal uprush" and his discussions of the subconscious parts of our mental functioning. I was already aware of the subconscious but I thought nobody else knew anything about it. During high school, I had found that if I read over a Latin passage or a geometry problem at night, when I woke up in the morning the passage would translate itself or the problem would be solved. I inferred that there must be some part of my mind working while I was asleep. Freud, the two psychologists by the name of Prince, and F. W. H. Myers opened the door for me into a world, which I had known existed but had not expected to find any possibility of sharing.

The negative side of my feelings about psychology were evoked by the work of the behaviorist J. B. Watson, who, I felt, certainly did not understand children at all. Other rigid, hardnosed psychologists to whose work I was exposed in the course of reading gave me the feeling that psychologists were not really interested in people and human life. Certainly the last person I would marry would be one of these narrow psychologists.

All of this is background for my startling introduction to Gardner Murphy when I was twenty-two. Ruth Munroe, a close Vassar friend with whom I was living in New York in 1924–25 while doing graduate work, talked about her brilliant teacher of the history of psychology at Columbia University. I was not too impressed since I had brilliant lecturers at Union Theological Seminary—two British professors in history, Moffatt and Foakes-Jackson, and a German lecturer on the Old Testament who dramatically made the prophets come alive in front of our eyes. I wasn't even impressed enough to attend a single lecture by Ruth's teacher. However, she insisted on bringing him over to tea. I heard to my amazement that he was spending part time at Harvard on psychic research and that Walter Prince was one of his friends. He also talked about F. W. H. Myers who had already thrilled me.

I was thunderstruck by this psychologist who bucked the establishment so courageously. Here was a pioneer (and my grandparents and father had been pioneers in their own way as well as forebears on my mother's side; being a pioneer was in my blood). I suppose my feelings leaked out, although I was quite reserved—Gardner's mother told me later that he had written her that he "met a very interesting girl at Ruth Munroe's but she kept running out to the kitchen to type her papers for Union." (I thought Ruth herself was personally interested in him as a possible husband. I didn't realize that she was practically engaged to John Levy, a psychoanalyst, and secretly wanted to bring Gardner into our circle.)

I did not refuse his invitation to a ferry trip across the Hudson, to hike along the Palisades, climb up Hook Mountain, and explore the woods across the river. We enjoyed each other and became good friends, as I thought, with many common interests in literature, history, and philosophy as well as nature, music, and art, a sense of tuning in to each other, and deep mutuality fed by our joint love of the poet Blake, Beethoven's Seventh Symphony, the philosopher Bergson, and their ilk. He was seven years older and seven inches taller, very established professionally, so that it didn't occur to me that he had any other interest than friendship. However, the next year while I was teaching in Baltimore to supplement my Union scholarship the following year, he kept coming down to visit; we had many more walks and talks until he finally exploded "What do you think I'm coming down here for? I want to talk about getting married." He was a completely different kind of psychologist from my image of the current hardnosed scientists who were not interested in human beings. After we were married, I finished my degree at Union, then taught comparative religion at Sarah Lawrence College for seven years. However, the combination of Gardner's kind of psychology and the stimulation of two irresistible and delightful children opened another door. And I joined Gardner in writing *Experimental Social Psychology* (1931), a pioneer integration of experimental work in social psychology.

CHILD DEVELOPMENT RESEARCH

In the 1930s, there was so much child psychology theory and research dealing with aggression and conflict that I again felt that people didn't understand children and that someone needed to do research on positive aspects of their social development, especially sympathy, since our children were both very empathic little people. Harold Coffman, a friend of Gardner's, said the Macy Foundation wanted some new ideas. I talked to President Kast about the need for a study of the beginning of sympathy. He listened with warm interest, then said, "That makes sense, go ahead and do the study and send me the bills." I was ridiculed by some of the nursery school establishment who said that of course children have to be socialized and that I wouldn't find any data on sympathy. However, there was no dearth of data and my book *Social Behavior and Child Personality* was published in 1937.

Because of my desire to be completely a mother I did not work full time until the children were in college. Knowing them well, along with their friends and schoolmates, was a joy to both Gardner and me, and also contributed enormously to my thinking about child development. During the depression years when jobs were scarce, it was possible to afford help for all the routine housekeeping work; this made possible time to visit the children's school, and know their teachers, as well as to spend time with our children.

Gardner and I had both been exposed to stimulating intellectual forces in New York. The year that we were married, we participated, along with our friend Margaret Mead, in a course given by Ruth Benedict in anthropology. Since I had already been deeply impressed by subcultural differences between my Iowa grandparents on my father's side and my mother's California family, the emphasis on the cultural setting of behavior was absorbed into my bones; it is impossible for me to write anything about development without attention to the subcultural context. Robert and Helen Lynd's study of Middletown strengthened this emphasis.

About 1934, the analyst Caroline Zachry initiated a study of adolescence and included Sarah Lawrence in a group of institutions cooperating in the study. As part of this, there were seminars with Erik Erikson, Erich Fromm, Fritz Redl, and other analysts. Erikson's report in the fall of 1935, not long after he had come here from Vienna, moved me deeply. He presented a play session with a small child and the delicate precision and empathy of his observation and direct, eminently logical inferences from his observations were impressive. Gardner and I also visited Henry A. Murray at his Harvard Clinic. We were thrilled with his comprehensive perceptive approach to "needs" and "press" and the creativity of his Thematic Apperception Test (TAT). This was close to the publication of *Explorations in Personality* (1938).

I had already been startled by the way in which some children projected personal anxieties onto pictures I had shown them during my sympathy study. In a 1934 meeting with Lawrence K. Frank—our close friend and neighbor in New Hampshire—and John Levy with children's drawings, I discussed my evidence of the children's projective reactions to pictures. Larry Frank remarked, "What you have is a projective method." Another friend, Ruth Horowitz, and I wrote the first paper on projective methods (1938).[1]

The combination of my own experiences with children's behavior and thinking, along with getting acquainted with Erikson's and Murray's work, led to my interest in studying child personality at the preschool stage with a variety of methods, and Lawrence K. Frank, then at the Josiah Macy, Jr., Foundation made this financially possible. Dr. Benjamin Spock, then a young psychoanalytically-oriented pediatrician, joined us once a week for discussions of the children. I decided to use Miniature Life Toys with normal children as an approach to the study of personality in young children. Also through the Zachry research, I got acquainted with Anna Hartoch, who demonstrated Rorschach analyses, and I decided to try the Rorschach on the youngest children—two-year-olds. She was a genius like Murray and Erikson and worked through the records with me with great sensitivity. Together with L. Joseph Stone and Eugene Lerner each studying different aspects of child personality, we produced the monograph *Methods for Studying Personality in Young Children* (1941a), which later I edited into a book at the request of Arthur Rosenthal of Basic Books. Along with the book on methods, I begged to have one book presenting all the material on an individual child, and he supported this. It became Volume II, *Colin: A Normal Child* (1956).

During the thirties I was also invited by Barbara Biber to cooperate in research at the Bank Street College for Teachers, where I had an opportunity to use Rorschachs and Miniature Life Toys with seven-year-olds. Bar-

---

1. H. A. Murray correctly questions the term "projective techniques" on the ground that this term assumes that unrealistic projections will always be given whereas quite realistic responses are common.

bara Biber and others of the stimulating Bank Street group became good friends (*Life and Ways of the Seven- to Eight-Year-Old*, 1952). And there were multidisciplinary conferences funded by the Macy Foundation where pediatricians, psychiatrists, and psychologists presented research findings and new concepts.

In the meantime, I decided that I did not want to be the kind of wife and mother who took long field trips, and without studies in India it would not be possible for me to continue the teaching of comparative religion at the level I would want to maintain. Having become so involved with children, I began in 1935 to teach courses dealing with human life and child development while we were also studying freshmen with a grant for studying development during the college years: with Ladd, *Emotional Factors in Learning*, (1944b) and with Rauschenbush, *Achievement in College* (1960).

During the thirties, through Ruth Munroe and John Levy, then, after he died, Bela Mittelmann, we met other psychoanalysts, Ernst and Marianne Kris, Heinz and Dora Hartmann, and René Spitz, among others, and Ruth talked about her analyst Paul Schilder—all people with rich, sensitive minds, warm responsiveness, and delight both in human life and in nature. Gardner was equally interested in and responsive to this group. At a 1936 conference at Swanscott we met Adolph Meyer, who, along with some others, deepened our awareness of biological contributions to personality. We also came to know David M. Levy whose originality and productiveness in studies of affect and relationships, mostly published in articles, have never been adequately appreciated. And later, among other refugees from Hitler's Germany, we became acquainted with William Stern and the Gestaltists Max Wertheimer, Kurt Lewin, as well as Fritz Heider, who with his American wife Grace became intimate friends. Kurt did not approve of my interest in psychoanalysis, but I was not deterred. All of these influenced my thinking about children.

When I started the research on sympathy, I thought it could be a Ph.D. dissertation and I might as well take the necessary courses for the doctorate at nearby Teachers College. I had the extraordinary good fortune of having Ralph Spence as a mentor on thirty points of individualized study in which I chose to read and write on Gestalt and psychoanalysis; the chairman of my research committee was Lois Meek (now Stolz), and A. T. Jersild, child psychologist, was a supportive advisor on my research. While of course I did not know enough to approach a psychoanalytic study of the sympathetic behavior I found, my discussion was sufficiently dynamic so that Susan Isaacs in London appreciated it before any Americans except Goodwin Watson. In general, the child development establishment ignored my work for a decade, but forty years later, some of the investigators of "prosocial behavior" regard my sympathy study as a forerunner.

During the war years, I was deeply interested in the reports of Anna Freud and Dorothy Burlingham on the coping patterns of children supported by the Foster Parents plan, evacuated from London to safety. I sent out a nationwide questionnaire to nursery school teachers on children's reactions to the war; this led to an article on children's reactions during wartime (1943).

Gardner and I had spent a summer session at the Institute of Child Welfare Research in Berkeley in 1938 and again after World War II in 1947, where I reviewed the Jones' data on young adolescents and prepared four case studies in order to persuade Harold Jones to publish an integrated study of one boy. I had many conversations with the Joneses and Jean Macfarlane, absorbing perspectives which deeply influenced my subsequent work. I also visited research programs at the University of Minnesota, the University of Iowa, and the Fels Research Institute in Yellow Springs, Ohio.

TO KANSAS

When in 1951 the Menninger Foundation in Topeka approached Gardner with an invitation to become director of research, he agreed to come in September 1952, if there was also a position for me. Sibylle Escalona promised to bequeath the unique records on infants she and Mary Leitch and their team had made from 1948 to 1951. This was an irresistible opportunity to study preschool children who had been well studied in infancy. Dr. Will Menninger asked what I wanted to do. I explained that while there were endless studies of pathology, no one had studied how normal children cope with their ordinary, everyday problems, and I thought this needed to be done. He said "Go ahead and do it, and I'll pick up the tab." Picking up the tab he did for the first year or so, then as my research group and secretarial needs expanded, I was urged to obtain grants to finance the work. The first N.I.M.H. site-visitor, John Benjamin, a brilliant psychologist, grilled me in a rather ridiculing way: "What do you mean by coping, what's the idea of studying coping in children and expecting a grant for it?" The term "coping" was not in the Psychological Abstracts Index at that time and, although it was a word which has been used in literary contexts and everyday discussion, it had never been the focus of research. After I had done enough explaining from my point of view, I became impatient and said, "I *know* this needs to be studied and if you and N.I.M.H. don't want to support it, you don't need to—I'll find somebody else to support it." He went back to Washington and, evidently, did support it because I received N.I.M.H. grants through 1969—the last grant being a contract initiated by Dr. Caroline Chandler who had become interested in our studies.

Our presentations at the American Psychological Association annual conferences in 1954 and 1955, then at the international conference in Brussels in 1957, introduced our studies of children's coping. My first book on this research, *The Widening World of Childhood*, was published in 1962. Escalona and Heider had written *Prediction and Outcome* (1959) comparing Escalona's predictions based on the infancy functioning of the children with their preschool patterns as we had recorded them. Numerous monographs and books used our data: I was determined that our study would not fail to be productive.

Along with the research, I had applied to the Topeka Psychoanalytic Institute for training as a special student. The combination of didactic work and analysis with a group of cosmopolitan minds opened new doors to the understanding of infancy and development. This was a period of brilliant analysts at the institute, including my training analyst Ishak Ramzy. Because of the combination of my focus on child development and my psychoanalytic training I was asked to teach at different times in several different psychoanalytic institutes.

I had also been involved in outside activities such as being chairman of the Preschool Committee of the Governor of Kansas' larger Committee on Retardation. Mobilizing social workers, pediatricians, and other workers with children, I got a vivid picture of the isolation and lack of resources for families to help retarded children in the rural areas of Kansas. Caroline Chandler, along with the analyst, Reginald Lourie, a psychoanalytically-trained pediatrician, were chairmen of a project to coordinate thinking about early child care, bringing together child analysts, psychologists, and pediatricians. This work led to three chapters by me in the book they edited with Laura Dittmann, *Early Child Care: The New Perspectives* (1968a).

Then came "Head Start." The concept of Head Start, of course, touched all my deepest interests in the needs of children, the possibilities of change, and ways of contributing to personality development. I participated at all levels, from that of national planning, training at the state level, and consultation one morning a week over three years with the local Head Start Center. And I was also involved in the planning for Parent-Child Centers, and some consultation and reporting on them. As a child, I had heard the phrase "poor white trash" and also, when I was five, my father had taken me on the trolley to churches where he was a visiting minister. I had seen dirty, poorly-clad children running along the street in front of saloons and was shocked by the contrast between their environment and the paradise that I had known in lovely eastern Iowa. I felt that something ought to be done about them and now, sixty years later, came my chance to help. I was excited about the response of the local Head Start Center—especially the growth of the children and of their mothers. I offered Jule Sugarman, then director of the Office of Child Development a manuscript based on detailed weekly notes as well as observations of day care and Head Start centers across the United States. Franc Balzer obtained the help of a gifted editor, Ethel Leeper, who joined in the preparation of ten booklets, *Caring for Children*, illustrated for the most part with photographs I had made. I am told that over 2,000,000 copies of these booklets were distributed and sold. About the same time L. Joseph Stone asked me to collaborate on a volume of reports on infants, *The Competent Infant* (1972b).

A very modest venture was a little book *Growing Up in Garden Court* (1974), based upon detailed records of the care and treatment of disturbed children in the Children's Hospital of the Menninger Foundation.

TO WASHINGTON, D.C.

In 1967, Gardner retired from the Menninger Foundation and accepted an invitation to teach at George Washington University while I accepted an invitation from Reginald Lourie to consult with an infant study at Children's Hospital in Washington. This involved both some training sessions and also, much later, some participation in and consultations with a program for high-risk infants and high-risk mothers, as well as other consultations.

In the meantime, I had begun to write a book on comprehensive treatment of a brain-damaged twelve-year-old girl, "Robin," who was not expected ever to be able to graduate from high school, but who did. She subsequently took nurse's aide training, is now taking care of babies in a nursery in a large hospital in Topeka, has bought a house, is driving a car, and living quite a normal life (*Robin: Comprehensive Treatment of a Vulnerable Adolescent*, with Cotter Hirschberg, 1982).

I had also worked ahead on integrating the research over the years of our longitudinal study in a book, *Vulnerability, Coping, and Growth*, with Alice Moriarty (1976), with the help of a superb editor, Jane Isay, at Yale University Press (she is now at Basic Books).

It is not possible in a short account to do justice to everything. A chapter in itself would be my experience in 1950, helping to plan the B. M. Institute of Child Development and Mental Health in Ahmedabad, India, and subsequent consultation with the Institute and members of its staff. This was a challenging experience which integrated in an unexpected way all my study and work with children and my background in the religions of India.

Presentations at conferences of various organizations concerned with children, the National Association for the Education of Young Children, the Association for Childhood Education, the Orthopsychiatric Association, the Association for Child Psychoanalysis, all included warm nourishing and stimulating contacts with caring people, as did lectures in the United States and abroad, and a presentation of one child, "Helen," at Hampstead Clinic, invited by Anna Freud.

It was natural after my basic training in child development and in psychoanalysis that I should want to bring the two together, feeling that child development needed to evolve a more dynamic approach and psychoanalysis needed to include a wider range of realities of childhood experience. This purpose led to a number of articles taking steps in this direction.

After Gardner's death in 1979, Marian Radke-Yarrow invited me to be a guest scientist in her Center for Child Health and Development at NIH. There I have enjoyed participating in seminars and consulting with young people engaged in prosocial research.

Whatever I have done has been fed by a wealth of experience with watching and listening to children in my own families, communities, and different geographic areas in the United States, observation of a hundred or more institutions and centers for children in the United States and around the world and sharing perspectives with people from different cultures as well as constant exchanges with Gardner and other friends. There are still many questions to be answered, many issues to be researched. The sciences of psychoanalysis and child development are both young, and I wish I had another lifetime to work on the problems in their integration.

REFERENCES

Adams, Henry. 1913. *Mont St. Michel and Chartres*. Boston and New York: Houghton Mifflin.

Bhagavad Gita. 1899. Eng. tr. London: Christian Literary Society for India.

Escalona, S. K. and G. M. Heider. 1959. *Prediction and Outcome*. New York: Basic Books.

Freud, S. 1921. *Group Psychology and the Analysis of the Ego*. Standard Ed. 18:67–143. London: Hogarth.

——1923. *The Ego and the Id*. Standard Ed. 19:3–66. London: Hogarth.

Kipling, R. 1898. *The Jungle Book*. New York: Macmillan.

Levy, David M. 1966. *Maternal Overprotection*. 2d ed. New York: Norton.

Murphy, L. B. *See* Representative Publications.

Murray, H. A. 1938. *Explorations in Personality*. New York: Oxford University Press.

Myers, F. W. H. 1903. *Human Personality and Its Survival of Bodily Death*. 2 vols. New York: Arno.

Prince, M. 1906. *The Dissociation of a Personality*. Rpt., Westport, Conn.: Greenwood Press, 1969.

Prince, Walter. 1915 and 1916. The Doris Case of multiple personality. *Proceedings of the American Society for Psychical Research*, vols. 9 and 10.

Spyri, J. 1902. H. White, tr. *Heidi*. New York: Crowell.

Watson, J. B. 1928. *Psychological Care of Infant and Child*. New York: Norton.

Representative Publications by Lois B. Murphy

1931.   With G. Murphy. *Experimental Social Psychology.* New York: Harper.
1937a. With G. Murphy and T. M. Newcomb. *Experimental Social Psychology.* Rev. ed. New York: Harper.
1937b. *Social Behavior and Child Personality.* New York: Columbia University Press.
1938.   With R. Horowitz. Projective methods in the psychological study of children. *Journal of Experimental Education,* 7:133–40.
1941a. With J. Stone and E. Lerner. *Methods for the Study of Personality in Young Children.* Monographs of the Society for Research in Child Development, vol. 7, series 30, no. 4. Washington, D.C.: National Research Council.
1941b. Social and emotional development from birth to maturity. *Review of Educational Research,* 11:479–501.
1943.   The young child's experience in wartime. *American Journal of Orthopsychiatry,* 14:10–21.
1944a. Childhood experience. In J. M. Hunt, ed., *Personality and Behavior Disorders.* New York: Ronald Press.
1944b. With H. Ladd. *Emotional Factors in Learning.* New York: Columbia University Press.
1952.   With B. Biber, L. Woodcock, and I. Black. *Life and Ways of the Seven- to Eight-Years-Old.* New York: Basic Books.
1960.   With E. Rauschenbush. *Achievement in the College Years.* New York: Harper.
1961.   Preventative implications of development in the preschool years. In G. Caplan, ed., *Prevention of Mental Disorders in Children.* New York: Basic Books.
1962.   *The Widening World of Childhood.* New York: Basic Books.
1965a. Factors in continuity and change in the development of adaptational style in children. *Vita Humana,* 7:96–114.
1965b. Psychoanalysis and child development. In I. G. Sarason, ed., *Psy-*

choanalysis and the Study of Behavior. Parts 1 and 2. New York: Van Nostrand.

1966.   Affective factors in learning of pre-school deprived children. Presentation at University of Maryland. Department of Education Conference, Oct. 25.

1968a.   Individualization of child care and its relation to the environment; Assessment of infants and young children; The vulnerability inventory. In Laura Dittman, Reginald Lourie, and Caroline Chandler, eds., *Early Child Care: The New Perspectives.* New York: Atherton.

1968b.   The interdependence of education and therapy with emotionally disturbed brain-damaged children. *Learning Disorders,* vol. 3. Seattle, Wash.: Special Child Publications.

1969.   Multiple factors in learning in the day-care center. *Childhood Education,* 45:311–20.

1970–1973. With E. M. Leeper. *Caring for Children.* DHEW Publications, Nos. 1026–30, 77-31031, 78-31035. Washington, D.C.: Department of Health, Education and Welfare.

1972a.   With C. Chandler. Building foundations for strength in the preschool years: Preventing developmental disturbances. In S. E. Golann and C. Eisdorfer, eds., *Handbook of Community Mental Health.* New York: Appleton-Century Crofts.

1972b.   With L. J. Stone & H. Smith. *The Competent Infant.* New York: Basic Books.

1972c.   Infants' play and cognitive development. In M. W. Piers, ed., *Play and Development: A Symposium.* New York: Norton.

1973a.   Coping, vulnerability, and resilience. In D. A. Hamburg, G. B. Coelho, and J. E. Adams, eds., *Coping and Adaptation: Interdisciplinary Perspectives.* New York: Basic Books.

1973b.   Some mutual contributions of psychoanalysis and child development. In B. G. Rubinstein, ed., *Psychoanalysis and Contemporary Science,* vol. 2. New York: Macmillan.

1974.   *Growing Up in Garden Court.* New York: Child Welfare League of America.

1976.   With A. E. Moriarty. *Vulnerability, Coping, and Growth.* New Haven: Yale University Press.

1978.   Roots of an approach to studying child development. In T. S. Krawiec, ed., *The Psychologists,* vol. 3. Brandon, Vt.: Clinical Psychology Publishing.

1979.   With C. Frank. Prevention: The clinical psychologist. In M. R.

Rosenzweig and L. W. Porter, eds., *Annual Review of Psychology*, vol. 30. Palo Alto, Calif.: Annual Reviews.

1981. Explorations in child personality. In A. I. Rabin, J. Aronoff, A. M. Barclay, and R. A. Zucker, eds., *Further Explorations in Personality*. New York: Wiley.

1982a. With C. Hirschberg. *Robin: Comprehensive Treatment of a Vulnerable Adolescent*. New York: Basic Books.

1982b. Psychoanalytic views of infancy. In S. I. Greenspan and G. H. Pollock, eds., *The Course of Life: Psychoanalytic Contributions toward Understanding Personality Development*, vol. 1. Washington, D.C.: U.S. Government Printing Office.

1982c. *The Home Hospital: How a Family Can Cope With Catastrophic Illness*. New York: Basic Books.

MARGARET IVES

How did I come to be a psychologist? Let us look at the record.

My paternal great grandmother was a Quaker whose life covered approximately the same period as that of Queen Victoria. She had nine children, yet she founded the first woman's club in Detroit and was instrumental in persuading the authorities to establish our beautiful city park on an island in the middle of the Detroit River. Also, I understand, she welcomed in her home escaping slaves on the road to Canada. She has written her reminiscences for my father, her grandson, which I hope to transcribe in permanent form.

On the other side of the family, my mother's father did not think girls needed a college education. So Mother graduated from "Normal School" (so-called then), taught school for awhile, saved her money, and departed alone for Europe at the age of twenty-three, so that she would be better able to teach French and German to high-school students. That was in 1896. And Mother, after spending time in Paris and Tours, went to Berlin, where she was admitted to the University of Berlin the first year they admitted women.

On the steamship Mother met an older woman, who, surprised that she was traveling alone, looked out for her and showed her around Paris. Later, back in the United States, Mother called on this woman while visiting Detroit. There she met the woman's son, who later became my father. They were married in 1901 and succeeded in having the word "obey" deleted from the Episcopal service.

I was the older of two children—the younger, a boy, Chandler Ives. It never entered my head that one of us was to be preferred over the other. I was older and therefore I should look out for my brother when necessary. Once, when I was about twelve, I knocked down the boy next door (my age) because he was fighting with my little brother. I explained afterwards that there was too much difference in size for me to allow that to go on. I had an advantage too. Nearly all the children on the street were boys and I happened to be a fast runner; I could run faster than any of them. I knew the boys didn't like it but there it was. Later on, at college, I made the track team. Our relay team broke unofficially the women's record at that time. It was not that we were faster runners than any women had been previously, but because members of the track team were for the first time permitted to wear shorts instead of wind-catching bloomers. It was decreed that the shorts must reach within four inches of the knee, but nevertheless I remember that the fences were lined with boys and young men watching us practice. Women in other sports, where speed was not so important, were still required to wear bloomers for awhile longer.

So I grew, considered a person who had a right to her own ideas and, so far as I can remember, never treated as other than an equal to my brother, Chandler. We were very close and the worst tragedy of my life occurred when he was drowned at the age of fifteen. He was at camp; the rowboat went down in a storm and he didn't make it to shore. That occurred during my freshman year in college, and it probably caused me to withdraw from social affairs and throw myself more than ever into my studies.

My father, Augustus Wright Ives, was a psychiatrist and professor of neurology and psychiatry at the Detroit College of Medicine, now the Medical School of Wayne University. When he discovered that I was interested in becoming a psychologist, he was strongly supportive. He said he had never learned much about behavior in medical school; he had gone to Vienna in 1903 to learn what he wanted to know. He thought psychology would be more to my liking than medicine and I agreed.

My mother had always wanted to go to college, but in spite of her study in Europe she had never attained a college degree. This was a handicap because the lack of credentials prevented her from returning to teaching later in her life. Vassar, one of the first colleges devoted exclusively to the education of women, was where Mother had always wanted to go. Its standards were high. She had no difficulty in persuading me that this was the college to attend. She registered me early and I do not remember any objections on my part.

There was strong motivation toward psychology in my Vassar experience. Margaret Floy Washburn was my professor and, in my freshman year, she was president of the American Psychological Association. She was the second woman to be so chosen and the last one for another fifty years. We were very proud of her.

She was reserved, an excellent teacher with many ideas of her own, but fundamentally a structuralist. We learned to introspect, describe our inner ideas and feelings as an "observer" in the laboratory. She had been one of

Edward B. Titchener's early students at Cornell and although John B. Watson, the father of behaviorism, was actively coming to the fore at that time, we never heard anything about him.

In my senior year, I did my first research, a study of emotional reactions to remembered situations. It was entitled "Memory Revival of Emotions as a Test of Emotional and Phlegmatic Temperaments" and was published in the *American Journal of Psychology* in 1925.

To my surprise, in looking back I find that I have never gone out to seek a job. My first one, on graduating from Vassar, was as a teacher in a continuation school in Elizabeth, New Jersey. The principal, Mrs. Hazen, came up to Vassar seeking two new graduates who had *not* had the typical preparatory education for teachers and who might therefore have new ideas. She wanted to remotivate the fourteen- and fifteen-year-old drop-outs, most of whom were working in factories—non-union garment factories—at an average wage of $7.50 per week. Two of us were chosen; we tried new things and learned a great deal. We even dared to take a small group into New York to see Shakespeare's *As You Like It*. They had read it in class and had a wonderful time. They came back wanting to put on a Shakespearean play themselves. Most useful later on was the ability to communicate with adolescent dropouts without either "talking down" to them or using words they could not understand.

During my teaching period an unusual opportunity came my way in 1926. The Equal Rights Amendment had first been introduced in 1923. My father's cousin, Margaret Whittemore, then vice president of the Women's Party, invited me to come to Washington to a meeting and demonstration. Because of the illness of the official delegate from New Jersey, I was asked on my arrival to substitute for her. So I joined the group who marched back and forth in front of the White House, carrying placards, and who had an audience with President Coolidge on behalf of ERA. Alice Paul, the eminent feminist, was the leader.

President Coolidge, as was his wont, replied to us briefly. He told us how, while governor of Massachusetts, he had worked for better conditions for women working in the factories and shops of his state. Did we want to reverse all that? That was the end of the interview.

I enjoyed teaching. I might have stayed longer in Elizabeth, but the unusually fine principal who had recruited us left in 1927 to accept a position on the Rutgers University staff. Her successor was, in my opinion, not so outstanding. In addition, educators from Columbia Teachers College came to instruct us in giving group tests to our students. I thought they "talked down" to us teachers as if we were not quite bright and I resented it. I decided I had better go back for more education, and soon I was on my way to graduate school to become a psychologist.

At first I considered becoming an industrial psychologist, a field which had come into prominence after World War I. I had lunch at their apartment in New York with Dr. Walter V. Bingham, an outstanding early industrial psychologist, and his wife, a Vassar graduate. He recommended Michigan as outstanding in his field. That was fine with me, an excellent university, near my home in Birmingham, Michigan. So I enrolled and am certainly glad that I did. But circumstances and my own preferences dictated that I did not become an industrial psychologist.

I entered graduate school at the University of Michigan in 1928. I found myself out of date, with behaviorism flourishing in some quarters. However, Dr. Walter B. Pillsbury, chairman of the department since 1903, had also been a student of Titchener. He taught the history of psychology, of which he had been an important part. His stories about other well-known psychologists made his course fascinating as well as informative.

When I was about to receive my master's degree in 1929, Dr. Pillsbury told me about an opening at the Wayne County Clinic for Child Study, associated with the Juvenile Court in Detroit. So I went for an interview with Elizabeth M. Hincks, Ph.D., and was offered the position. Dr. Hincks, also a Vassar graduate, had obtained her Ph.D. from Harvard in 1924 and then had gone to Geneva, where she was analyzed by Jung. She was, in my opinion, way ahead of her time.

Fortunately for me, I entered upon my duties at the clinic just two months before the 1929 stock market crash. I stayed for three years, the first two under the close supervision of Dr. Hincks. The third year I was more independent. There were no internships in those days, but everything was carefully scrutinized. The duties of the psychologist included testing or assessment of children, both delinquents and dependents, and often of their parents as well. We did "personality interviews" and psychotherapy with the children, wrote detailed reports to the Court, and frequently appeared as witnesses. The procedure in the Court was very informal; except in serious cases, the judge was often not present.

In addition to four psychologists in the clinic, there were four social workers and four secretaries. We did a thorough examination of each child referred. There were also two consultant psychiatrists who came in once or twice a week to see cases referred to them. Once a week there were staff conferences, at which each case was presented and a decision made on what we would recommend to the Court.

In the fall of 1932, I returned to graduate school at the University of Michigan, assisted by a fellowship from Vassar. Salaries in those depression days were small and I needed money; so I applied and was granted the fellowship. I spent another three years full time at Michigan, during which I was busy and happy. I became acquainted with outstanding psychologists who were my teachers, among them Dr. Pillsbury, Dr. Burton Thuma, Dr. Martha Colby, Dr. Carl R. Brown, and Dr. Norman R. F. Maier. My major professor was Dr. Brown and I assisted Dr. Maier in the laboratory. My first experience with the idea that I shouldn't expect much because I was a woman occurred when I considered applying for the University Fellowship at Michigan for assistance during my last year there. I was told by various colleagues that I had no chance of being chosen because a psychologist had received it the year before and was "a woman too." Nevertheless I thought it would do no harm to try.

I heard nothing from the university. Finally, in mid summer, I received a letter telling me that if I did not wish to accept the fellowship, I should at least let them know. I had never received their letter, which, it was discovered later, had never left the registrar's office. So, after all, I was granted the fellowship.

I had passed my preliminaries and was beginning my research when the husband of Jack Schott, one of my Michigan classmates, offered me a position as his associate. He was Emmett L. Schott, Ph.D., the chief psychologist at the Henry Ford Hospital in Detroit. I hesitated; I would be forty miles from Ann Arbor and had only begun my dissertation, which was in experimental psychology, not in clinical. (Few were in clinical in those days.) But the depression was not over; I had had Juvenile Court experience and the offer was tempting.

So for the next three years I shuttled back and forth to Ann Arbor on weekends and spent every spare minute on my research. Finally I took two months' leave of absence to finish my dissertation and once again was fortunate to be asked to stay with the Norman Maier family in Ann Arbor. I had been a student of Dr. Maier, had served as his assistant in the laboratory, and had known his wife, Ayesha, slightly when she had been a young girl living in Birmingham, my home town. I had also baby-sat for the Maiers with their son, Richard, now an associate professor of psychology at Loyola University in Chicago. In June 1938, I received my Ph.D. degree.

The experience at the Ford Hospital was excellent. Dr. Thomas J. Heldt, psychiatrist, was chief of the department of neuro-psychiatry and was one of the first to employ psychologists on a general hospital staff (in 1926). Psychologists participated in almost all aspects of the work of the department except the prescription of drugs. We saw patients of all ages and in all diagnostic categories, from babies being placed for adoption to seniles, from normals to psychotics. I was very glad that I had studied neuroanatomy in the medical school at Michigan, because I was working very closely with the neurologists and learned the basics of what is now known as neuropsychology. Psychotherapy comprised much of my work in addition to assessment. We went on daily ward rounds, sat with patients recovering from electroshock therapy (EST), and took social histories. (There were no social workers; Henry Ford did not want any.)

One surprising development came early during World War II, when many physicians were entering the service. I was asked by Dr. Heldt to be responsible for approving all departmental diagnoses for indexing. I demurred; I was not a physician. He said he would check my work, but I know that he did not always do so. It was embarrassing when I had to report to the neurologist that I believed his resident had diagnosed the patient's lesion on the wrong side. Thank goodness I was right.

There was no discernible discrimination on the basis of sex among my colleagues at the hospital, but I noticed significant change in my status when I had received my Ph.D. The title "Doctor" was very important there.

However, there was serious discrimination among management personnel. Henry Ford would have no women physicians on his staff; there were two women Ph.D's, a chemist and I. The lay superintendent said outright that women should not be paid as much as men and he paid no attention to my chief's recommendation in this matter. I received 60 percent of the salary of the male psychologist, Dr. Schott, and no raise at all when I received my degree. Furthermore, the superintendent's office sent a note saying that I should continue to punch the time clock because I was a woman. I refused. I won on the time-clock matter, but not with regard to salary; so I decided to leave.

As part of my search for a new position, I took an unassembled Civil Service examination. More than a year later I received a letter from Isabelle V. Kendig, Ph.D., asking if I would be interested in a position as her associate on the psychology staff at Saint Elizabeths Hospital in Washington, D.C. She was the chief psychologist for that large and famous federal hospital. I came to Washington in January 1943. Dr. Kendig left in 1950 and I became chief in 1951.

At first at Saint Elizabeths I taught psychology to the student nurses, supervised psychology students, and tested maximum security patients in the John Howard Hall. It was only later that I did much psychotherapy, first with nurses, later with patients, especially the forensic patients. I gradually became a frequent witness in the Federal Court. Monte Durham was my patient (the Durham Rule). [1] I was a witness in the "Jenkins case," when the case, being tried by Judge Curran, was thrown out of court because the psychiatrist testified that she had based her diagnosis on the results of the psychological tests and the judge did not consider psychologists competent to make a diagnosis. On appeal, the case was eventually heard by all nine judges, sitting en banc in the Court of Appeals. Psychology won seven to two in 1962 and thereafter we were considered expert. The next time I was a witness in court the judge reminded me that I was no longer to give my "impression" but was to make a diagnosis.

The training program for interns in psychology did not really get started until 1947, although we had had students before that. After I became chief, the program continued to develop and grow and was one of the first few approved by APA. Much of its success is due to its director, my colleague Margaret Mercer, Ph.D.

The psychology branch grew. In 1943, there were two psychologists and two students. When I left in 1973, there were nearly forty psychologists, many of them doing research under the auspices of NIMH (the National Institute of Mental Health). But shortly before I retired, unitization [2] took place and my job changed its title from "Director of Psychological Services" to "Associate Director for Psychology." This was a staff rather than a line position and, in my opinion, less challenging.

From 1956 to 1966, while I was at Saint Elizabeths, I was chair of a rating panel for psychologists, under the U.S. Board of Civil Service Examiners. We rated all applicants, nation-wide, who applied for a Civil Service status in psychology, except for the Veterans Administration. I think this led to better prepared psychologists on Civil Service lists, but there is no longer any such committee. My position there probably led to my being asked to serve on a Civil Service committee organized to recommend revision of Civil Service standards for psychologists. Later, in 1971, when the licensing law for psychologists had finally been passed for the District of Columbia, I served for six years on the D.C. Board of Psychologist Examiners.

1. Monte Durham became famous later because the "Durham Rule" was named for him as a result of the decision in his case in the Federal Court for the District of Columbia that a defendant is not guilty if it can be shown that his criminal behavior is "the product of mental disease or defect." This became law in June 1954, largely as a result of the efforts of David Bazelon, eminent lawyer and judge.
2. "Unitization" refers to the concept, then widely being tried, of dividing large institutions into more or less autonomous units. At Saint Elizabeths each unit had its own psychiatrist in charge and a chief psychologist, social worker, nurse, etc. Staff was recruited by each unit and D.C. patients were housed according to the section of the District in which they lived. Saint Elizabeths became more like a group of small hospitals, all in one geographical location.

During much of the period at Saint Elizabeths I taught one class, usually assessment, at the George Washington University (1946–1970), where I attained the rank of professorial lecturer. I was appointed by Thelma Hunt, M.D., Ph.D., who is an outstanding woman of my generation. She first became a member of the George Washington faculty in 1928, was for many years chair of the department of psychology, and is now emeritus professor. Currently she is in private practice in D.C. as a clinical psychologist. She also has the distinction of having been the first president of the D.C. Psychological Association.

An aspect of my career that I consider unusual is that most of the recognition I have received has come since I reached my sixties. Before that, I was working, learning, teaching, trying to build and improve the psychology branch at Saint Elizabeths Hospital, but was, I think, little known nationally. I had, to be sure, received my Phi Beta Kappa and Sigma Xi keys when I was at Vassar and the University of Michigan, respectively, had had fellowships which have been mentioned, and had been awarded the diploma of the American Board of Professional Psychology (ABPP) in 1948. Way back in 1938, I had been president of a now defunct group, the Detroit Psychology Club, and from 1952 to 1955, I had been secretary-treasurer of the International Council of Psychologists. That was it.

Then in 1963, I was elected secretary-treasurer of the Division of Consulting Psychology (13) of APA, was twice its council representative and president in 1967–1968. In 1970, I was president of the Division of Psychologists in Public Service (18), and in 1975 of the D.C. Psychological Association. The U.S. Department of Health, Education, and Welfare honored me with its Superior Service Award in 1964 and I received the Harold M. Hildreth Memorial Award for psychologists in public service in 1974. Finally, in 1980, the American Board of Forensic Psychology gave me its first "Distinguished Psychologist Award" for my "pioneering efforts in forensic psychology." This grew out of my testimony in the Jenkins case. I feel deeply indebted to these organizations for their recognition.

After April 1973 I was supposedly retired; I had a few patients and one student to supervise because she was not yet eligible for licensing in Virginia. I kept reasonably active in psychological affairs. Then, in January 1977, the Board of Trustees of the American Board of Professional Psychology invited me to serve as executive officer, supposedly a part-time position. This was a challenging and interesting job, replete with problems involving all of psychology. The present concern over credentialling, over the definition of a psychologist, over the identification of and differentiation between specialties in psychology, and, most important in my position, how do we define excellence. I attended the meetings of APA's Board of Professional

Affairs and was invited to other meetings concerned with these matters. Most of all I tried to stress the importance of excellence and of the ABPP diploma. I spent four years as executive officer, retiring again on May 1, 1981, just in time to embark on a trip to China as a participant in a "People to People International Mental Health Project."

The trip to China was a fascinating, unparalleled experience. The "People to People International" was started by President Eisenhower with the purpose of increasing the knowledge of one country's people about another. We were a group of thirty-eight people from all over the United States, all of whom were in some way involved with mental health. There were psychologists, social workers, nurses, educators, mental health association officers, and even a librarian from a hospital library. Strangely, there were no psychiatrists.

It was a strenuous trip; we were kept busy morning, noon, and evening. There were no "afternoons at leisure." We visited seven cities in seventeen days: Guangzhou (Canton,) Beijing (Peking,) Tianjing (Tientzin,) Nanjing (Nanking,) Suzhou (Soochow,) Shanghai, and Guilin (Kweilin.) We needed to learn the Chinese names, which have been changed from the Western convention.

We visited a university, hospitals, schools, a day care center, a steel factory, a commune, and the Children's Palace in Shanghai, where children go for play and recreation after school. Also there was plenty of sightseeing: the Great Wall, the Forbidden City (no longer forbidden,) the Ming tombs, caves, the zoo, and trips on the rivers, where we saw not only one of the great harbors of the world at Shanghai, but beautiful scenery, especially the strangely shaped mountains on the Li River near Guilin. I took many pictures, both slides and movies, and so did nearly everyone else.

Most interesting were the people, especially the children and young people. We saw two performances of Chinese acrobats, who were indeed remarkable. Many of the leaders whom we visited in the various institutions spoke good English, told us what they were doing and answered our questions with apparent frankness and in some detail. They always served tea. The young people, most of whom seemed to be studying English, gathered around us in large numbers in the streets wherever possible, or in the "Friendship" stores where we were taken to shop. We met them wherever we visited. They wanted to practice their English and ask questions; seemed well informed and very friendly. (This seems an amazing change from what must have been the case during the recent "Cultural Revolution," which they now characterize as a great mistake.) These young people evidently want to go places and do things—in contrast to the Russians who seem resigned to their fate and do not expect to be allowed to go anywhere.

The weather was excellent for the most part, but nevertheless there was something in the air which made all of us contract coughs and bad colds. Nearly everyone had to take at least one day off and remain in bed. (I missed the caves.) This, combined with the strenuous program, the fourteen-hour trip across the Pacific with no stopover and a nine-hour time change brought many of us back exhausted, if not ill. But it was worth it.

I must not close this section without telling about our oldest colleague on the trip. Hildegarde Durfee, Ph.D., a retired psychologist, aged eighty-five, now living in Vermont. She carried a cane, but went everywhere with us, climbing many stairs and even going up on the Great Wall. The Chinese, who respect the elderly, were most helpful and solicitous, as well as amazed when they learned her age.

To sum up this account, I think I have had a good life. Most of the time I have been content and involved in my career and have been generously treated by colleagues of both sexes. However, my list of publications is embarrassingly small; I have not written as much as I had hoped and planned or should have done. Despite my degree in experimental psychology, I have not carried on significant post-doctoral research.

Although I have and have had many friends, I must admit that at times I am lonely. Unfortunately I never married and therefore have not had the family life in adulthood that most people have. It was a disappointment not to have a husband and children and it is difficult to explain to myself or others why I did not marry. Just before I retired from Saint Elizabeths, my young cousin, aged eighteen, who was having adjustment difficulties, came to live with me in Alexandria and was here for three years. Later her younger sister joined her and both attended college. This was a rewarding experience for me and I think for the girls as well.

Now that I am older, I think that if I wanted to advance in a career, it is probably best that I remained single. Had I married and raised a family, I think I know myself well enough to believe that I would have thought it best for the children that I stay at home most of the time, especially when they were young. Had I married young, I might never have completed a doctorate. Many, of course, do both successfully, but I am thinking about myself and contemplating how I would have behaved fifty years ago. As it is, I did complete a doctorate while holding down a full-time job forty miles from the university. So who can say what might have happened? Now, at any rate I have a full and interesting life; I travel frequently and widely, have more time to visit museums, art galleries, and concert halls, read more extensively, and have a small private practice as well.

Representative Publications by Margaret Ives

1925. With M. F. Washburn, et al. Memory revival of emotions as a test of emotional and phlegmatic temperaments. *American Journal of Psychology*, 36:459–60.

1938. The flight of colors, following intense brief stimulation of the eye. Dissertation, University of Michigan. Ann Arbor: University Microfilms.

1946. Interrelationship of clinical psychology and psychiatry. *Journal of Clinical Psychology*, 2:146–50.

1965. With Arthur H. Brayfield, et al. Testimony before the Senate Subcommittee on Constitutional Rights of the Committee on the Judiciary. *American Psychologist*, 20:898–901.

1970. Psychology at Saint Elizabeths Hospital, 1907–1970. *Professional Psychology*, 1:155–58.

MILDRED B. MITCHELL

On December 25, 1903, in Rockford, Illinois, Dr. Hoye, the family physician of Bessie Warner and Louis Biglow Mitchell, was called away from his Christmas dinner to deliver their first child, me! Before I was two years old, my family moved to Harvard, Illinois, where my father operated the town power plant and *Harvard* became a part of my vocabulary at an early age. After two years, we moved back to Rockford where I lived until I graduated from Rockford College. The majority of Rockford residents were the children or grandchildren of Swedish immigrants if they were not immigrants themselves. My parents bought a house in a neighborhood where all but one elderly couple spoke English. Their daughter and her family lived next door to us. It was here with my two brothers and three sisters, including twins ten years younger than I, that I was raised. A few years ago, I learned that my twin sisters had been made to feel very inferior when the teacher asked all the students to tell their nationality. All the other children gave a nationality of some northern European country, mostly Sweden. When my sisters said they were Americans, the teacher said they couldn't be. Everyone came from somewhere.

All of our grandparents were dead long before I was born, but we had great uncles on both sides of the family who were veterans of the Civil War (now called the War between the States) and we knew relatives who had fought in all American wars since then. Later we learned that we also had ancestors who fought in the American Revolution. We never learned the year they migrated to the British colony in America nor from where they came. It is highly probable, however, that they came from the Protestant part of the British Isles because we were raised very strictly in the Presbyterian church (the Church of Scotland). This belief was reenforced when I saw "Mitchell" on all the London buses because a Mitchell was treasurer of the bus line when I was there in 1932. I was always proud to be an American. With this patriotic background, it seemed only right that I, too, should serve my country, so when the Army decided to have a woman's auxiliary, I took the first examination given in Minnesota (1942). Although I was accepted,

I was not called up immediately. In the meantime, I heard the Navy was going to commission women. When I went to the Navy Recruiting Office in Minneapolis, the Navy petty officer told me the Navy would *never* commission a woman. I might become a yeoman (secretary) but never a commissioned officer. How wrong he was! In less than a year, I was a Lieutenant (jg) in the Bureau of Naval Personnel with a *male* yeoman. I was delighted with the Lieutenant (jg) commission. Most men as well as women officers were midshipmen for six months and then commissioned as ensigns. Later I learned that men who were students with me at Harvard and Yale were commissioned as Lieutenant Commanders. I was always overage for grade. As a result, I did not become a Lieutenant Commander for fourteen years, after it became known that I helped select the first seven astronauts.

As a child, I never heard of a psychologist. I started school at the age of five and had such a wonderful teacher I wanted to be a teacher just like her. From then on, I told everyone who asked me what I was going to be when I grew up, that I was going to be an old maid school teacher. (At that time any teacher who married was immediately discharged.) Living at home as an undergraduate with a house full of noisy younger siblings and a mother who believed it was her duty to train me to be a good housewife, reenforced my earlier career choice of old maid school teacher. After the stimulating social life in Washington and New York during World War II, however, the prospect of returning to Minneapolis alone as a civilian seemed dull, except for the job. An Army Lieutenant, Ira Spear, whom I had met at a dance in Washington came home to New York after serving in the Normandy invasion and the Battle of the Bulge. I had been transferred to New York while he was overseas and neither his family nor I had heard from him for six months. He sent me huge boxes of flowers for three days straight before I learned who was sending them. He began taking me to plays, ballets, boating, swimming, and mountain climbing. We found we enjoyed many of the same things. After the American Psychological Association meetings in Philadelphia in 1946, I told him I had been recruited by the Veterans Administration (V.A.) to return to Minnesota to open the psychology department at the V.A. Mental Hygiene Clinic at Ft. Snelling. His first comment was, "You can't go!" By then, however, he knew I was too independent to turn down a job that paid almost three times what I was making at the Domestic Relations Court in New York City, so he said, "I'll go, too." The last of December I went to Minneapolis, bought a house, and on January 2, 1947, began work as the first chief clinical psychologist at Ft. Snelling. Six weeks later, Ira left his job as accountant at the American

Cancer Society headquarters and came to Minneapolis. I took a half-day leave from my job and we were married in the judge's chambers in the Minneapolis Court House.

When I entered Rockford College at the age of sixteen (1920), I was undecided whether to major in mathematics or history. In my sophomore year, I took a course in general psychology because it was required for a teaching certificate. The professor was Dr. Benjamin Van Riper, a philosopher with a Ph.D. from Boston University. I enjoyed his course so much I took his course in abnormal psychology the next semester. His reading list included Morton Prince's A *Dissociation of a Personality* (Prince 1906). I was so fascinated by it that I read everything I could find on hypnosis and started experimenting informally, on every willing subject I could find. On Memorial Day, Dr. Van Riper took our small class on a field trip to the state insane asylum in Elgin, Illinois. I was terrified but entranced by the paranoid schizophrenic who hugged the wall and glared at us as he followed us through a large ward.

My junior year, I took the only other psychology course that was offered, educational psychology, which was required for a teaching certificate. The education professor who taught it, told us that mathematics and philosophy were the most difficult subjects and that males did better in them than females. Undaunted I went on to major in mathematics to have something I could teach with a B.A. degree and to take all the philosophy courses offered. All three of my mathematics teachers in college and one in high school were women, so I saw no reason why I could not teach mathematics. Some years later, however, when I applied for a job teaching high-school mathematics, the superintendent told me frankly he only hired men to teach mathematics. Much as I liked mathematics, I could not see myself getting a Ph.D. in mathematics. All the mathematical problems seemed to have been solved already. I enjoyed the philosophy courses, especially the philosophy of religion, philosophy of science, and ethics. Philosophy seemed to be a more promising field for getting a Ph.D. No philosophical problems seemed to have been solved.

After receiving a B.A. degree from Rockford College in 1924 with a major in mathematics and minors in philosophy, speech, and education, I taught high school mathematics and dramatics in Missouri and Arkansas. Then a friend asked me if I would go to Columbia University or Harvard summer school with her. I told her I would not go to Columbia, but I would go to Harvard. We arrived in Cambridge shortly before classes began. We had no trouble registering for Dr. Frederick Wilhelm Brinkmann's graduate course

Famous Problems in Geometry. We soon learned that not all the problems in geometry had been solved. We spent our afternoons and many evenings studying in Widener Library.

Before summer school was over, I decided to stay in Cambridge to get an M.A. and hoped eventually to get a Ph.D. in philosophy. A few weeks before the fall term opened, I resigned my teaching position. When I went to register, I discovered, being a woman, I had to register at Radcliffe and pay my tuition there. The first day of fall classes, I found there were also other differences between being a Harvard summer school student and being a Radcliffe student. As a graduate student, I was assigned a cubicle in the stacks of Widener Library, where Harvard undergraduates were not allowed, but when I tried to enter the building after 6:00 P.M. I was stopped because I was a woman.

As I had assumed, there was no problem being accepted as a graduate student. Radcliffe simply asked Rockford College to send them a copy of my credentials. Because the four-day preliminary examinations (prelims) in philosophy at Harvard included a one-day examination in advanced general psychology, I registered for a course in it with Dr. Frank Pattie. I also registered for three courses in philosophy the first semester and four the second semester.

One night shortly afterwards, I attended a play in Harvard Yard. By chance I sat next to Dr. Leonard Carmichael, the first Ph.D. in psychology I had ever met. I spent several delightful hours with Dr. Carmichael learning all about the men with whom I intended to study that year, including Pattie who had been one of his students at Princeton. Then Dr. Carmichael told me something that not only led me to change one of the courses I had registered to take the first semester, but all the courses I had registered to take the second semester and my vocational goal. He told me Dr. Morton Prince had retired from Tufts Medical School and was going to teach a course at Harvard in clinical abnormal psychology. I was ecstatic at the possibility of studying with the author of A *Dissociation of a Personality*.

At that time (1926), psychology was still part of the philosophy department at Harvard. The chairmanship of the department alternated between a psychologist and a philosopher. It was a philosopher that year, so I went to him and readily received permission to take Prince's course instead of one of the philosophy courses for which I had registered.

Not wishing to miss a word Prince said, I chose a front seat in his class. I learned later that I was sitting between Prince's two assistants, Henry Murray, M.D., and Helge Lundholm, Ph.D., who was also working at McLean Hospital. (He later introduced me to the Rorschach cards which he was using there with his patients.) I found Prince to be a charming elderly gentleman and his lectures to be as fascinating to me as the first book of his I had read. I continued my informal experimenting with hypnosis and reported my results to Prince before each class. One day with a big grin, he shook his finger at me and said, "Miss Mitchell, you are a very dangerous woman." I was amused at this because I knew he was poking fun at those who were afraid to be hypnotized. They believed hypnotists had some occult power so they could make people say and do things they did not want to do. He obviously appreciated my enthusiasm for his course and for hypnosis and for my willingness to cooperate with him in class demonstrations. At the end of the semester, he permitted me and three men, including David Shakow, to register for a research course with him. He divided us between his two assistants. I was assigned to Lundholm. Since he was working at the hospital and I had found an excellent subject who was also working during the day, we did all our research at night. Emerson Hall, which contained the psychological library and classrooms as well as the laboratories, was locked at 6:00 P.M. After I had waited a long time in a blizzard for a man with a key to come along and let me into the building, Lundholm told me to go to Edwin Garrigues Boring's secretary and pick up a key to the building. When I asked her for a key, she told me to come back the next day. The next day, she took me into Boring's private office where he was pacing the deck. He asked if I were a Radcliffe student. I replied that as a woman, I had had to register at Radcliffe, but every cent of my tuition had been sent over to Harvard for I was taking all my academic courses at Harvard. The only course I was taking at Radcliffe was aesthetic dancing, a non-credit course. He paced and paced and reiterated that I was a Radcliffe student. I got no key! All semester in spite of snow, sleet, or rain, I waited in front of Emerson Hall for some man with a key.

Soon after Boring refused to give me a key, Mrs. Lundholm began accompanying her husband to Emerson Hall whenever we were working there. Ostensibly, she came to help us record our results. Although we had no electronic recording equipment in those days, Lundholm and I had not been having any difficulty recording our data. Since Mrs. Lundholm was very compatible, I did not say anything because I thought she was just trying to be helpful. It was not until five years later (1932), after I happened to see Lundholm in the elevator of the Eiffel Tower in Paris, that I learned there had been more to Mrs. Lundholm's presence in Emerson Hall than I had suspected. Lundholm told me Boring had written him a letter that ought to be framed, but he refused to tell me what was in it.

Twenty-four years after Boring refused to give me a key to Emerson Hall,

I published "The Status of Women in the American Psychological Association" as the lead article in the *American Psychologist* (Mitchell 1951). A few months later I received a letter from Boring enclosing a copy of the manuscript he had written in response to my article, so I could write a rebuttal if I wished. I was in no condition to write a rebuttal. His letter reached me in the V.A. Hospital, Minneapolis, where I was seriously ill with double pneumonia. He seemed to think that he and Alice Bryan had written all that needed to be said about the "woman problem." He said the reason women did not get anywhere in APA was because they would not work more than forty hours a week. That aroused my adrenalin to the point I was able to sit up in bed long enough to answer his letter. I reminded him that he had done everything he could to keep me from working more than forty hours a week and that I still remembered standing out in a blizzard waiting until some man with a key came along to let me into Emerson Hall. I also reminded him that the psychological library and Widener were both closed to me after 6:00 P.M. Boring wrote back that the *Zeitgeist* was not good for women at Harvard in 1927. He enclosed a revised version of his manuscript (Boring 1951). I was not exactly elated with it, but I felt no need to write a rebuttal. In today's *Zeitgeist*, I might have written a rebuttal to *American Psychologist* instead of a letter to Boring, but at that time I was satisfied with the catharis I got from expressing my feelings to him which I could not do as a student.

Refusing to give me a key was not the only way Boring discriminated against women. The first semester I was at Harvard, taking two courses in psychology and two courses in philosophy, I was invited to attend the philosophical colloquium (a regular meeting of students, research fellows, and some faculty to discuss their research and theories), but not the psychological colloquium. The second semester, although I was taking four courses in psychology, including Boring's history of psychology, I still was not invited to attend the psychological colloquium.

In June 1927 I received an M.A. in philosophy. It was then necessary to replenish my diminishing bank account. I became a professor of mathematics and education in a small Presbyterian college in the hills of Kentucky. The new president of the college had just received an M.Ed. from Harvard. In order to get an "A" rating from the state for the three-year preparatory school that was part of the college, he needed a principal who was not also the president of the college. As professor of education, he gave me the job of principal as a little additional duty. For $1,000.00 a year and a small room and board in the dormitory, I taught twenty hours of mathematics, education and psychology a week. I also tried to teach the football players and their coach that the players should at least register at the college and make at least a "D" in some of their subjects. The president and I learned a great deal about the culture of the hills. We both felt lucky to still be alive at the end of the year and were happy to return to Harvard.

I had been accepted at Yale but without any financial assistance. Then an elderly friend in Cambridge wrote that she was having great difficulty getting a live-in female cook to please her and she was afraid to stay in her large house alone. She offered me a room and some meals very reasonably if I would just come back to Harvard and stay with her. Since I wanted very much to take Frederic Wells' course at Boston Psychopathic Hospital, I was glad to accept her offer. The first year at Harvard when I decided to continue in psychology instead of in philosophy the second semester, I had asked Wells' permission to take his course in clinical psychometrics at Boston Psychopathic Hospital. It was the only one (there were none at Yale and few, if any, elsewhere) which gave psychology students an opportunity to work with mental patients, to learn to give tests, and to cooperate in research projects. Wells preferred that I begin the course in the fall, so I waited.

When I returned to Harvard, Boring was officially on leave. He secluded himself in his office writing his *History of Experimental Psychology* (Boring 1929). Diane Selling, a Radcliffe senior, and I were invited to attend the psychological colloquium. The second semester, Boring was back on duty and lost no time getting the psychological colloquium back the way he wanted it. He found Selling in the psychological library. He told her the psychological colloquium was very dear to his heart and he did not believe that men could discuss things frankly in the presence of women. He asked her to tell me. Although I thought his stated reason for not wanting us was asinine, I was not sorry to have the time to spend on something else. Actually, I had not found the meetings of much interest. Boring was struggling to keep psychology "pure" and I was more interested in the unacceptable "applied" research. As Burrhus Frederic Skinner wrote in the second volume of his autobiography (Skinner 1979), the men argued a great deal and I, the only graduate woman, did not say much. The next semester, when I entered Yale as a graduate student, I was immediately given a master key to the old chemistry building which housed the psychology department, including my private office where I could conduct my research, and the psychological library. Furthermore, I was welcomed to the Yale equivalent of the Harvard psychological colloquium. The second semester I was elected co-chairman of the group. The following year, Boring was invited to speak to our group.

The Yale psychological department had just moved into the beautiful new Institute of Human Relations building adjoining the Yale Medical School. I felt very smug when Boring said he felt like the poor relations.

Although Boring caused me great frustrations, he was not all bad. He was by no means a mentor, but he did teach me some things that greatly influenced my future. Now that I have told you about the frustrations he caused me and some sequelae to them, let me go back to my first year at Harvard and tell you some of my pleasanter experiences with him. Boring did not refuse to have women in his classes as Leonard Troland did. At the time Boring refused to give me a key, I was taking his history course. He gave me a high enough grade that I attained the "A" average I needed to get my M.A. in one year. Boring was a good, formal lecturer, but he was very tense. He frequently paced the deck as he presented material from the book he was writing (Boring 1929). I enjoyed his vignettes, especially the one of his mentor, E. B. Titchener, whom he described as an English psychologist who taught German psychology to American students for many years without becoming an American citizen even though, as a foreigner, he had to pay more each year for his hunting license. He described Leonard Carmichael as an up-and-coming young experimental psychologist. His vignette that affected me most, however, was the one of Mary Whiton Calkins. He said she had worked at Harvard with William James, before there was a Radcliffe College, and done everything a man would have done to get a Ph.D., but Harvard refused to give her one because she was a woman. Later, when Radcliffe was founded, Radcliffe offered her a Ph.D. She refused it, saying she did her work at Harvard and she did not want a Radcliffe Ph.D. I decided then and there I did not want a Radcliffe Ph.D. either. It had always rankled me to have to register at Radcliffe and give my money to Radcliffe. I now had a B.A. from Rockford College and would soon have an M.A. from Radcliffe College. I had stayed at home and gone to Rockford College, then a private woman's college, because they gave me a scholarship and the coeducational university of my choice would not take girls under eighteen years of age. I did not want to wait two years.

In addition to courses with Prince and Boring my second semester at Harvard, I took an interesting course in problem children with Walter Fenno Dearborn in the Harvard Graduate School of Education where women were not only welcome, but were even given Harvard degrees. I also took Edward Stevens Robinson's course in learning. He was an exchange professor from the University of Chicago that semester. Robinson had a profound influence on my future. He was a very friendly, relaxed, informal lecturer with a good sense of humor. One day in class he said he wished one of us "hypnotic nuts" would do some work on retroactive inhibition and hypnosis. That sounded interesting to me and I did not think anyone could qualify better than I, as a "hypnotic nut." The next semester Robinson went to Yale as an exchange professor from the University of Chicago for one semester, but stayed until he was killed by a bicycle.

While at Harvard, I also took a seminar with Walter Samuel Hunter on animal behavior. He came over from Clark University to give this course. He had considerable influence on my future. It was a small class so we sat informally around a table. I was the only woman. Hunter seemed to be very critical of everyone else's work. Skinner (Skinner 1979), who was also a student in the course, found him very unfriendly. I felt that if I could do work to please him, I could be sure it was good. One day in class I was talking enthusiastically about Wolfgang Köhler's *Mentality of Apes* (Köhler 1926). Hunter critized Köhler severely saying Yerkes had done the same experiments. I had not read Yerkes' work so I could not rebut him intellectually. In what I suppose all the men thought was a typical female emotional reaction, I replied, "Well I like Köhler, anyway!" Hunter laughed and said he liked Köhler, too. He was a very nice man. Hunter was the editor of the new journal, the *Psychological Abstracts*. He asked for volunteers to abstract articles written in French and German. Skinner (Skinner 1979) wrote that he volunteered because Hunter said it would give us exposure. That did not impress me, although *Psychological Abstracts* went to all members of APA and our surnames and initials were printed at the end of each abstract. I volunteered because I needed practice in reading German, in order to pass my German examination for my Ph.D. German had been eliminated from all Rockford schools during World War I and was not taught again until my senior year in college. The abstracting was successful for I passed my language examinations. I continued to write abstracts until the *Psychological Abstracts* began requiring authors to furnish their own abstracts in the middle 1960s.

In 1931 when I received my Ph.D. from Yale and delivered my first paper at APA, Hunter was president of APA and remained on the Board of Directors for years when it was dominated by academic experimental psychologists. They generally did not consider applied psychology as "pure" or psychologists who practiced it worthy of becoming Fellows of APA. In 1938, when I returned from my first trip around the world, Hunter recommended me for a job as psychometrist at the Psychopathic Hospital at the State University of Iowa. I was deeply involved in applied research, training senior medical and graduate psychology students, and working with patients in the hospital and clinic there when APA changed its membership classifications from member and associate to fellow, member, and associate. Hunter presented my name to the board for fellow status on the basis of the six articles (Mitchell 1932a and b, 1933a, b, and c, and 1934) I had published in the field of learning, half of which had been published in the *American Journal of Psychology*. Boring had taught us that one's status in APA depended on the number of articles published in that journal. He apparently was right because I became one of the first fellows in spite of my contamination in hospitals and clinics.

After my second year at Harvard, Robinson helped me get a scholarship at Yale to work with him on retroactive inhibition and hypnosis. I found no sex discrimination in the Yale Graduate School psychology department. Catherine Cox Miles gave a course on sex differences, which I audited a few times. It was the only psychology course taught by a woman anywhere I studied. Half the Ph.D.s in psychology granted at Yale the two years I was there were given to women. One each to male and female in 1930 and two each in 1931. Harold Saxton Burr let me attend his courses in the Yale Medical School, neuroanatomy and the Neurological Clinic. When I tried to take a course in psychiatry, however, the psychiatrist whose name I do not recall, refused to let me register for the course. He said women would spoil his stories. The only other problem I had because of my sex, resulted from some superb treatment. My second year at Yale I was given half the money given to the psychology department for university fellowships, although the catalogue definitely stated that Yale graduates (who were men) were given preference for them. The other half was divided between two men, one of whom was Robert Sears who became president of APA in 1951. In addition I became a "reader," which involved grading papers for undergraduate courses. As a woman, I was not permitted to attend undergraduate classes. I thought I could do a better job if I knew what they had been taught.

When I arrived at Yale, Robinson told me Clark Hull, who had been working on hypnosis at the University of Wisconsin, was coming to Yale and he was interested in the work I had done with Prince at Harvard (Lundholm 1928). Robinson suggested that I might prefer to work with Hull because Hull knew more about hypnosis than he did. Hull objected, however, because he did not wish to be accused of stealing students, so I remained officially Robinson's student but actually did more work with Hull than with Robinson. My first year at Yale I ran two student volunteer subjects for my proposed dissertation on retroactive inhibition and hypnosis. The results were promising. The following year I was given the fellowship to continue my research. Unfortunately, we soon ran into a threat of legal difficulties, so all hypnosis at Yale was abruptly ended. One down!

Hull had a theory that anything that could be done by hypnotic suggestion (Hull 1933) could be done just as well by waking suggestion. I tried it, but it did not work. The results were negative, so not acceptable for a dissertation. Two down!

While having subjects memorize lists of three-digit numbers, I had become interested in the kinds of errors made. I took my suggestion to analyze the errors to Robinson and he accepted it. I received my Ph.D. in 1931 as planned.

There were no Ph.D.'s in clinical psychology in 1931, but I had chosen abnormal psychology as my field of special interest for my prelims. I had taken all available related courses at Harvard including Wells' full year course at Boston Psychopathic Hospital, Dearborn's course in problem children at the Harvard Graduate School of Education, and Prince's course in clinical abnormal psychology. At Yale I had taken Harold Saxton Burr's courses in neuroanatomy and in his Neurological Clinic at the Yale Medical School.

Before I graduated from Yale, Robinson referred me to two jobs. One was in a Friends secondary boarding school, not far from New Haven and New York. The other was a teaching job in a small woman's college in the south. He advised me against the teaching job. He said, as a woman, the best I could hope for in teaching was a professorship in a woman's college and even there the department heads were almost always men.

After a year and a half in the boarding school, Wells referred me to the New Hampshire State Hospital. That launched me into a rather long career in mental hospitals and clinics in seven states. It included training many psychologists as well as medical and other personnel and opening new psychology departments.

As I have already pointed out, when I was a student there was very little training available in what we now know as clinical psychology. I had to grow up with the profession. I visited and learned from other psychologists who willingly shared their knowledge *free*. I visited David Shakow at a Massachusetts mental hospital and Grace Kent at a Massachusetts state school for feebleminded. I had known Shakow when we were both students of Prince at Harvard. He had collaborated with Grace Kent on the Kent-Shakow Formboards. He referred me to her. When I moved to New York (1937), Clairette Armstrong let me work with her briefly at the Court of Domestic Relations. I worked briefly with Emily Burr in her Guidance Center for Girls, I helped Harriet Babcock with her Mental Efficiency test and I worked about a year with David Wechsler when he was developing the Wechsler-Bellevue, the first individual adult intelligence test. I had met Armstrong when she gave a paper at an Eastern Psychological Association meeting at Yale while I was a student. I introduced myself to her. She needed a place to change her clothes before the dinner meeting, so I took her to my apartment. She introduced me to her friends Burr and Babcock. A woman who was working with me at the New Hampshire State Hospital, after studying at Yale and working at Bellevue with Wechsler, introduced me to Wechsler during some psychological meetings at Dartmouth College. Later I attended many workshops including some with Bruno Klopler, Marguerite Hertz, and Samuel Beck. Armstrong saw to it that I joined all the right organizations and attended their meetings.

When I joined APA in 1931 and gave my first paper (on hypnosis) at Toronto, APA had less than 2,000 members and no divisions, the dues were less than $5.00 a year and they included the *Psychological Bulletin*, the *Psychological Abstracts*, and the *Annual Directory*. There was no registration fee for meetings. APA officers were elected at the annual meeting. The meetings were small enough that everyone could attend the annual dinner. Members could easily find old friends and make new friends. There was no employment service, but information about jobs circulated among friends. No one dreamed of a child care center. Few students or women psychologists were married. Men psychologists usually left their wives home with the children.

Before I was married, I felt free to accept a job anywhere and move on short notice. Most of the jobs I have had, I have obtained when I was not actively seeking employment but learned about from friends or administrators I met by chance at meetings or social events. Some I got through recommendations of former professors (the Ivy League "Old Boy" system). I changed jobs frequently because, as a woman, I often found myself in dead-end jobs or where men less qualified than I were given the higher paying jobs when openings occurred. As a result, I could not resist a job that sounded more challenging. For instance, I could not resist the challenge of opening departments in: the U.S. Employment Service in New Hampshire as vocational director and counselor of juniors (1936); psychology departments in two state hospitals in Iowa (1939); the U.S. Naval Hospital, Bethesda, Maryland (1943) and the V.A. Mental Hygiene Clinic, Ft. Snelling, Minnesota (1947).

When I went to Ft. Snelling, I was given a civil service grade rarely given to women because there was a scarcity of men clinical psychologists to fill the many new jobs created by the Veterans Administration at the end of

World War II. Before the war, men had avoided low paying clinical and counseling jobs usually held by women. At Ft. Snelling I had more trainees than any V.A. Chief in the country, but never had a promotion to a higher grade that was being given to men. I was told the reason was because I was not supervising any Ph.D.s. Trainees did not count! I was doing the work of three men psychologists who had fewer trainees. After serving ten years as a chief clinical psychologist at Ft. Snelling and at the V.A. Center in Dayton, Ohio, a male counseling psychologist from a state university was brought in as chief of the psychology department at the grade higher than I had.

A couple of years later, after working on a national research project in the V.A. Tuberculosis Hospital that was part of the Dayton V.A. Center (Mitchell 1959b), I attended a Miami Valley Psychological Association meeting at which some officers from Wright-Patterson Air Force Base spoke about the need for more psychologists at the base. I went out to the base to talk to the chiefs of the two psychology branches. They were impressed by my qualifications, but after working for years as a clinical psychologist, I could not get excited about the type of research in which they were involved. One of them told me that the Stress and Fatigue Section of the Biophysics Branch had had a clinical psychologist, but she had left. I went over to see what they were doing. I found two psychiatrists and two M.A. psychologists. All were Air Force captains; at that time I had an equivalent rank in the Naval Reserve. They were doing research on isolation and evaluating men for unusual missions including Air Force high altitude balloonists and Navy frog men. This sounded more exciting than anything I had done since working with Prince at Harvard, so I immediately put in a request for a transfer there (August 1958). I was deeply involved in research on *Time Estimation and Disorientation in Isolation* (Mitchell 1962a) when the astronaut selection program interrupted it.

For six weeks in February and March, 1959, I worked long hours six days a week with the thirty-one astronaut candidates from whom the seven Mercury astronauts were chosen (Mitchell 1963a and b and 1967). We examined five a week except for the last week we examined six. They came to the base on Sunday mornings and left the following Saturday afternoon. On Saturday afternoons those of us who had been working with them all week met to rank them until we had them ranked one to thirty-one. The candidates were all of superior intelligence, had graduated from military test pilot schools, and most of them had graduated from engineering colleges as well. They had been selected by their services as the best pilots. Although we gave them intelligence tests and various personality tests, we were most interested in their emotional adjustment and their ability to work efficiently under severe stress. For instance, I gave each of them different forms of a battery of six repetitive tests before and after sitting in a heat chamber at 130 degrees for two hours, and before and after being in the high altitude chamber at the equivalent of 65,000 feet for an hour and then at 100,000 feet if they did not pass out. After it became known that I had been involved in the astronaut program, the Navy ignored my overage for grade and I was promoted to Lieutenant Commander, my first promotion in fourteen years! By 1962 NASA had opened at Houston with larger facilities. I was not interested in transferring to Texas.

I was invited to meet with a small group of men from American Aviation (now Rockwell International) who were interested in research in bionics. (My definition of bionics is the science of things that behave like living organisms.) A few days later, the mother of the medical student who was working with us for the summer, invited me to a cocktail party at her home. There I met a colonel who was chief of the Electronic Technology Laboratory. He was interested in having a bionics branch in his laboratory. When he learned I had degrees in mathematics, philosophy, and psychology and had taught biology, he thought I was made for bionics. He told his superior, an Air Force General, about me. The General told him if he could get me, he could have his bionics branch. I immediately applied for a transfer on base. I became the first person officially assigned to bionics. I became a research psychologist (engineering). It was in this classification that I received my first civil service promotion. Before retiring, I spent five exciting years monitoring Air Force contracts in bionics in universities and industry from coast-to-coast.

Through personal contacts at a cybernetics meeting at the University of South Florida that I was invited to attend as a representative from WPAFB, I was able to return to my first vocational goal of teaching and finally to get a job in Florida. (The V.A. had promised me I could transfer to Florida or Georgia if I would just go to Minnesota and get things started there. After five years I was transferred south, to southern Ohio.) I became an associate professor of psychology at the University of Tampa full time for two years. Then through the head of behavioral sciences at the new University of South Florida, whom I met beside the swimming pool at a local psychology association party, I became a part-time lecturer at South Florida for three years. After that, I did part-time consulting and occasionally took a private patient (which I had done occasionally since the 1930s) until 1977. This gave me time to pursue my hobbies of world travel, lecturing, dramatics, and swimming. Before coming to Tampa, I had been around the world twice and have been around twice since as well as on many other tours to unusual places on all the continents, including Antarctica and to many islands in all the oceans.

Since the secret classification was lifted on the astronaut selection program, I have literally given hundreds of lectures about it, usually without pay, to all kinds of groups and all ages of students. In 1962 I spoke about it at a symposium jointly sponsored by the American Psychological Association and the International Council of Psychologists at the meetings in St. Louis (Mitchell 1963a and 1967). As an undergraduate, I had a minor in speech, was a member of the intercollegiate debating team and acted in plays and dance dramas every year. Later I spoke at many meetings, so I did not hesitate to accept invitations to speak about the astronauts or bionics for the Air Force. Some of my speeches have been published, and quoted in *Pravda* in Moscow (Mitchell 1959d, 1962b, 1963a, b, 1964, 1967). During the last ten years, I have done volunteer lecturing for the American Cancer Society and for a school enrichment program in the Hillsborough County public and private schools. At first, in the enrichment program I lectured and showed slides only about the astronaut selection program, but as teachers learned of my world travels, I have received more and more requests to give lectures and show colored slides I have taken in many parts of the world.

In 1982 I am still active in many organizations, often serving on boards, including the Reserve Officers Association, the Retired Officers Association, the American Association of University Women, the local Harvard Club and Yale Club. I try to keep physically fit by walking or swimming daily. I enjoy going to plays, working with a senior citizen theater group, reading, and traveling whenever I can find a luxury tour that goes places I have not been. That is no longer easy.

After having many jobs, it became a chore to prepare a *vita*. I began to think that if I were a Hindu, I would pray that in the next reincarnation I would go to only one college, have only one job, and live in only one place. But that would be a dull life! I have strong empathy for the twenty-eight-year-old seaman I examined for the court in New Hampshire. (The chief psychiatrist for the state and I examined all major criminals in the state before they went to trial.) He was charged with first degree murder. He admitted he got in a fight with a man in a bar and killed him. He told me he did not care if they did hang him; he had done more things and seen more of the world in his twenty-eight years than most people in eighty years

Certainly I cannot claim to have made any significant contribution to psychology, but I believe I have had more exciting jobs and seen more of the world than most psychologists.

REFERENCES

Boring, E. G. 1929. *A History of Experimental Psychology*. New York: Century.
———. 1951. The woman problem. *American Psychologist*, 6:679–82.
Hull, C. L. 1933. *Hypnosis and Suggestibility: An Experimental Approach*. New York: Appleton-Century.
Köhler, W. 1926. *The Mentality of Apes*. London: K. Paul, Trench, Trubner.
Lundholm, O. H. 1928. An experimental study of functional anesthesias as induced by suggestion in hypnosis. *Journal of Abnormal and Social Psychology*, 23:337–55.
Mitchell, M. B. *See* Representative Publications.
Prince, M. A. 1906. *A Dissociation of a Personality*. Longmans.
Skinner, B. F. 1979. *The Shaping of a Behaviorist*. New York: Knopf.

Representative Publications by Mildred B. Mitchell

1932a. Retroactive inhibition and hypnosis. *Journal of General Psychology*, 7:343–59.

1932b. Retroactive inhibition and waking suggestion. *Journal of Abnormal and Social Psychology*, 27:336–41.

1933a. Errors in the memorization of numbers. *American Journal of Psychology*, 45:1–16.

1933b. Alleged warming-up effects. *Journal of Experimental Psychology*, 16:138–43.

1933c. The effect of serial position in the continuous memorization of numbers. *American Journal of Psychology*, 45:493–94.

1934.   Anticipatory place-skipping tendencies in the memorization of numbers. *American Journal of Psychology*, 46:80–91.

1939.   With O. L. Tinklepaugh. Monthly and weekly weight cycles in women and their relations to behavioral and physiological functions. *Journal of Genetic Psychology*, 54:3–16.

1941a. The Revised Stanford-Binet for adults. *Journal of Educational Research*. 34:516–21.

1941b. Irregularities of university students on the Revised Stanford-Binet. *Journal of Educational Psychology*, 32:513–22.

1942.   Performance of mental hospital patients on the Wechsler-Bellevue and on the Revised Stanford-Binet Form L. *Journal of Educational Psychology*, 33:538–44.

1943.   The Revised Stanford-Binet for university students. *Journal of Educational Research*, 36:507–11.

1944.   The clinical psychologist in a naval hospital. *Psychological Bulletin*, 41:561–64.

1947.   Careers in applied psychology. *Conference on Science and Centennial Commemoration of the Charter*. Rockford, Ill.: Rockford College.

1948.   Review of *Twentieth-Century Psychology*. New York: Philosophical Library, 1946. *Journal of Clinical Psychopathology*, 9:590–93.

1949.   Prejudices in hiring. *Personnel Journal*, 28:265–66.

1950.   With H. F. Rothe. Validity of an emotional key on a short industrial personality questionnaire. *Journal of Applied Psychology*, 34:329–32.

1951.   The status of women in the American Psychological Association. *American Psychologist*, 6:193–201.

1952.   Preferences for Rorschach cards. *Journal of Projective Techniques*, 16:203–11.

1953.   Can't the men take it? *Reserve Officer*, 29:22.

1954.   Station report, Dayton, Ohio. *Newsletter for Psychologists in Tuberculosis*, 1:5–6.

1955a. Hospitals now conducting psychotherapy groups, VA-GM, Dayton, Ohio. *Newsletter for Psychologists in Tuberculosis*, 2:20–21.

1955b. Group procedures with tuberculosis patients. *Newsletter for Psychologists in Tuberculosis*, 2:35–37.

1959a. With Z. A. Piotrowski. Mental development of a hydrocephalic. *Training School Bulletin*, 55:71–72.

1959b. The best doctor in the hospital. *American Review of Tuberculosis and Pulmonary Diseases*, 79:533–36.

1959c. "Personal liberties" threatened? *Science*, 130:66 and 106.

1959d. Liberal arts in orbit. *Alumna Rockford College*, 36:7–9.

1960.   Review of *Longitudinal Statistical Analysis*, by Nathan Goldfarb. Glencoe, Ill. Free Press, 1960. *Personnel Journal*, 39:237–38.

1961a. Review of *Test Construction* by Dorothy Adkins Wood. Columbus, Ohio: Charles E. Merrill, 1960. *Personnel Journal*, 39:329.

1961b. Review of *Psychological Testing* (2d. ed.), by Anne Anastasi. New York: Macmillan, 1961. *Personnel Journal*, 40:178–79.

1961c. Trends toward multiple authorship in scientific publications. *Journal of Psychology*, 52:125–31.

1962a. *Time Estimation and Distortion in Isolation*. USAF, ASD-TDR-62–277.

1962b. Progress report on bionics, Aeronautical Systems Division. *National Aerospace Electronics National Conference Proceedings*. Dayton, Ohio: IRE.

1963a. Seleção de astronautas. Arquivos Brasileiros de Psicoténica. 15:5–10. (Traducão e adaptacão por Huberto Schoenfeldt.)

1963b. Bionics for space travel. *Alumna Rockford College*, 41:3–5.

1964.   Bionics for space travel. *New Research Frontiers in Physical Electronics*. Ann Arbor: University of Michigan Press.
1967.   How the big 7 were selected. *Twenty-Fifth Anniversary Clients Conference*. New York: Klein Institute.

EUGENIA HANFMANN

I was twelve years old when the Russian revolution shattered the life of my country and my family and erased all thoughts of the future. During the years of civil war and famine, our concern was to stay alive today and tomorrow. We moved from place to place in search of safety, shelter, and food. I worked now and then so as to have a ration card. My school attendance was sporadic, my plans for the future nil. When, after the end of the Civil War, we left Russia for Lithuania, my father's country of birth, the return to a relatively normal existence seemed a miracle.

There was much catching up for me to do. I worked intensively for a year to get a Lithuanian high-school diploma. In 1923, I entered the University of Jena, at the time one of the few German schools that admitted foreigners—mostly members of Jewish minorities of Latvia, Lithuania, and Poland seeking higher education in pre-Hitler Germany. My interests and abilities were clearly in the field of humanities, but no one discipline stood out as my choice. In a Russian university I would have entered the historico-philological faculty, as my mother had done in her time, and studied a wide range of humanistic disciplines, but in the German system, I had to choose only a few. For two years I took a variety of courses, not getting seriously involved in any and not learning much. These lecture courses involved no grades, no exams, no class discussions. Eventually I made psychology my main field, with philosophy, education, and English my minors.

Psychology *was* one of my early interests; it was taught in Russian high schools, and I had done some reading in it on my own (I have a vivid memory of reading William James' short *Psychology* during a bombardment of Kiev, trying not to take notice of the explosions). Yet more weighty reasons than these early beginnings determined my choice. The professor of psychology—an Austrian Jew and a socialist—welcomed foreigners in his labs and seminars, as most of his colleagues did not. He was interested in his students and generous with his time. My relationship with Professor Peters transformed my school life. Outside I often felt a stranger, a person without country and without rights, but within the Psychological Institute,

I found companionship, intellectual stimulation, and warmth. My teacher was an eclectic, keenly curious about a wide variety of issues, averse to abstract theorizing, careful in his methods. In assigning a thesis problem to me, he took into account my interest in the psychology of thinking and in systematic introspection. I went to work in earnest. In spite of one false start, I completed my experimental project on the formation of visual associations within a reasonably short time; it proved publishable (Hanfmann 1927). I passed my doctoral examination in 1927.

My degree in psychology did not indicate an intention to pursue a career in this field. In Europe at that time psychology had no application except in academia; yet university positions were few and all but closed to the likes of me; German faculties did not welcome foreigners. In Lithuania, I had citizenship rights but did not speak the language. Nor was my self-confidence equal to supporting such aspirations. Professors were held in high esteem in Germany, and my scholastic ability, as shown by my record, was good but not outstanding. On getting the degree I tried to secure a position as a language teacher in Latvia or Lithuania. Failing in this, I took a clerical job in Riga and was happy to start working: my father was in poor health and needed relief from his financial burdens. A year later, during my vacation trip to Jena, Peters put it to me, emphatically, that being well fitted for an academic career, I should start on it without further delays. He promised to sponsor me throughout and for a start offered me an assistantship at his institute. "You won't earn much, but at least you will be doing real work instead of wrapping herrings." It was books, Russian classics, not herrings, but be that as it may, I was overjoyed and made a commitment to psychology then and there. Peters did not remain my mentor for long, but he became later a lifelong friend.

During the next years, I did some teaching and published a study pertaining to the intellectual development of children (Hanfmann 1930). In 1930 Peters recommended me as a research associate to Kurt Koffka, a German Gestalt psychologist working in the United States at Smith College. The job was for a limited period. Peters was confident that by the time I returned the social democrats would have regained power in Thüringen; this should facilitate my promotion. Less optimistic than he, I succeeded in obtaining a visa enabling me to stay in the States. When the work with Koffka was over, I was glad to be able to do so: the depression seemed preferable to Hitler. By then I had had two stimulating productive years in Koffka's small research setting, a bit of an ivory tower. I continued doing research in cognitive and developmental psychology (with Dembo 1933a; Hanfmann 1933b, 1935b, 1936), enlarging my perspective through first-hand acquaintance with various theoretical approaches, with the views of Koffka, Fritz Heider, Kurt Lewin. The new social environment also proved thought-provoking both for me and for my colleague Tamara Dembo, another new arrival from Europe. Though some of the novelty was puzzling, most of it was enjoyable: the loveliness of the New England countryside, the affluence of the students' life, the faculty's youth, informality, and friendliness.

Appreciation, however, was one thing, employment another, particularly during the depression. Having gotten no replies to my hundreds of applications to colleges, I was facing a choice between taking any job I could find and accepting help offered by friends. At this point, through the mediation of Maria Rickers-Ovsiankina, along with Dembo, I was rescued by David Shakow, then head of psychology at Worcester State Hospital. By hiring me to do a psychologist's work for an attendant's remuneration, he gave me a chance to acquire first-hand knowledge of the clinical field, an area that had been absent from my training.

The hospital—then at its height—supported many training and research programs; it proved a fascinating school. Given free rein, I roamed the wards, observing the routines and talking to patients, pursuing the course of those who interested me most, learning from staff and seminar meetings. I was introduced to psychoanalysis and to the Rorschach test by experts arriving in droves from Europe. Although I did some testing, I was mostly occupied in research. I studied in detail individual cases of cognitive malfunctioning (Hanfmann 1939c; with Goldstein & Rickers 1944b), including a highly informative case of agnosia. With Tamara Dembo, I made a study of new patients' reactions to the hospital, which has some practical applications (with Dembo 1934, 1935a; Hanfmann 1945; and with Ladieu & Dembo 1947). I began a systematic study of schizophrenic thinking (Hanfmann 1939a, 1939b), which soon led to a contact with Kasanin, a psychiatrist who wished to sponsor a continuation of experimental work with schizophrenics done by the talented Russian psychologist Vygotsky (Hanfmann 1968b; with Kasanin 1937 and 1938). He obtained a grant and engaged me to do the work; the result was a joint monograph on conceptual thinking in schizophrenia (with Kasanin, 1942), which was viewed as an important contribution to the field and led to much further experimentation (Hanfmann 1941, 1944a); years later, after the war, the Russian psychologist Luria persuaded me to prepare for publication in English Vygotsky's seminal book *Thought and Language* (Vygotsky 1962).

But to return to my time of apprenticeship:

The years spent in Worcester and with Kasanin in Chicago increased my familiarity with the American scene. I had met people from all walks of life, had done some applied work, had published in English. I felt ready for a teaching position. In 1939 I obtained one at Mt. Holyoke through the mediation of a friend who was vacating. The years in hospital settings had initiated a shift in my interests from cognition as such to its pathology, then to the study of personality, its dynamics, its disturbances, their treatment. In the next decade these interests were further developed through some aspects of my work, my personal analysis, and my association with Robert White, Andras Angyal, Grete Bibring, and Abraham Maslow.

This development, however, was not continuous. The years at Mt. Holyoke were relatively barren. I enjoyed the few courses where I could use my firsthand knowledge of a field to get the students involved. Yet I often had to lecture to a politely uninterested audience, using prescribed textbooks which endlessly discussed nature-nurture, or other unproductive dilemmas. I did not try too hard to improve the situation: during the anxious years preceding and following the start of the war, my concerns were less with my work than with helping my brothers and my mother to escape from Europe to settle in the States. Most of my young male colleagues soon left for war work. Then a call came for me, too: a mysterious invitation to commit myself, sight unseen—but in company with some people I knew—to important work in Washington. (The chairman was greatly aggrieved by my request for a leave of absence. Worried about the fate of my five courses, he dreamt that a brooding hen had abandoned her nest with its five eggs.)

The Assessment Program of the Office of Strategic Services, designed by Henry Murray and located on a large estate in Virginia, was a very unusual enterprise. The evaluation of people volunteering for service overseas was carried out by carefully selected teams of psychologists and psychiatrists, using a wide range of imaginative methods, of interviews, and of situational tests especially created for this purpose. The work went on from early until midnight, with high morale, a high level of group functioning, and a great deal of learning taking place. Our subjects were not the kind of people whom we study in our usual clinical work: here we were dealing with stable people, many of them successful and satisfied with their lives. Maladjustments were not absent, but my reaction to a large segment of this group was admiration for the way people can be at their best, for their immeasurable resources. We found robust health even in many of those whose childhood misfortunes might well have crippled them; this called for a revision of our theories. The demanding conditions of the staff's life and work led us to discover our own qualities, as people and as "evaluators." In the matter of assigning ratings to abstract variables (such as "emotional stability") I could not be worse, but I greatly enjoyed the intensive free-wheeling interviewing and was able to obtain rich material from most subjects. I was also judged to be good at perceiving patterns in this material and synthesizing all data into comprehensive individual portraits; I was emerging as a clinician. The great frustration of the OSS job was having to burn, at the end of the war, all our records and notes. Instead of looking for answers to the intriguing questions of personality theory in the stories of the many hundreds of men I had interviewed, I had to be content with contributing a few chapters to the book by the OSS staff, *Assessment of Men* (The OSS Assessment Staff 1948) and discussing in several articles the nature and function of various methods of personality study (Hanfmann 1948, 1950, 1952, 1953a, 1956b; and with Getzels 1953b).

On returning to "civilian life," I did not want to continue at Mt. Holyoke; I let it be known at meetings that I was looking for a new job. Recommendations by my colleagues at the OSS led to a lectureship in clinical psychology at Harvard. My first year there was also the first year of the Department of Social Relations, which combined an excellent clinical program, headed by White, with social psychology, sociology, and cultural anthropology. The climate of the new department was invigorating, and I entered it with zest. I taught courses on theories of personality and seminars on projective techniques; I took part in a multidisciplinary study of opinions and personality (Hanfmann 1951). I enjoyed teaching the mature postwar graduate students and helping undergraduates to design honor theses pertinent to their personal concerns. But my interests and activities were clearly shifting from academic to clinical work. I started doing some therapeutic work with children and adults. When in 1952 Abraham Maslow invited me to start a counseling service for students at the young Brandeis University, I left Harvard and eventually invested all my energies in this job, my last and longest lasting one. Before I left Harvard, however, I had a chance to do a job of clinical research as part of the project on the Soviet social system conducted by the Russian Research Center. In this project, Soviet citizens, displaced in large numbers to Europe in the course of the war, were used as informants about life behind the Iron Curtain; the clinicians were charged with doing an intensive personality study of a large sample of these respondents. This was a true reunion with my past. I met, face to face, people similar in many vital ways to those I knew in my childhood, but who had suffered catastrophes and hardships and were still leading the insecure life of the displaced. I had had no illusions about the Soviet state, but the reality conveyed through these interviews proved worse than the worst fantasy; yet most of the people we studied had fully preserved their humanity. I conducted the study with the help of a colleague, Helen Beier, a talented clinician and an old friend. The results were published in a series of articles (with Beier 1956a and 1958a; Hanfmann 1955b, 1957; with Inkeles & Beier 1958b; with Getzels 1955a) and later in a book of case histories entitled *Six Russian Men: Lives in Turmoil* (with Beier 1976).

To turn now to my last job. Maslow's backing enabled me to do all that was needed to make psychological counseling available and acceptable to all students; they came to view it less as help for the ill than as emotional education for the well. The service was very effective as long as its financing was adequate. I had a chance to develop my therapeutic skills, learning a great deal from my insightful clients (Hanfmann 1960, 1980; with Jones, Baker & Kovar 1963). I also learned much from preparing for posthumous publication (with Richard M. Jones) the book *Neurosis and Treatment: A Holistic Theory*, by Andras Angyal, the Center's first consultant (Angyal 1965). It is an outstanding work, greatly stimulating not just for theoreticians and practitioners but for students and laymen as well (Hanfmann 1965 and 1968a). My early psychoanalytic orientation was greatly modified by this influence and by my own experiences as a therapist. The gratifying stretch of work at Brandeis was not without its major setback. The Brandeis president, before resigning his post, carried out his early plan to bring the Center in line with the medical model: he transferred it to the Health Services and placed a psychiatrist in charge. This resulted in years of malfunctioning and struggle, but the reduction of my duties under the new regime enabled me to write and publish my second book on college counseling (Hanfmann 1978). At present, we are back to employing a psychologist as director, a woman who ably safeguards many of the Center's achievements; I can function there comfortably as consultant and a teacher of the interns we train. I also continue to engage in the private practice of psychotherapy.

The anxieties which beset the beginnings of my career resulted from social upheavals that struck at men and women alike. Sex discrimination was not evident in any of the work settings I was part of; it remained outside, as in the case of rejection of women students by most German professors. Like many professional women, I was often a minority member in my jobs, sometimes a minority of one. I wanted to have some female companionship at work and did everything I could to obtain it. I was very happy to find Thelma Alper at Harvard, but I was aware that the minority position had its advantage. Being one of a kind, one stands out from the group, one commands attention; at times I received more recognition than was due me for my work. This insight did not prevent me from enjoying the bonus. I took my minority position to reflect the low percentage of women in my profession, and though I realized that some men's high valuation of my contribution may have been due to their low expectations of women, I recall only one concrete instance that suggested to me this dynamic. A rather arrogant colleague, impressed by one of my articles, told me that he knew I wrote good case histories, but had not expected me to be so good at theory. Some similar conception of a woman's place in research may or may not have been at work when an extremely ambitious colleague of mine forgot—to his advantage—a verbal agreement we had made about our respective publication rights.

Institutional discrimination did touch my life once, but luckily caused no harm. At the end of my first year at Harvard, my chairman told me, beaming, that the department had unanimously recommended a three years' reappointment for me. Shortly afterward, he told me, with a long face, that the dean had turned down the request. His reason? The three years' appointment would have entitled me to be present at faculty meetings, and no woman had ever attended a meeting of the Harvard Faculty of Arts and Sciences! Then it is high time one did, I told the chairman (although I personally would be content to renounce the privilege). The dean had a different solution: he guaranteed me three successive yearly appointments. In the course of those three years, the terms of a donation made for establishing a chair at Radcliffe made it mandatory and feasible to appoint to full professorship a prominent woman historian. Given this precedent, my next reappointment was a regular three years' one. I attended *one* faculty meeting—just to confirm my suspicion that I had not been missing much. This change, by the way, is the only clear instance of women gaining ground in academia which I have personally witnessed; my friends on the affirmative action committees tell me that nothing spectacular has happened on this front. The memory of my first reappointment, and of some other incidents highlighting the anomaly of "a woman at Harvard," has stayed with me as a story of absurd anachronisms with which to regale my friends.

My attitude of not anticipating discrimination and being slow to discover it in the wider environment may have resulted from the nature of my early experiences. My family belonged to the progressive Russian intelligentsia, a thin social layer in which women were no longer looked down upon. The women of this class had struggled for emancipation in the second half of the last century and had made some major gains. My father hoped that I would enter the medical profession because it was considered a very good one for women. One of my aunts was a highly successful physician, as was the mother of my best friend. I also knew other professional women, both married and single. My mother was a part-time teacher. I disliked being left during her absences in the care of ever-changing governesses, but accepted it as a fact of life; I knew my mother was not happy to stay at home. When later in life I met women who genuinely enjoyed both their children and their housework, my feeling of shock at this anachronism vied with my feeling of envy for those children. More important perhaps than the nature of role models was the fact that the early sex-role typing I encountered lacked the rigidity and the strong emotional charge which I was later to observe in this country. No dolls were forced on me. In school I took carpentry and was readily given the tools I wanted; when one of my brothers went through a period of dressing as a girl, no one was upset. In my environment, men were not forbidden to express feelings; they kissed and embraced; male dancers were not viewed as effeminate. My parents' willingness to make sacrifices for the children's education was extended to sons and daughter alike. I knew I would have to earn my living, but I felt no pressures either for or against marriage: it was up to me, or to fate.

My staying single was not due to a deliberate decision: it had its roots in the unhappy experiences caused by the breakup of my parents' marriage. When I became aware later of the various anxieties and conflicts underlying my avoidance of marriage, I tended for a while to overestimate the advantages of the married state and its value as an index of "normal adjustment." I was disabused of these notions after participating in a study of Vassar alumnae, twenty years after graduation. I found no lesser incidence of neurotic disturbance in the married majority than among those remaining single, many of whom in fact had developed into interesting, non-stereotyped people. I realized that my not raising a family had given me freedom to make use of the opportunities that came my way—even though I have been greatly involved in the lives of my large family and of my friends and have often given personal matters priority over the professional ones.

These personal realizations eventually gave me some understanding of the feminist movement, which I originally lacked. In my first years here I met several women of my age who effectively combined family and profession, and did so without the extensive domestic help which had made this possible in Russia. I probably overestimated the incidence of such women in the general population, or underestimated the amount of the strain they were feeling. It was the results of a research project that gave me a glimpse of the tensions existing in many American marriages. In studying the attitudes of the Russian displaced persons by means of semi-projective tests, we asked them, and an American comparsion group as well, to discuss some briefly outlined social situations. In one story a couple is discussing a job the husband has been offered in another city; he wants the job, but his wife, satisfied with *her* job, prefers to stay where they are. What will they say and decide? The Russian men had the couple discuss the situation without much heat, in terms of the advantages of each job and each location, of the feasibility of weekend visits. To my astonishment, the Americans took the situation greatly to heart and treated it as an instance of the battle between the sexes. They strongly insisted on the precedence of the husband's rights and wishes; they even felt that a man's self-respect would be undermined if the woman did not give in.

The study was done in 1950. When, in the sixties, Betty Friedan's book signaled the beginning of the feminist movement, I recalled this early glimpse of smouldering marital resentments but I remained puzzled about their causes. I failed at first to relate the eruption of the feminist protest to what I, myself, have observed: such as the distress of many college girls, if by the time of graduation they were not married or at least engaged. I kept wondering why activist women would not join forces to fight, first and foremost, the dangers threatening the whole of mankind, instead of fighting to improve their own situation, which, in the case of middle-class women, seemed tolerable to me, at least as compared with that of some other minorities. The answers came from the reminiscences of some of my feminist friends and some women patients. They had early experienced some demeaning treatment by their environment under circumstances strongly suggesting that what was wrong with them was their sex; or they had been pressured to implement some exalted ideal of womanhood, demanding the devaluation and suppression of their abilities, interests, their genuine wishes. No wonder that for them the fight for women's rights was truly liberating and took precedence over other social causes, which some of them felt would also benefit from women acquiring more power. Strong personal motivation is an important root of ideologies and social movements (as well as of choices of profession), a condition of their vigor and success. The exaggerations and distortions to which all ideologies so easily fall victim can be effectively counteracted if the participants are aware of their personal motives—the whole range of them. Psychology—and in particular women psychologists—has an important role to play in helping both the proponents and the opponents of the feminist movement to achieve these liberating insights.

REFERENCES

Angyal, A. 1965. *Neurosis and Treatment: A Holistic Theory.* New York: Wiley.
Hantmann, E. *See* Representative Publications.
The OSS Assessment Staff. 1948. *Assessment of Men.* New York: Rinehart.
Vygotsky, L. 1962. *Thought and Language.* Cambridge: MIT Press, New York: Wiley.

Representative Publications by Eugenia Hanfmann

1927. Die Entstehung visueller Assoziationen. *Zeitschrift für Psychologie*, 105:147–94.

1930. Ueber das Bauen der Kinder. *Zeitschrift für Kinderforschung*, 36:255–334.

1933a. With T. Dembo. Intuitive halving and doubling of figures. *Psychologische Forschung*, 17:306–18.

1933b. Some experiments on spatial position as a factor in children's perception and reproduction of simple figures. *Psychologische Forschung*, 17:319–29.

1934. With T. Dembo. The value of an orientation letter for newly admitted patients. *Psychiatric Quarterly*, 8:703–21.

1935a. With T. Dembo. The patient's psychological situation upon admission to a mental hospital. *American Journal of Psychology*, 47:381–408.

1935b. Social structure of a group of kindergarten children. *American Journal of Orthopsychiatry*, 5:407–10.

1936. On the factors underlying a phenomenon discovered by Hering. *Psychologische Forschung*, 21:132–41.

1937. With J. Kasanin. A method for the study of concept formation. *Journal of Psychology*, 3:521–40.

1938. With J. Kasanin. An experimental study of concept formation in schizophrenia. *American Journal of Psychiatry*, 95:35–48.

1939a. Thought disturbances in schizophrenia as revealed by performance in a picture completion test. *Journal of Abnormal and Social Psychology*, 34:249–64.

1939b. A qualitative analysis of the Healy Pictorial Completion Test II. *American Journal of Orthopsychiatry*, 9:325–29.

1939c. Analysis of the thinking disorder in a case of schizophrenia. *Archives for Neurology and Psychiatry*, 41:568–79.

1941. A study of personal patterns in an intellectual performance. *Character and Personality*, 9:315–25.

1942. With J. Kasanin. Conceptual thinking in schizophrenia. *Nervous and Mental Disease Monographs*, vol. 67.

1944a. Approaches to the intellectual aspects of personality, *Transactions of the New York Academy of Sciences*, Series 2, 6:229–35.

1944b. With K. Goldstein and M. Rickers. Case Lanuti: Extreme concretization of behavior due to damage of the brain cortex. *Psychological Monographs*, 57 (4):1–72.

1945. Older mental patients after long hospitalization. In O. Kaplan, ed., *Mental Disorders in Later Life*. Stanford: Stanford University Press.

1947. With G. Ladieu and T. Dembo. Studies in the adjustment to visible injuries: Evalution of help by the injured. *Journal of Abnormal and Social Psychology*, 42:1469–192.

1948. Projective techniques in the assessment program of the Office of Strategic Services. In American Council on Education, *Exploring Individual Differences*.

1950. Psychological approaches to the study of anxiety. In P. Hoch and J. Zubin, eds., *Anxiety*. New York: Grune & Stratton.

1951. The life history of an ex-alcoholic. *Quarterly Journal of Studies on Alcohol*. 12:405–43.

1952. William Stern on "Projective Techniques." *Journal of Personality*, 21:1–21.

1953a. Concept formation test. In A. Weider & D. Wechsler, eds., *Contributions towards Medical Psychology*, vol. 2. New York: Ronald Press.

1953b. With J. W. Getzels. Studies of the sentence completion test. *Journal of Projective Techniques*, 17:280–94.

1954. With R. J. Dorris & D. J. Levinson. Authoritarian personality studied by a new variation of the sentence completion technique. *Journal of Abnormal and Social Psychology* 49:99–108.

1955a. With J. W. Getzels. Interpersonal attitudes of former Soviet citizens as studied by a semi-projective method. *Psychological Monographs*, 69 (4):1–37.

1955b. Boris, a displaced person. In A. Burton and R. E. Harris, eds., *Clinical Studies of Personality*. New York: Harper.

1956a. With H. Beier. Emotional attitudes of former Soviet citizens as studied by the technique of projective questions. *Journal of Abnormal and Social Psychology*, 53:143–53.

1956b. The Non-Projective Aspects of the Rorschach Experiment. III. The point of view of the research clinician. *Journal of Social Psychology*, 44:199–202.

1957.   Social perception in Russian displaced persons and an American comparison group. *Psychiatry*, 20:131–49.

1958a.   With H. Beier. The mental health of a group of Russian displaced persons. *American Journal of Orthopsychiatry*, 28:241–55.

1958b.   With A. Inkeles and H. Beier. Modal personality and adjustment to the Soviet socio-political system. *Human Relations*, 11:3–22.

1960.   Psychologische Probleme Amerikanischer Studenten. *Psychologische Beiträge*, 5:374–82.

1963.   With R. Jones, E. Baker, and L. Kovar, *Psychological Counseling in a Small College*. Cambridge: Schenkman.

1965.   Holistic theories of neurosis. *Science and Psychoanalysis*. Vol. 8. New York: Grune & Stratton.

1968a.   Andras Angyal. *International Encyclopedia of the Social Sciences*. New York: Macmillan and Free Press.

1968b.   K. Goldstein and L. Vygotsky. In M. Simmel, ed., *The Reach of Mind: Essays in Memory of Kurt Goldstein*. New York: Springer.

1976.   With H. Beier. *Six Russian Men: Lives in Turmoil*. Quincy, Mass.: Christopher.

1978.   *Effective Therapy for College Students*. San Francisco: Jossey-Bass.

1980.   Psychological work in colleges: The criteria of our usefulness. *Proceedings of the 29th Annual Conference of the Association of University and College Counseling Center Directors*.

MOLLY R. HARROWER

My task in this joint venture, as I see it, is to provide enough autobiographical material so that my perspective on women in psychology will emerge meaningfully from my actual experiences. Hence I begin with my British background and education, which differs considerably from the American way of life. I grew up in England and, following strict tradition, was shipped away from home at age ten to a public school (private school in this country), remaining there except for two months' vacation each year until I was eighteen. This early banishment is supposed to further independence of spirit! Unlike America, where, in the normal course of events, girls from such a school would go on to college, opportunities for higher education for women in England were, and are, minimal by American standards. The few hundred vacancies in women's colleges each year were obtained through competitive examinations. And since it was not until the next stage of traditional education, namely a year abroad learning to speak French and German, that it occurred to me that I wanted to go to a university, admittance along regular lines was impossible. I was squeezed into London University by the back door, as a journalist student, permitted to audit, among other things, a course in psychology by the famous woman professor Dr. Beatrice Edgell.

Edgell had been trained in Germany, an innovation for British women at that time, under Oswald Külpe, taking her Ph.D. in 1906. Külpe was a psychologist of the Würzburg School, who made important contributions to association theory in the early nineteen hundreds. I was challenged by Edgell's excellent mind, vowed to switch somehow to psychology, a move which she strongly endorsed. She arranged for me to work toward the academic diploma in psychology, ironically, a post-doctoral specialty but requiring no specific entrance examination, so I was free to take it. I worked under Edgell's guidance for two years.

However, the post-World War I depression had caused acute financial problems in my family, and technically degreeless, but full of fervor, I was job hunting and landed a position as girl Friday to C. K. Ogden, a unique scholar, free-lance psychologist, linguist, the inventor of Basic English and in the words of an article appearing on him in *Life* in 1957 "one of the most eccentric of all English eccentrics." Working for him was an education in itself.[1] What is important in the chain of events in my erratic education was the fact that Ogden was publishing Kurt Koffka's *Growth of the Mind* and Wolfgang Köhler's *Mentality of Apes* in the prestigious *International Library of Philosophy, Psychology and Scientific Method.* (These two books, incidentally, are foundation stones in the development of Gestalt psychology.) Hearing that I wanted to go to America to study, he promptly wrote recommending me to Koffka, suggesting that I be appointed to the newly founded research laboratory at Smith College, which Koffka had been invited from Germany to direct.

The research laboratory, which Koffka headed over a period of six years and to which I was appointed, included at various times Fritz and Grace Heider, Tamara Dembo, Eugenia Hanfmann, Alexander Mintz, and a Chinese psychologist I Huang, a truly international group. We were all set to work on various Gestalt-oriented projects. I was put to work on the perceptual problem, the nature of gamma movement (Harrower 1929b), and worked with Koffka on problems of his choosing relating to the interrelation of form, color and brightness (Koffka 1931, 1932a).

After two years of work with Koffka, I was invited to hold a temporary position in the department of psychology at Wells College in Aurora, New York, a challenging first year of teaching. No sooner back to Smith when again another interruption. The position of senior lecturer at Bedford College was vacant owing to the sudden death of Dr. Victoria Hazlett. Professor Edgell issued an unusual invitation to me to fill this position for a year. Somewhat loath to return to England and interrupt my work at Smith, it was felt by all concerned to be too important an opportunity to miss.

The invitation to these two positions, together with my publications, resulted in Koffka's being able to arrange with the Graduate Committee for me to take a Ph.D. at Smith. Since Smith College was not a higher degree granting institution I had taken no courses—for none were available—and there was much confusion and concern over setting up this examination. In order that it be taken with full seriousness, Edwin Boring from Harvard, Arnold Gesell from Yale, George Humphrey from Canada, a member of the Smith psychology department Harold Israels, and Koffka were corralled as examiners. All Ph.D. examinations have a crisis nature attached to them, but the irregularities of my English degreeless background added to the general excitement for me, and stress for all concerned. For example, no one

1. I have written more about C. K. Ogden in Harrower (1978).

seemed to know whether a candidate should be isolated during the five days of written examinations. Thus, to be on the safe side I was secluded in Dean Marjorie Nicolson's house, with meals brought on a tray, so that I did not leave the premises!

My dissertation dealt with the relative facility with which completed or incompleted jokes were remembered: Expressed in Gestalt terminology I was studying conceptual rather than perceptual units (Harrower 1932b).[2] Boring told me years later he had placed my dissertation in the number three slot in the framework of ten Harvard Ph.D. candidates, so the turmoil may have been worth it!

The years at Smith College held much in addition to the work experience with Koffka, invaluable though that was. There were all sorts of student and faculty activities which were available to me. With my British heritage and an intimate knowledge of the Gilbert and Sullivan operas I was asked to direct a student performance of the *Mikado* and acted in the faculty's production of *Trial by Jury*. I got to know many students and faculty members. I lived for the first year, as a representative from a foreign country, in one of the large dormitories. In my second year I was put in charge of one of the smaller dormitories acquiring a beautiful suite of rooms as recompense for my supervisory services. During my final year I was in charge of the graduate house with graduate students from France, Italy, Germany, Poland, and Egypt, together with students from other parts of the United States.

The outdoor life possible in the New England fall will always remain a vivid recollection. Excursions into the surrounding country were almost unbelievable to someone brought up within the confines of greater London.

In 1934, equipped academically, and with the full blessing of the Gestalt psychologists to go forth and teach, one of those personal experiences which I believe influences almost everyone's life pattern occurred for me. A close friend subjected to unusually severe surgical procedures emerged post-operatively with what I would now describe as personality changes. Thus I decided to seek a way of using my psychological training to deal with patients rather than perception or abstract studies of thought processes.

This same year, therefore, I submitted a proposal to the Rockefeller Medical Foundation which, in essence, suggested that an experimental psychol-

2. My dissertation was published, as were all the articles from the Smith College Research Laboratory, in two places. In a special series *Smith College Studies in Psychology* in the United States and in the *Psychologische Forschung* in Germany. Because the publication of the *Psychologische Forschung* was terminated by the Nazis in the 1930s the reader who wishes to know more about the studies of color and organization, gamma movement and organization in higher mental processes (the remembering of jokes) will find excellent summaries in Koffka's *The Principles of Gestalt Psychology*, pp. 106–305 and 591–647.

ogist be allowed to work in a hospital for the purposes of research on patients suffering from the impacts of various surgical traumas. To my delight and surprise the Rockefeller Foundation decided to back this, at that time a highly unusual proposition.

However, at the same time as the Rockefeller Fellowship was granted I was offered the position of director of students at Douglass College, part of Rutgers University. After much soul searching I took this job for three years, partly because of its financial benefit and partly to make a final decision as to whether I wanted to break away from the established academic order, to follow my all absorbing interest on an uncharted course. Fortunately I was told by the foundation that I could reapply at a later date with the full expectation that the fellowship would be available. The years at Douglass College were a valuable experience in the satisfactions and problems of college administration and student counseling. In my free time I wrote my first book, *The Psychologist at Work*, with an introduction by Koffka.

But after the three years I was more than ready to pick up my fellowship. In the meantime Dr. Alan Gregg had tracked down two major hospitals where a Rockefeller psychologist would be welcomed. Massachusetts General in Boston, under the direction of Dr. Stanley Cobb, was one of them. Dr. Cobb was a neuropsychiatrist with analytic interests who was open to a wide spectrum of new ideas. The Montreal Neurological Institute under the internationally known brain surgeon Dr. Wilder Penfield was the other.

Boston under Dr. Cobb would have, in many ways, been the easier transition from the academic to the medical. Stanley Cobb was far more aware of psychological problems than most physicians at that time, but in the interview with him a disconcerting thing happened. Dr. Cobb hardly said a word for over an hour and I poured out my story becoming more and more apprehensive every minute! A silent reception always meant for me disapproval, so that I interpreted this as disinterestedness. As a matter of fact, it was nothing of the sort. Dr. Cobb had a severe stuttering problem and did not wish to expose me to that at the time of my decision-making. Years later when we got to know each other well we laughed at how these twists of fate had influenced my decision.

My choice, after several days spent in interviews in Montreal, was to go to the Neurological Institute with Dr. Penfield. Looking back I see that my work, as I now understand it, began at this moment, for I became a clinician with experimental interests or, otherwise stated, an experimentalist with clinical awareness.

Penfield at that time had developed a brain operation whereby he hoped to cure persons with epileptic seizures. In an eight- to nine-hour operation, with the patient fully conscious, the brain itself was exposed, electrical stimulation was applied to various parts of the cortex, until the seizure was produced artifically. Whereupon that part of the brain, which triggered the attack, was excised.

As Penfield's psychologist, my task was to sit under the drapes with the patient, while the exposed brain was worked on by a team of surgeons. A highly unusual experience, which, particularly at the beginning, I found almost as stressful as did the patient.

The research material available in Montreal was tremendous. My first studies dealt with patients who, despite large removals of the cortex still showed no change in I.Q. but, conversely, demonstrated an almost uniform personality pattern, through the Rorschach test. The Rorschach then became part of diagnostic examinations in cases where cerebral pathology was suspected (Harrower 1939, 1940a, 1940b, 1941).

It was in Montreal, however, that for the first time in my life I came head on with prejudice against women. Only a few women were on the entire McGill University faculty; no women were allowed to enter the Faculty Club. When three of us finally made the grade in regard to the Faculty Club, we were met with this sign: "Ladies are asked to pass as quickly as possible to the quarters allotted to them, and under no circumstances to linger in the hall or on the stairways."

In 1939 Canada entered World War II. This event brought about a big shift in my work assignments: The Rorschach and the Projective Techniques had proved of unquestioned value in the medical setting of the Royal Victorian Hospital and Montreal Neurological Institute. In addition to daily examinations of patients I had been asked to administer the Rorschach to entering medical students of McGill. As soon as I suggested to Dr. Penfield that these methods could be employed to screen out individuals with acute psychological problems in recruitment centers as well as on an academic campus, he endorsed an application to the National Research Council of Canada for funds to adapt the Rorschach method into a group procedure. The funds were immediately forthcoming and I was able to appoint an assistant, Mathilda Steiner, to work with me. It was a pressured experimental study to prove the effectiveness of the group method. We had to equate the results obtained from the traditional individual method with a group presentation of the Rorschach cards now presented as slides. This method was published in detail in articles and in book form and continues to this day to be actively used (Harrower and Steiner 1943a, 1945 and Harrower 1943b).

This is one of the points where a few more personal details are pertinent. Not long after arriving in Montreal, and after a whirlwind courtship, I married Dr. Theodore Erickson, a neurosurgeon at the Institute. We were married from the Penfield house. The physicians and the other fellows from the hospital were like family members, for I had become part of the cohesive and congenial group of those privileged to work at the Neurological Institute.

Our married life while in Montreal was one in which we were both dedicated to our specialties, putting in long hours of work, but one of great camaraderie with other young marrieds on the staff. Skiing parties, amateur theatricals, and endless evenings of discussions on politics and professional problems are stamped on my memory.

In 1941 my husband was appointed neurosurgeon to the University of Wisconsin's Medical School. It was, of course, an excellent opportunity for him, but presented extraordinary difficulties for me. I was faced with the nepotism ruling, which makes it impossible for two members of the same family to hold positions. This was in sharp contrast to the opportunities in Montreal where I had built up from scratch a department of clinical psychology. I had been able to appoint assistants, publish freely and contribute to the national problem by developing a technique which was being widely used in Canada. I had had, in fact, the type of collaboration with neurosurgeons, neurologists, psychiatrists, and internists which had allowed clinical psychology as a profession to begin to emerge.

While it was true that what I had left behind had taken roots, I was faced with no position, salary, or funds to carry on research. However, what I had achieved stood me in good stead. With the United States shortly to enter the war, the group Rorschach procedure, successful in Canada, when presented to medical and military personnel in the States, evoked interest. Dr. Frank Fremont-Smith, medical director of the Josiah Macy, Jr., Foundation, had received sufficient feedback from Canada to realize the potential usefulness of the group method. I was, therefore, independently funded by the Macy Foundation, thereby circumventing the nepotism ruling, and was able to accept invitations for consulting jobs involving the establishment of group procedures in recruitment centers, hospitals, and the Services.

Working with what turned out to be top military brass during the war made possible, at war's end, a private practice of psychodiagnostics, for many of my wartime military medical colleagues returned to overloaded psychiatric practices and needed in their own work the psychodiagnostic evaluations which they had utilized in the Services. Thus, when I decided to live and work in New York City after a divorce in 1945, a means of livelihood was immediately available. Independent practice, research grants, and consulting fees allowed me to bypass the more competitive situations inherent in academic advancement and from then on, to function outside the traditional job market.

By 1950 private practice of psychodiagnostics had reached the recognized status of a profession. The well-known social historian Harold Lasswell summarized it this way: "When a basic need of the general public meets up with a new technique which can relate to this need, we have the birth of a new profession." [3]

What have I wanted to do with my life as a psychologist? The most general way I can state this would be that I have been interested in making psychological insights, psychological awareness, psychological methods, part and parcel of health care in general, be it physical or emotional. Clearly this interest found expression in the Neurological Institute in Montreal where a better understanding of the peculiar difficulties of brain-injured patients could be studied in conjunction with medical colleagues.

This same interest found expression in a different way in the years 1947–50. The Surgeon General of the Army appointed mental health teams to teach in three big Army hospitals for a month each summer. The teams consisted of four psychoanalytically-oriented psychiatrists, an internist, a psychologist, and a psychiatric social worker. Our task was to make available to senior Army medical officers the basic psychosomatic and psychological approach to medicine. The team on which I served was headed by Dr. Lawrence Kubie—an outstanding psychiatrist—and, as our detailed reports to the Army showed, psychology had been given equal time and equal responsibility in the total program.

Based on the actual questions asked me by the military physicians during these classes, I wrote an explanatory textbook on the projective techniques. Interestingly enough, the questions asked by the physicians were no different from those asked by psychology students, as I found out in my years of teaching at the University of Florida where I used this book as an introductory text (Harrower 1952b)

You could say that this same interest found expression in 1954 when I originated, with the financial backing of the Josiah Macy Foundation, a conference on psychological and medical teamwork in the care of the chronically ill. I had the responsibility of choosing the thirty participants from various disciplines, a task requiring considerable knowledge of the field.

3. In 1952 Yale University sponsored six public lectures on new developments in the mental health field. The words quoted were used by the Chairman Harold Lasswell when introducing me.

I co-chaired the event with Dr. Paul Holbrook, an internist with wide experience in chronic diseases. It was also my task to edit the proceedings and see them published in book form (Harrower 1955a).

In 1958, in somewhat the same way, this interest was sufficiently pressing so that I decided to stop practice for almost five years and concentrate on a long-term follow-up study of 1,600 patients on whom I had a full battery of psychological tests given before these patients entered psychotherapy. These patients had been referred to me by as many as 276 different therapists over a twelve-year period. My questionnaire sent to the therapists requested them to evaluate the patients that they had referred in terms of the degree (on a four-point scale) of the psychological improvement, or lack of it, subsequent to their therapeutic experience.

What emerged from this study was the fact that a patient's mental health potential, or psychological strength as reflected in the pre-therapy psychodiagnostic testing, correlated significantly (at the .01 level) with the degree of improvement as measured independently by the therapist. The psychologically richer personality gained more from therapy than did those with less psychological potential. To him that hath it shall be given![4] (Harrower 1965c, 1969a and 1969b, and Luborsky 1962).

Who have been the most influential people in my psychological adventure?

From a galaxy of interesting scientists and clinicians whom I have come in contact with I choose, rather arbitrarily, three: Professor Beatrice Edgell, a woman who had gone her own way in an era of far greater restriction than we have known; Koffka, for his attitude to science, his meticulous care over experimental work, and his capacity for relentless and rigorous thinking. I would also choose Dr. Alvan Barach, professor of clinical medicine at the College of Physicians and Surgeons, who became my psychoanalyst. Barach was a truly Renaissance man, a novelist and a poet in addition to his medical specialty. He has been called the father of oxygen therapy, writing over 300 articles on his research into breathing difficulties. Barach, having been analyzed himself, took one or two patients a year and I was fortunate enough to be one of them.

The flexibility of Barach's therapeutic methods struck an answering chord in me and much of my experimental attitude to therapy flourished as a result of his endorsement of original trends I may have shown in analysis. By this I mean my use of the patients' responses on the Rorschach, Sentence

4. Dr. Lester Luborsky recently wrote me "The sounder the emotional health of patients to begin with the more they seem to benefit from treatment. In psychotherapy as in finance the rich get richer. I see that we clearly think alike on this issue."

Completion, TAT as associative material in therapy (Harrower 1956, 1960). Later, the use of poetry by classical authors and the patients' own poems within the therapeutic sessions (Harrower 1972a and 1972b), or the use of written sessions rather than face-to-face interview (Harrower 1965a and 1965b).

What did analysis mean in my life, and did I change as a result of it?

It was an exciting experience, and one that allowed me to be explicit about my feelings, and rejoice in my happiness. What the therapeutic work enabled me to do was to avow a quality in myself that others had noticed, but for which I did not take full responsibility. Here is an example of an expression of joyousness:

> I am so happy that I burn the people who pass me
> Particularly those who have also known ecstasy
> And are on good terms with laughter.
> But even the people who live on the shady side of the street,
> The people who pull down the curtains on life
> The people who cover the parlor carpet with newspaper
> In case it should fade.
> Even they look up as I pass, and say
> Why, the sun is pleasant this morning,
> Quite spring like.

And I *do* consider happiness a responsibility, not a luxury:

> Happiness is a responsibility
> It is an inward barometer
> Of well being of body and mind
> And their inter-relation
> It is a precise indicator, a balance
> Exact and intricate
> Reflecting interaction and timing of ever changing
>   needs and desires
> It is an exquisite, a fantastically delicate instrument,
> To be treasured
> To be lived by
> With full realization of every minute of fulfillment,
> Exultantly and without apology.

I wrote many poems during my analysis, some of which have been published (Harrower 1946, 1969a).

But enough of poetry! I will be more specific and concrete. I have first to distinguish between different phases of my analytic work. To begin with, I had a few, vitally important, emergency sessions in 1944 while I was caught in the turmoil of indecision surrounding the question of my first husband.

Then, once established in New York after the finality of the divorce, and at the point where I was starting my practice, I embarked on regular sessions which lasted for over a year. Toward the end of this phase I passed over into what would be considered a period of training for my own therapeutic work. It had become clear to me by that time that I intended to work as a therapist as well as a diagnostician in my practice.

The conditions under which a person enters any form of therapy are of great importance. There must be a feeling of need. By that I mean the individual must be vulnerable, and admit that vulnerability. When I entered I was unhappy. Even more appropriate I, who had not known that there was such a thing as fear, was experiencing acute anxiety. I could not predict when a massive apprehensiveness would overwhelm me. I was not able to make a basic choice. I was indeed ripe for treatment!

But these initial sessions also contained a very positive experience. I was able to respond quickly, able to face insights, and leap forward. I dealt with my inability to move from the pseudo security of my home and gathered a more honest understanding of my role in the situation. Once the hidden aspects of the problem had been forced into the open, I developed the single-mindedness necessary to make the move. I was free of anxiety.

Did I change much? I am sometimes asked. That is harder to answer and probably better observed from the outside. I had the feeling rather of being restored to a more appropriate self, than of changing.

My recollections are more in terms of sudden insights, rather than behaving or acting differently. I saw, for instance, how I had for years associated my father's silences as disapproval of me rather than the result of his own shyness. I saw how this belief had become ingrained and was an inhibitory influence on my spontaneity particularly in professional meetings where I would hold back from speaking. I suspected condemnation unless overtly reassured. Gradually I came to see situations for what they actually were.

My training sessions were an opportunity to discover how I could with ease and enjoyment relate to persons who came for help. I saw that I could never learn rules which were to be played out correctly on a therapeutic chess board. My strength lay in trusting my natural reactions. When I had reached a point of solidarity and belief in my own ways of working, and could defend them, Barach gradually disclosed his own ideas which were remarkably similar.

What kind of support did I experience?

Certainly in the early days I would say 100 percent from my parents, even though they had never expected to have a professionally oriented daughter, and even when, in order to achieve my ends, I had left my home in England and come to the States. During the struggling years, probably more than usual support from mentors, Koffka, Kurt Goldstein, Wilder Penfield, Alan Gregg, Frank Fremont-Smith, all of whom provided not only opportunities for work, but expressed their belief in what I hoped to achieve.

The strongest emotional support came from my second husband, Mortimer Lahm, whom I married in 1955. Remarriage was for me a very important step. The ten years which had intervened since my divorce had enabled me to develop a life-style of my own. I felt solid as a person, my friends were legion, and the opportunities for genuine contributions in the field of mental health ample. Did I want to change this life? For it would have to be changed if I was at this time to live into the kind of marriage I envisaged.

Mortimer and I had been good friends for some time, and he, a widower who had had a happy marriage, had no doubts at all about the married life he envisaged for us. But I was still haunted by the thought that perhaps I was not really cut out for the role of the traditional wife.

I need not have worried: Mortimer took as much interest in my work as I did. In fact, it was possible to achieve, during our years together, the kind of combination of independence and dependence that I had always longed for.

When I spoke of making changes in my routine were I to remarry, I had some very concrete steps that I felt I must take. The first major decision was to turn down an offer to head up psychological research in a large medical center. Another change was to give up projects involving long trips and take only those that could be done from home base. There was no question of giving up being a psychologist, but I have always felt that in order to avoid exhausting conflicts, one must have some indisputable priorities in one's life, which automatically take precedence and obviate recurring choices, as situations arise. As far as I was concerned, being married to Mortimer took preference over any offer or any plan which would have made our joint life more difficult to achieve.

Our life followed a pattern dictated by Mortimer's business responsibilities. He was able to get away for two months in the winter and we discovered an ideal and relatively unknown town on the east coast of Florida to which we went regularly, year after year. In the summers, when Mortimer had to remain in New York, our Long Island cottage provided a haven on weekends. One memorable summer we explored Italy together.

This segment of my life was unquestionably the high point in richness of living, and Mortimer's death was the most difficult and tragic experience I have had to face. But I have emerged to enjoy profoundly my academic life of teaching and research, and another "family" of close personal friends.

Over all I have experienced very little conflict in the merging of the personal and the professional, a problem which I think has troubled many women. One reason may lie in the fact that since 1945 my office has been in the same house or building as my home. This is important to me. The office rooms have personalities of their own, but have been separated only by a door or a landing from the rest of the house or apartment. Thus I have shuttled back and forth, both literally and figuratively, without noticing the transition. I do not think of "myself" as distinct from my psychological interests. There is really no "living" versus "working" in my life. I want to bring to the office anything that has become the residue of intense living, conversely, there is no such thing as "shop talk" being banished from my home.

Conflict as I have known it, however, seemed much more to be related to the clash between science and patient care. I experienced this acutely in my work in Montreal, especially when my job was to sit with the fully conscious patient during brain operations. In 1938 I wrote in a letter: "I believe the strain is really too much for anyone who sees both sides, the human and the scientific. The surgeon's salvation lies in the fact that he doesn't have to consider the patient as a person."[5]

I experienced this conflict again as the research director in the Manhattan Children's Court in 1954 when some experimental situations needed for our research required withholding possible benefits from "control" subjects.

I have at times been asked about my sources of strength and my style of functioning. The strength which I have is related in some ways to my powerful interest in what I am doing, to genuine enthusiasm which I am able to express, and energy, which I am told I have. I clearly draw strength from the results of the self-knowledge gained in analysis, particularly in avoiding unnecessary anxiety. Perhaps most important is the constant awareness that there are close friends who are convinced that what I stand for, and am doing, is something worthwhile.

My style of functioning I think is guided entirely by what I would call "listening to what I *want* to do." It is the antithesis of the Protestant work ethic—because I feel forcing oneself to work is counter-productive.

I know I am thought of as a very energetic and active individual. However, I feel myself quite differently, and on first taking the Rorschach as a

5. The surgeon's observation on this same problem can be seen in a recent book, *Brain Surgeon*, by Laurence Shainberg (1979).

totally naive subject, the animal seen on Card 8 was a sloth! With this self-assessment by my unconscious I totally agree.

Reviewing some of the things which have happened to me, I come to thoughts on prejudice in regard to women, and to the accusation that women are considered second-class citizens. To shut one's eyes to the fact of discrimination would be ridiculous, and it is true that some institutions, at various times, have put senseless obstacles in my way. Perhaps as a result of my rather ingrained independent way of functioning, I have bypassed a lot of problems. It is possible that academic or institutional careers per se result in women facing more built-in prejudices. But if one's primary interests and needs are to work in areas which provide challenges, one may be less vulnerable.

At any rate, I would have to say that I cannot think of a single instance during the fifty years in which I have considered myself a psychologist in which vital and worthwhile psychological interests, or projects, were aborted or made impossible because of my sex. I have made detours, yes, but never been basically frustrated.

REFERENCES

Harrower, M. R. *See* Representative Publications.

Köhler, W. 1927. *Mentality of Apes.* New York: Harcourt Brace.

Koffka, K. 1928. *The Growth of the Mind.* New York: Harcourt Brace.

—— 1935. *The Principles of Gestalt Psychology.* New York: Harcourt Brace.

Luborsky, L. 1962. The patient's personality and therapeutic change. In H. Strupp and L. Luborsky, eds., *Research in Psychotherapy*, vol. 2. Washington, D.C.: American Psychological Assn.

Shainberg, L. 1979. *Brain Surgeon.* New York: Lippincott.

Representative Publications by Molly R. Harrower

1929a. *Plane Jane.* New York: Coward McCann.
1929b. Some experiments on the nature of the gamma movement. *Psychologische Forschung*, 13:55–63.
1931.   With K. Koffka. Colour and organization, part i. *Psychologische Forschung*, 15:145–92.
1932a. With K. Koffka. Colour and organization, part ii. *Psychologische Forschung*, 15:193–275.
1932b. Organization and higher mental processes. *Psychologische Forschung*, 17:56–120.
1934.   Social status and moral development of the child. *British Journal of Educational Psychology*, 4:75–95.
1936.   Some factors determining figure-ground articulation. *British Journal of Psychology*, 26:407–24.
1937.   *The Psychologist at Work.* London: Kegan Paul; New York: Harper.
1939.   Changes in figure-ground perception in patients with cortical lesions. *British Journal of Psychology*, 30:47–51.
1940a. Personality Changes Accompanying Cerebral Lesions. i. Rorschach studies of patients with cerebral tumors. *Archives of Neurology and Psychiatry*, 43:859–90.
1940b. Personality Changes Accompanying Cerebral Lesions, ii. Rorschach studies of patients with focal epilepsy. *Archives of Neurology and Psychiatry*, 43:1081–1107.
1941.   Psychological studies in patients with epileptic seizures. In Wilder Penfield and Theodore C. Erickson, *Epilepsy and Cerebral Localization.* Springfield, Ill.: Thomas.
1942.   Kurt Koffka: 1886–1941. *American Journal of Psychology*, 55:278–81.
1943a. With M. Steiner. Directions for administration of the Rorschach group test. *Journal of Genetic Psychology*, 62:105–17.

1943b. Large scale investigation with the Rorschach method. *Journal of Consulting Psychology*, 7:120–26.

1943c. With M. Steiner. Modification of the Rorschach method for use as a group test. *Journal of Genetic Psychology*, 62:119–33.

1943d. A multiple choice test for screening purposes (for use with Rorschach cards or slides). *Psychosomatic Medicine*, 5:331–41.

1943e. The Rorschach method in the study of personality. *Annals of the New York Academy of Sciences*, 44:569–88.

1944. The use of the multiple choice test (Rorschach) in the military services. *War Psychiatry*. Proceedings of Second Brief Psychotherapy Council. Chicago: Chicago Institute of Psychoanalysis.

1945. With M. Steiner. *Large Scale Rorschach Techniques*. Springfield, Ill.: Thomas.

1946. *Time to Squander, Time to Reap*. New Bedford, Mass.: Reynolds.

1947. Hysteria; Neurotic depression in a child. In A. Burton and R. E. Harris, eds., *Case Histories in Clinical and Abnormal Psychology*. New York and London: Harper.

1948. The evolution of a clinical psychologist. *Canadian Journal of Psychology*, 2:23–27.

1950a. The most unpleasant concept test. *Journal of Clinical Psychology*, 3:213–33.

1950b. Results of psychometric and personality tests in multiple sclerosis. *Association for Research in Nervous and Mental Diseases*, 28:451–70.

1951a. With Jane Kraus. Psychological studies on patients with multiple sclerosis. *Archives of Neurology and Psychiatry*, 66:44–57.

1951b. Visual aids in presentation of test material. *Journal of Projective Techniques*, 15:380–87.

1951c. The pastor and the clinical psychologist. *Pastoral Psychology*.

1952a. The application of clinical psychological tests to a fuller understanding of somatic disease. *Bulletin of the New York Academy of Medicine*, 28:573–91.

1952b. *Appraising Personality*. New York: Norton. 2d ed., New York: Franklin Watts, 1964; 3d ed., New York: Simon & Schuster, 1968.

1953a. *Mental Health and MS*. New York: National Multiple Sclerosis Society.

1953b. The group Rorschach. In Arthur Weider, ed., *Contribution toward Medical Psychology*. New York: Ronald Press.

1954a. Clinical aspects of failures in the projective techniques. *Journal of Projective Techniques*, 18:294–302.

1954b.   The measurement of psychological factors in marital maladjustment. *Texas Reports on Biology and Medicine*, 12:72–85.

1955a.   Editor. *Medical and Psychological Team Work in the Care of the Chronically Ill*. Springfield, Ill.: Thomas.

1965b.   Who comes to court? *Journal of Orthopsychiatry*, 25:15–25.

1956.   Projective counseling: A psychotherapeutic technique. *American Journal of Psychotherapy*, 10:74–86.

1957.   Screening . . . for what? The relevant use of psychological tests in medical education. *British Journal of Medical Psychology*, 30:19–26.

1958a.   *Personality Change and Developments as Measured by the Projective Techniques*. New York: Grune & Stratton.

1958b.   Why you like the people you like. *Vogue*, August 1.

1959.   The contribution of the projective techniques to psychiatric diagnosis. In *Progressive in Psychotherapy*. New York: Grune & Stratton.

1960.   With P. Vorhaus, M. Roman, and G. Bauman. *Creative Variations in the Projective Techniques*. Springfield, Ill.: Thomas.

1961a.   The independent practice of clinical psychology. In W. Webb, ed., *What Psychologists Do*. New York: Holt.

1961b.   *The Practice of Clinical Psychology*. Springfield, Ill.: Thomas.

1963a.   Psychological tests in the Unitarian Universalist ministry. *Journal of Religion and Health*, 2:129–42.

1963b.   Psychodiagnostic and personality testing. In *Encyclopedia of Mental Health*. New York: Franklin Watts.

1964.   Mental health potential and success in the ministry. *Journal of Religion and Health*, 4:30–58.

1965a.   A clinical psychologist looks at short-term therapy. In Lewis Wolberg, ed., *Short Term Psychotherapy*. New York: Grune & Stratton.

1965b.   Clinical psychologists at work; Differential diagnosis. In B. Wolman, ed., *Handbook of Clinical Psychology*. New York: McGraw-Hill.

1965c.   *Psychological Testing: An Empirical Approach*. Springfield, Ill.: Thomas.

1965d.   Therapeutic communications by letter-notebooks and recorded transcriptions. In Leonard Pearson, ed., *The Use of Written Communications in Psychotherapy*. Springfield, Ill.: Thomas.

1966a.   Changing roles and changing responsibilities. *Clinical Psychologist*, 20:11–14.

1966b. *Manual for Harrower Inkblots.* 3d ed. Beverly Hills, Calif.: Western Psychological Services.

1968.   Research on the patient. In *New Directions in Mental Health.* New York: Grune & Stratton.

1969a. Poems emerging from the therapeutic experience. *Journal of Nervous and Mental Disease.* 149(2):213–23.

1969b. Projective classification. In *New Approaches to Personality Classification.* New York: Columbia University Press.

1971a. Notes on the Koffka papers. *Journal of the History of the Behavioral Sciences,* 7:141–53.

1971b. Koffka's Rorschach experiment. *Journal of Personality Assessment,* 35:103–21.

1972a. Projection, play and poetry. *Journal of Personality Assessment,* 36:507–24.

1972b. *Therapy of Poetry.* Springfield, Ill.: Thomas.

1974a. Women in independent or free-lance practice. *International Understanding,* 9/10:88–96.

1974b. The therapy of poetry. In *Current Psychiatric Therapies.* New York: Grune & Stratton.

1975.   With Caroline B. Thomas and Ann Altman. Human figure drawings in a prospective study. *Journal of Nervous and Mental Disease,* 161:191–99.

1975–1976. Variations on the theme: Artist as therapist, therapist as artist. *Voices,* 11:5–9.

1976a. Were Hitler's henchman mad? *Psychology Today,* 10:76–80.

1976b. Rorschach records of the Nazi war criminals: An experimental study after thirty years. *Journal of Personality Assessment,* 40:341–51.

1977.   The Rorschach and self-understanding: The instruction-insight method. *Journal of Personality Assessment,* 41:451–60.

1978.   Changing horses in mid-stream: An experimentalist becomes a clinician. In T. S. Krawiec, ed., *The Psychologists: Autobiographies of Distinguished Living Psychologists,* vol. 3. Brandon, Vt.: Clinical Psychology Publishing.

1980.   Last hour. *Voices,* 15:9–11.

1983   *Kurt Koffka: An Unwitting Self-Portrait.* Gainesville: University Presses of Florida.

MARGARET J. RIOCH

I feel impelled to begin this presentation by telling you a little bit about myself that is autobiographical in nature that I think bears on my professional experience as a woman. I was born in 1907 in Paterson, New Jersey. When I was twelve, my family moved to a nearby suburb and I attended high school in Ridgewood, New Jersey. I was brought up in an exceedingly feminine household, or I should say rather in an exceedingly female household. My father had died when I was a year old in 1908—I do not remember him—and my mother moved back thereupon to *her* mother's house and never remarried. My grandmother was an exceedingly dominating old lady whom I never liked. She had, in addition to my mother and two married sons, two daughters who never married and who were obviously under her thumb. Her own husband had died quite early when my mother was a very young woman. All three of her daughters, including my mother, were teachers of various kinds. They and my grandmother constituted the family in which I was the only child. Needless to say, there was not a great deal of money around. One aunt was rather nondescript, but one was delightful. She told me tales of old sagas and fairies, and she played most charmingly with children. I was very fond of her and in many ways tried to follow in her footsteps.

As a child and as a young girl, it seemed to me very natural that a woman should have a profession. In fact it would seem to be unnatural for a woman *not* to have a profession of significance and importance to her. Marriage, on the other hand, did *not* seem so natural. Although I found men attractive and, indeed fascinating, I did not marry until I was around thirty. Although I tried, assisted by medical advice, to become pregnant and although I wanted to have children, I did not have any, which I regret.

All this is by way of explaining some of my later attitudes and problems, or lack of them, as a woman.

My first areas of specialization did not include psychology at all, but were philology, literature, and philosophy. I had been educated, not surprisingly, at women's colleges: Wellesley and Bryn Mawr. In those days it was not so

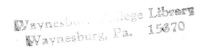

hard as it is now to enter graduate school. For me the question of where one could get a large scholarship was of prime importance, and that decided me for Bryn Mawr. My first jobs were teaching German, first at Wilson College and then at Wellesley where I first knew Dr. Thelma Alper, who later became professor of psychology at Wellesley.

My professors in college were always role models for me and I aspired to be one of them. It never occurred to me that I could not. I had always been a good student and had been on the whole well treated in school, college, and graduate school. One summer I had even ventured into a large, city university, namely Columbia, in New York City, where my teachers and more than half of the students were men. Everything went all right for me there too. Some of my graduate work was done in Europe, in Frankfurt-am-Main, Berlin, and Basle, where the students and professors were mostly men. I never felt it to be a disadvantage that I was a woman, though I was well aware that in the generation before me it had been a hard struggle for women. I remember thinking that the presidents of women's colleges should be women so long as there were no women presidents of men's colleges. I also remember thinking, with the arrogance of youth, that women, and particularly I, had to be a little better than the average man in order to stay equal. That seemed to me to be quite all right since I was quite sure that I *was* better than the average man. That there was a gross injustice here, I preferred to overlook. I took it for granted that the "great" people about whom I studied and whose books I read, were almost all men. My closest woman friend in my twenties, Dr. Edith Helman, a professor of Spanish and French at Simmons College in Boston, was a brilliant and very successful professional woman who was also an excellent cook. I remember at the time of my marriage saying to her that she was the only woman I felt comfortable with in discussing mundane, household matters. I think with other women it felt degrading to betray an interest in things like cooking and interior decorating. I should be superior to such things.

Soon after my marriage, my husband, who was on the faculty of the Harvard Medical School at the time, was appointed professor and head of a new department of neuropsychiatry at Washington University in St. Louis. Of course, we moved from Boston to St. Louis. It never occurred to me to raise any questions about this, although it meant for me giving up a job and a promising career. Today a woman would probably at least question whether or not to leave Boston.

It was not exactly easy to shift from being a career woman, quite independent in every way, to being simply "a wife," occupied with moving, getting settled in a new community, and finding a place among the wives of the medical faculty, some of whom had jobs and careers, but many of whom did not. My husband, a neuroanatomist who later also became a psychiatrist, was very busy with his new department. I soon found out that Washington University in St. Louis had a policy which I then understood to be for the purpose of protecting against nepotism and unfair use of influence by families, but which now seems to me to be unfair to women as well as sometimes to men. In any case they did not want to hire wives of men who were already on the faculty. That meant that there was no hope of my getting a job there so long as my husband was employed in the medical school. I did a little more desultory investigation of the teaching field in St. Louis and then gave it up.

Gradually I began to realize that my real interest lay in psychology. This dawned on me slowly over a long period of time. In college I had been turned off by psychology. Although the professor, Dr. Eleanor McKinnon Gamble, was a very lovable person, the subject matter as it was then taught, seemed to have little or nothing to do with me and *my* psychology, which was of prime importance to me, as I think it is to many other young people. The compartmentalization of "me" into sensation, perception, emotion, will, and God knows what else, seemed not to be relevant to my experience of "me" at all. It was only later that I realized that my interest in literature and philosophy had been at bottom a psychological interest. Fortunately marriage gave me leisure and financial security enough to pursue graduate work in psychology, and so I did. I received an M.A. from Washington University. My first research had to do with the Rorschach test, which was then just being introduced into the United States. I went to New York to take private lessons from Dr. Emil Oberholzer, who had been a colleague of Hermann Rorschach and who was himself really a poet and an artist in his Rorschach interpretations. Dr. Oberholzer was a friend of my sister-in-law, Dr. Janet Rioch, a psychoanalyst in New York, and I had met him through her. He was a bit contemptuous of American developments, but my familiarity with European culture stood me in good stead with him and he turned out to be a very stimulating and perceptive teacher. A mutual friend told the story of taking him her own Rorschach without telling him it was hers, but also inserting one response which was not really her own, but which she had "stolen" from someone else because it was so "original." He was not at all complimentary about her test, but when he came to the "stolen" response, he stopped, and said in a surprised and puzzled way that this response, though quite delightful, clearly did not belong in the test. This was the kind of artistic detective work which characterized his approach and which made him an enviable interpreter whom I tried to emulate.

I found that my interest was in the qualitative rather than the quantitative aspects of psychology and it did not take me long to find out that I wanted to be a clinician. I also took private lessons from Dr. Sylvan Tomkins, then at Princeton University, in the Thematic Apperception Test and its interpretation. At that time, before World War II, psychologists were considered to be primarily diagnosticians and experts in psychological testing. I found myself particularly drawn to the projective techniques, especially the Rorschach and TAT. Only later, after we moved from St. Louis to the Washington area, and specifically to Rockville, Maryland, did I find that I wanted to work also as a psychotherapist.

After some initial question about whether I would be too absorbed in a job to be a good wife, my husband became very supportive of my endeavors and he has been consistently an important source of support. If we had had children I am sure it would have been more complex, but I did not find it too difficult to work and still manage a household, so that I think he has not been worse off than other men.

After about five years in St. Louis, my husband decided to return East to work at the Chestnut Lodge Sanitarium in Rockville, Maryland, which boasted at that time a very distinguished staff, including Dr. Fromm-Reichmann and Dr. Sullivan as a consultant. My husband became a staff psychiatrist, but never joined the Psychoanalytic Institute. After a few years he became director of the division of neuropsychiatry at the Walter Reed Army Institute of Research where he remained until 1970. This was a research division, spanning everything from neuroanatomy to psychiatry and it was very appropriate to his varied interests.

Again without questioning I went along and found my own niche in the Community Mental Hygiene Clinic in Rockville and, later, as psychologist at Chestnut Lodge, where I was the only psychologist ever permitted to do therapy in that very medically, psychoanalytically-oriented hospital. This was a part-time position and I began to do part-time private practice, starting with diagnostic testing, particularly projective techniques, and gradually doing more and more psychotherapy. My psychotherapy has a psychoanalytic orientation, and, of course, I have been psychoanalyzed myself over several years. My major teachers were Harry Stack Sullivan and Frieda Fromm-Reichmann.

Dr. Sullivan was an outstandingly stimulating, challenging teacher. He was also at times abrasive and intimidating. At such times it was hard to imagine, but nonetheless true, that with patients in trouble he could be warm, supportive, and so obviously competent that it was confidence inspiring. At the same time it was almost impossible to deceive him. He was ruthless in insisting upon truthfulness insofar as a patient could tolerate it. He himself could tolerate a great deal, which helped patients to be honest too.

I had the privilege of knowing him not only as a teacher in various courses, but also of going to him for private supervision, which he conducted in his house in Bethesda, a house overgrown with day lilies and overrun by large numbers of cocker spaniels who bit the students they or he did not like. I also knew him socially, since my husband and I were part of the group around Chestnut Lodge and the Washington School of Psychiatry where he taught. He could be delightfully entertaining or aloof depending upon his mood.

Dr. Frieda Fromm-Reichmann was a very different sort of person. She was very approachable and tended to see the positive side of things and people. I knew her too socially and as a teacher at Chestnut Lodge and the Washington School of Psychiatry. She seemed to be always the therapist and I used to say that her many cures of very sick and not so sick people were in part, at least, a matter of her will power. She made it very clear that the patient *would* get well, willy-nilly. She was also a very practical arranger of people's lives. If a guest came from out of town, one might find oneself commandeered to entertain him or her for lunch or dinner without even realizing that one had been commandeered. She was a very tiny woman and it sometimes seemed anomalous that she should be so powerful. Many people thought of her as seductive. At Chestnut Lodge she was the "mother" and, as is often the case with real mothers, she was often in the middle of fights and dissensions.

To come back to my own work, I have done chiefly individual psycho-therapy, though I do sometimes see couples. Family therapy interests me in principle, but I have no experience with it in practice.

I have always been interested in psychotherapy as a craft or an art. I have never been able to interest myself very much in theory or traditional research in this field and I find myself supporting young graduate students in their complaints about the stupid and insignificant dissertations they have to write to get their Ph.Ds. What I really mean by psychotherapy as an art or a craft is that each session is for me a new event and a new challenge. Not that there is no continuity with previous sessions. But rarely do I have an agenda. It is much more a fresh experience in which I wait to see what the patient will bring. In this it is something like a dance in which my steps have to mesh with his or her steps. I do sometimes take the initiative, but more often the role is a following one. Sometimes I have to explain to a patient that that is to his advantage. One of the things which students have to learn, I find, is to keep quiet and to value the potential silences. Usually students have been taught to "reflect" whatever the patient is feeling, or they are driven by anxiety and social convention to respond to whatever the patient says. It is not, I think, that I undervalue *my* role in the therapy, but I try both implicitly and explicitly to let the patient see that it is *his* life, and *his* session.

In addition to doing psychotherapy I think I have made two main contributions to the field of psychology which I will try to talk about in terms of what they have represented for me as a woman.

The first is a project which I conducted, together with Dr. Charmian Elkes, at NIMH in 1960–62, which was called A Pilot Project in Training Mental Health Counselors. We also did follow-up studies and I did a second project in the Childrens Hospital of Washington, D.C. The idea for the original project came to me à propos of a conversation I had with Dr. Fritz Redlich, then chairman of the Yale department of psychiatry. It was somewhere in the 1950s and he said, thinking of the problems as they were then: "Where in the world would we get enough gifted people to be psychotherapists and to work for little money?" It came to me then or shortly afterward that the answer to that question was easy. One could use one problem to solve another. The one problem, of which I was keenly aware, was that women, whose children were more or less grown, were in dire need of an activity to take the place of child-rearing which had often been for them both absorbing and time-consuming. When the children no longer needed them, they were left feeling unused, unneeded, and empty. I knew from my personal acquaintances that many of these women were intelligent, perceptive, and potentially very good therapists. The second problem, which Dr. Redlich and others raised, was that there was a great need at that time for low-cost psychotherapy. My idea was that for many intelligent women whose husbands were at the height of financially successful careers—doctors, lawyers, etc.—the financial rewards were not very important. You will remember that this was back in the 1950s. Not long after that, Dr. David Hamburg, now of Harvard, gave me the opportunity to come to NIMH as research psychologist. I had known David Hamburg first when as a very young man he worked in my husband's division at the Walter Reed. Later he went to NIMH and became director of the division of adult psychiatry. When he asked me to come on his staff, this seemed like just the right chance and the right setting to get evidence that middle-aged women, of the kind I envisioned, could prove themselves to be competent therapists. I planned that they would become professionals, and this fitted with the idea of Dr. Lawrence Kubie, who was also a friend of mine, and at that time director of research at the Sheppard and Enoch Pratt Hospital in Towson, Maryland, that there should be a new profession called psychotherapy with its own special training, which would not be identical with that for psychiatry, psychology, or social work.

Actually I think that the project we did at NIMH had a greater impact throughout the country on the development of paraprofessionals. And that is all right with me too. But the intention was to develop professionals and we thought that we provided as rigorous "proof" as one can get in this fuzzy field that the women we trained were as good as the traditional "professionals." The training program continued at Johns Hopkins in a small way until 1980. But I must admit that if a woman of thirty to forty comes to me now for advice, I suggest that she enter one of the established professions. There is too much need for a "union card," especially these days, for most women to embark on a non-traditional venture. Anyway it was great fun to do the training and to administer and write up the project. And the seven women (actually there were eight trainees, but one has since unfortunately died of cancer) we trained had a twentieth anniversary of the beginning of the project in the spring of 1980. We commented at this "reunion" that everyone looked *very* well preserved and relatively young. It was gratifying to see that they all felt fulfilled and satisfied with their lives. They had all worked for at least four years at paid jobs after completing the project. After that, one dropped out since her husband wanted her to travel with him too often to make regular work possible for her. She has remained active, however, in the mental health community. Another trainee has now joined her husband in retirement, but five are still working full time.

In 1963, after the training part of the project was over, it came to me in a sort of revelation what it had been all about. This may seem to be obvious, but it is not strange that the person who does something does not know what he or she is doing. Anyway I suddenly saw, around 1963, that I had wanted to prove that women after the menopause could still be creative. Of course, that included me too. I believe we proved it—if indeed such a thing needed proving or could be proved by a pilot project. But the eight women themselves were most gratifying to work with and they did, each one, grow and develop and become more creative as they were given opportunities to do so.

My third area of interest in psychology has been the A. K. Rice Institute. My history with this organization goes back to 1963 when I went to Leicester, England, to participate as a member in a group relations conference conducted by the Tavistock Institute of London and directed by Dr. A. Kenneth Rice. He was an anthropologist by training, and had become an active member of the staff of the Tavistock Institute. He had earlier been an officer in colonial Africa where his liberal convictions and lack of sympathy with racial prejudice made him unpopular with the British colonial administration at the time. He had also been a consultant to industry in India with the very rich Sarabhai family which is known for its connections to Gandhi, and he had worked in many other places as a consultant to business and to other organizations. He was already the author of several books and the creator of important concepts having to do with organizations and management. He was enormously attractive personally—articulate, entertaining, brilliant, and clear both in conversation and in writing.

I went to the Tavistock group relations conference in Leicester at the recommendation of an English friend of mine who said that if I considered myself a psychologist and did not know of this important work, I ought to shut up shop. Anyway I went, along with Dr. Morris Parloff from NIMH. It was a deep and significant experience and left a profound impression upon me. At the end of it, I asked Kenneth Rice and his second in command, Dr. Pierre Turquet of the Tavistock Clinic, if they would consider conducting such a conference in the United States. They said they would, but we agreed it would be safer to conduct a conference first in England in the summer, when many Americans go to Europe anyway, to test out whether there would be enough real interest. In the meantime, in the summer of 1963, I went to Bethel to find out whether we already had an indigenous product of this kind right here. The whole attitude, the philosophy, the principles, and what one could learn, seemed to me quite different from what I had experienced in England so that I felt sure I would be bringing a new injection into the American bloodstream. The conference we planned with the Tavistock was conducted in the summer of 1964 in England. I coralled twenty-five Americans and the Tavistock people collected twenty-five Europeans, many of whom were business types, and we held what was for me the second conference.

In June 1965 we held the first American group relations conference at Mt. Holyoke College. It was under the sponsorship of the Washington School of Psychiatry, for my old friend Fritz Redlich had become interested, and the Tavistock Institute of London. Informally the Walter Reed, through my husband, lent us a great deal of support, but as a government agency it was considered wiser that it should not be named as an official sponsor. Three British staff members came over; Kenneth Rice, as director; and Pierre Turquet, who was his friend and colleague, a psychoanalyst from the Tavistock Clinic; and Dr. John Sutherland, who was director of the Tavistock Clinic.

Of the three people from Tavistock who helped us to get started, two are now dead and the third, Dr. Sutherland, is now retired but still working in Edinburgh.

My own relationship was particularly close to Kenneth Rice, whose untimely death in 1969, was an occasion of grief and mourning for many people. Since my college days there is no one I regard so much as my teacher, mentor, and in many ways a role model. I admired particularly the discipline with which he held to any task he took on, but particularly that of conference director.

Actually, without bragging very much, the whole thing came about through my initiative, and continued so for some years. I have gradually handed it over to younger people. There is now a national organization with five local centers in Washington, Texas, the Midwest, Missouri, San Francisco, and one developing in the Northwest and also one developing in Rochester, New York. I was at first executive director of the national organization and chairman of the executive committee of the Washington-Baltimore Center. After the death of Kenneth Rice in 1969, the organization was renamed in his honor, the A. K. Rice Institute. It has suffered many ups and downs and the local centers are sometimes turbulent and not always very stable financially. The group relations conferences we run, which have so far been our chief activity, are copied more or less faithfully from the Tavistock model. The staff does not teach, but "offers opportunities for learning." The task of the members is to study interactions in the "here and now" and what they learn is up to them and is judged by them. The staff does not concern itself with individuals, but keeps its attention focused on the group, singling out one individual *only* when he or she is representing something or speaking for the group. The message seems to get across that everyone is responsible for the whole group even when he or she expresses a dissenting opinion. The consultants, that is the staff members, are often seen to be grim and distant, since they refuse to become involved in individual relationships with group members. Actually they usually feel very strongly how the group is pulling them this way and that way and, as they become experienced, they are able to use these experiences in the service of the group's learning. They are both active and passive, active in that they work at studying the group's behavior and at making important interventions which the group usually finds *very* important, perhaps more important than they really are. And passive in that they are like a mirror, wiped clean as possible of personal concerns, and reflecting back to the group what their projections are of authority figures as embodied in the consultant, a young man or an old woman, of the same race or a different one from theirs. As a person who is both active and passive, the consultant is in a sense hermaphroditic and must allow for both traditionally masculine and traditionally feminine qualities to be projected upon him.

I have often asked myself deeply what is the nature of my fascination with this kind of work that I have devoted so much time and energy to, both in the conferences we run and the administration of the organization. I think that my fascination with this is with the kind of ambiguity of being both active and passive which I have just mentioned. It is also with the secret power that is never flaunted and can therefore never be rebelled against, for if one rebels one is met not by opposition but simply by an interpretation. This secret power that one can exercise while at the same time denying it and insisting that it is the members who have the real power, is a great and fascinating thing. The "hermaphroditic" quality of consultants seems to suit me very well, and to fit with the family in which I grew up, independent and self-sufficient women, who nevertheless longed for the unattainable man.

There is one piece of research which I have never done but which intrigues me; and that is the question of what becomes of girls who are brought up without fathers. I cannot account for it except by coincidence, but I seem to have been blessed with a disproportionate number of patients who were girls brought up without fathers. I trust I will be forgiven for the lack of statistics in my never undertaken study, but I have observed that these are women who are externally quite feminine; they do not go in for masculine types of clothes; but inwardly they are tough; if one is friendly, one calls them strong; if unfriendly, one calls them hard. They also have some sort of romantic or poetic streak. They are interested in philosophy or religion or poetry or music; at the same time they are pretty practical.

Just to illustrate that I fit into this category very well, and at the same time to come back to my work with groups, it may be worth noting that the power that consultants wield is somewhat akin to that of the Zen master, who has no real power to make his disciples do anything, but who nevertheless exercises an enormous influence over them, so that they supposedly stand and literally freeze waiting in front of his door for admission. His power seems to lie in the fact that he refuses to exercise power. At its deepest level Zen and "systems theory," which is the theory on which we base our group conferences, both have to do with the merging of the one and the all. Occasionally a group shudders at the place where it has found itself. I think one might say it is a place without the boundaries that we are used to in our everyday skins. Occasionally I have been moved myself to say that I am the group and the group is me. Sometimes I have known that in a group I went down into a deep tunnel-like death and the reward was deeper and greater communication between me and the group. It is this, I think, which

Christian religious people speak of as the Way of the Cross. It is a sacrifice which seems to be inevitable when I take upon myself willingly the responsibility for the whole group. There is no longer a bad choice between mine and thine because mine is thine and thine is mine.

This past fall I took a course given by a young woman, Dr. Faith Gabelnick, in the Washington School of Psychiatry. It was entitled "Lives of Women": and the intention was that through reading autobiographical and other writings we could gain special insights into the feminization process and understand better how gender identity and sex role functioning worked. At the end of the course I found myself saying that some of the things we read had been second-rate and that the really great women writers were not preoccupied with women's issues. I think there is a lot of room for debate about who the really great women writers are, but I had in mind particularly Isak Dinesen who is one of my heroes. I did not know at that time something which I have come across recently. Isak Dinesen, in her "Daguerreotypes and Other Essays," has one entitled "Oration at a Bonfire, Fourteen Years Late" which was to be apparently given to a group of feminists. She tells at the beginning that she at first declined to speak saying, "I cannot accept this assignment for I am not a feminist." "Are you against feminism?" asked the lady who was interviewing her. "No, I can't say that I am that either." "How do you stand upon feminism?" was the next question. "Well, I never thought of it," she answered. "Well, think of it now," answered her questioner. Isak Dinesin goes on to say, "That was a good bit of advice, which I followed, even though things did not go so quickly that I got around to giving the oration. . . . When I endeavor to untangle the whole matter for myself I usually begin at the bottom and ask 'Why are there two sexes?'" While commenting that a scientist could probably give a better explanation, she goes on to say essentially that in her opinion the existence of two sexes serves the function of each one being an inspiration to the other. She emphasizes the difference between the two sexes in that a man is known for what he *does*, and a woman for what she *is*.[1] I think I am in general in accord with her.

In this paper I have emphasized what I *do*, in other words the masculine component. I find it very difficult if not impossible to put into words what I am, or for that matter, what any other woman is. And I suspect that this along with other really important matters, has to remain in the realm of the unspoken, unless perhaps it can be said in poetry.

1. Isak Dinesen, *Daguerreotypes and Other Essays*, Chicago: University of Chicago Press, pp. 66 ff.

Representative Publications by Margaret J. Rioch

1941. Trans. On the psychology of so-called process of abstraction, by Egon Weigel. *Journal of Abnormal and Social Psychology*, vol. 36.

1949. The use of the Rorschach test in the assessment of change. *Psychiatry*, 12:427–34.

1953. With Jarl H. Dyrud. Multiple therapy in the treatment program of a mental hospital. *Psychiatry*, 16:21–26.

1954. The mosaic test as a diagnostic instrument. *Journal of Projective Techniques*, 18:89–94.

1959a. With Ardie Lubin. Prognosis of social adjustment for mental hospital patients under psychotherapy. *Journal of Consulting Psychology*, 23(4):313–18.

1959b. Trans. Buddha and the intuition of the universal, by Hubert Benoit. *Hibbert Journal*, vol. 57.

1960a. The meaning of Martin Buber's "element of the interhuman" for the practice of psychotherapy. *Psychiatry*, 23:133–40.

1960b. Three questions in pastoral counseling. *Journal of Pastoral Care*, 14(2):104–7.

1962a. With Arden A. Flint. An experiment in teaching family dynamics. *American Journal of Psychiatry*, 119(10):940–44.

1962b. A training program in mental health counseling for middle-aged women. *Journal of the American Association of University Women*, May.

1963a. With Elkes, Flint, Usdansky, Newman, and Silber, NIMH pilot study in training mental health counselors. *American Journal of Orthopsychiatry*, 33:679–89.

1963b. Review of *Experiencing and the Creation of Meaning*, by Eugene T. Gendlin. *Psychiatry* (August), vol. 26.

1964a. The fiddlers of X. *Psychotherapy*, 1(2):88–90.

1964b. A late career experiment. *Wellesley Alumnae Magazine* (January), pp. 92–93, 108–9.

1965. With Charmian Elkes and Arden A. Flint. Pilot project in training mental health counselors. U.S. Department of Health, Education and Welfare, Public Health Service Publication No. 1254.

1966.   Changing concepts in the training of therapists. *Journal of Consulting Psychology*, 30(4):290–92.

1976a.   With Reginald S. Lourie and Samuel Schwartz. The concept of a training program for child development counselors. *American Journal of Public Health*, 57(10).

1967b.   Memories of Dr. Daisetz Suzuki. *The Eastern Buddhist*, N.S. 2(1).

1967c.   Pilot Projects in training mental health counselors. In Emory L. Cowen, Elmer A. Gardener, and Melvin Zax, eds., *Emergent Approaches to Mental Health Problems*. New York: Appleton-Century-Crofts.

1970a.   Group relations: Rationale and technique. *International Journal of Group Psychotherapy*, 20(3):340–55.

1970b.   Should psychotherapists do psychotherapy? *Professional Psychology*, 1(2):139–142; and in *Journal of Contemporary Psychotherapy*, 3(1):61–64.

1970c.   The work of Dr. Hubert Benoit. *Theoria to Theory*, 4:43–58.

1970d.   The work of Wilfred Bion on groups. *Psychiatry*, 33:56–66; and in Sagar and Kaplan, eds., *Progress in Group and Family Therapy*. New York: Brunner/Mazel, 1972.

1970c.   Trans. Various songs and poems for the programs of the Theater Chamber Players.

1971a.   "All we like sheep . . ." (Isaiah 53.6) Followers and leaders. *Psychiatry*, 34(3):258–73. The Frieda Fromm Reichmann Memorial Lecture.

1971b.   Gruppenmethodesn. Das Tavistock-Washington-Modell. *Gruppendynamik: Forschung und Praxis*, 2:142–52.

1971c.   Two pilot projects in training mental health counselors. In Robert R. Holt, ed., *New Horizon for Psychotherapy*. New York: International Universities Press.

1972a.   Comment on Henry Ezriel, Experimentation within the psychoanalytic session. *Contemporary Psychoanalysis*, 8(2):246.

1972b.   Comment on Silvano Arieti and Sally Lorraine, The use of the therapeutic assistant in the treatment of the psychotic. *International Journal of Psychiatry*.

1972c.   Comment on Ira M. Steisel, article in *Professional Psychology* (Fall), pp. 334–335.

1975a.   Review of *Lâcher Prise*, by Hubert Benoit. *Psychiatry* (August), vol. 38.

1975b.   Review of *Encounter Groups: First Facts*, by Morton A. Lieberman, Irvin D. Yalom, and Matthew B. Miles. *Psychiatry*, 38:196–97.

1976a.   The A. K. Rice intergroup exercise as a reflection of society. *Journal for Personality and Social Systems*, 1(1):1–16; and in Gordon Lawrence, ed., *Exploring Individual and Organizational Boundaries*. New York: Wiley, 1979.

1976b.   With Winifred Coulter and David Weinberger. *Dialogues for Therapists*. San Francisco: Jossey-Bass.

1976c.   Review of *Love and Ecstasy*, by Arthur B. Colman and Libby Lee Colman. *Psychiatry*, 39:101–102.

1976d.   Why I work as a consultant in the conferences of the A. K. Rice Institute. *Journal of Personality and Social Systems*, 1(41):33–50.

1977.   Trans. Various poems for a concert at the Phillips Gallery and for Mildred Allen Taub.

1980a.   Advanced learning in a small group. *Journal of Personality and Social Systems*, 2(2–3).

1980b.   The dilemmas of supervision in dynamic psychotherapy. In Allen Hess, ed., *Psychotherapy Supervision: Theory, Research and Practice*. New York: Wiley.

THELMA G. ALPER

To understand my final career choice necessitates a long backward look into the major factors which influenced it. When I first began to give serious thought to what I would do after graduation from Wellesley, I found myself being drawn more and more to the possibility of making use of my undergraduate major, German. I realized, for example, that I probably would be able to teach German at the secondary-school level without much further training. Yet I was not sure that this was what I really wanted to do. Besides, the specter of the small demand for German in my own high school for several years following World War I gave me pause. How easy would it be to find a job, especially if I did not go on to graduate school? As it turned out, both a job, but not in German, and the chance to start graduate work unexpectedly came my way right after graduation. But the retrospection must start well before my college days.

Thinking back now I recognize that the most important single factor influencing the course of my development was the support and guidance given me by my sister, Bertha. Ten years older than I, she was my most significant role model. She was brilliant, socially outgoing, and remarkably empathic. As I was growing up in Chelsea Massachusetts, I was certain that I would never match her achievements. But I was also certain that I could count on her to help me over the rough spots of growing up in a very achievement-oriented, but not at all a college-oriented, Jewish family. It was she, not my parents, who insisted that I follow the college preparatory track in high school, and that I subsequently attend a four-year liberal arts college. She, herself, had settled for the business track and had graduated, at age sixteen, valedictorian of her class. After high school, she quickly entered the business world and was soon launched on a highly successful business career.

In my junior year of high school, my sister began urging me to consider which college I would like to attend. In the end, the choice was more hers than mine. Since my academic record this far had been good, I was informed by my high school principal that I was eligible for admission to Radcliffe College and that it would not be necessary for me to take the

College Entrance Examination. Not having to take these exams appealed very much to me. But no one in the family, other than I, favored Radcliffe. My mother preferred Simmons College, where she felt I would get "a practical education." My sister held out for Wellesley, a four-year, live-in, liberal arts college, and my father, having a high regard for the soundness of her judgment, agreed with her. But since none of my friends was headed for Wellesley, I was somewhat reluctant to accept her choice. Yet the die was cast. I took the College Boards in June 1925, and in September 1925, I entered Wellesley, a shy, socially immature, seventeen-year-old adolescent.

At first, I disliked Wellesley intensely. Lacking my sister's social adaptability, I was very lonely. Besides, at this time, I thought that I would like to end up as a kindergarten teacher. But if, in fact, kindergarten teaching was to be my career choice, wasn't I in the wrong school? Wellesley's Education Department offered no courses in this field. Given the freedom to choose, I would have preferred to leave Wellesley well before the end of the first semester. But my sister wanted me to stay on, at least until the end of the school year.

As the year progressed, I began to feel less negative about Wellesley. The German courses I was taking were very stimulating. Having had four years of German in high school, Wellesley had allowed me to skip the 100-level introductory courses and move directly into several 200-level literature courses. Most of these were taught by the chairman of the department, Miss Natalie Wipplinger. Her scholarliness and almost other-worldliness began to fascinate me. In short, I remained at Wellesley and majored in German. In June of 1929, I graduated with General Honors.

In the pre-crash days of 1929, job offers of all sorts were plentiful. I received several in my major field. One, for example, was to teach German at Wheaton College, another to serve as a translator in an out-of-town publishing firm, and a third to work in the foreign language department of the Yale Library. I turned them all down. My sister had died the preceding December, and I was needed at home.

In my sophomore year at Wellesley, I had enrolled in the required semester course in introductory psychology. I admired the instructor, Miss Eleanor Acheson McCullough Gamble, a close friend of Miss Wipplinger. But the subject matter of the course did not interest me. Neither did the two or three more advanced courses I later took in the department. It was all so cut-and-dried, so unchallenging, so dull. Clearly, in those days psychology was not one of the strong departments in the college. Yet in May 1929, when Miss Wipplinger asked me if I would be interested in serving as

Miss Gamble's assistant, I accepted with alacrity. For one thing, it would enable me to live at home, close to my sister's delightful two-and-one-half-year-old son, and to assist in his care. Moreover, I would also be able to begin graduate work at Wellesley, if I wished to do so, tuition-free.

Miss Gamble was rapidly losing her eyesight and needed someone to be her girl Friday, to help her work up her lectures, to grade her exams, and to translate some of the studies in the German psychological literature which interested her at this time. For me, a tailor-made job paying the munificent annual salary of $500.

At the end of that first year, I was promoted from assistant to Miss Gamble to assistant in psychology, with no increase in salary but with more time for graduate work, an opportunity to try my hand at teaching discussion sections in the introductory course and to start some research on my own. All of these I enjoyed very much.

The next few years were very full and happy, and I was in no hurry to move on. I had married Abraham T. Alper in April of 1932, and I was quite content just to maintain the *status quo* as far as my job was concerned. In June of 1933, I was awarded the M.A. degree. But during that summer Miss Gamble died and with her death, as I later learned, I lost my main support in the department along with any chance of early promotion. I finally realized that if I was to stay in psychology, I would have to go on to the Ph.D. My husband was all for it, but I wanted to be sure that this was what *I* really wanted. His enthusiastic support throughout the difficult years that followed sustained me. I could not have managed without him.

But to back up a little. In the summer between my junior and senior years at Wellesley I had naively walked into the Judge Baker Guidance Center in Boston and offered my services to Drs. Healy and Bronner, the co-directors of the center, gratis. As it happened, they desperately needed someone to do some testing and they took me on, assuring me, and I suspect themselves, that I could learn how to administer and score a Binet in less than a week. I had as yet never even seen a Binet. My first testee was a fifteen-year-old girl who had been picked up by the police charged with prostitution. The court remanded her to the Judge Baker for intelligence testing. She terrified me. She was twice as tall and twice as broad as I. She was also very angry. But we both gradually relaxed and were somehow getting through the Binet. We had started with the vocabulary test. She did reasonably well until we came to the word "scorch." "It is what my father drinks," she said. She giggled, so did I. Thinking that my Bostonian pronunciation of the word might have misled her, I spelled it out for her. She stuck to her original definition. More giggling, but somehow we completed the test. This was my first exposure to clinical work and thanks to Miss Louise Woods, the staff psychologist, I learned a great deal in my six-week stint at the Judge Baker. But it would be almost another ten years before I would seek out further training in a clinical graduate program and another twenty years before I would join the Judge Baker staff on a part-time basis.

Four years after completing my M.A., I finally admitted to myself that I was in a dead-end situation in my work at Wellesley and that the time had come to accede to my husband's urgings to explore what the Boston area had to offer in clinically oriented graduate courses in psychology. It was clear that if I was to go on with graduate work, it would have to be in the Boston area for this was where my husband had recently started up his law practice. It was also clear that if we were to keep ourselves afloat financially in those depression days I should remain, at least temporarily, in my Wellesley job.

Around this time several members of the English department at Wellesley were asking for help for a growing number of freshmen, poor readers and "abominable" spellers. I decided to take up the challenge. The Harvard Graduate School of Education offered the courses I would need: remedial reading, test construction, and advanced statistics. Armed with the knowledge gained from these courses, and a new college-level spelling test, *The Wellesley Spelling Scale*, devised earlier in collaboration with a Wellesley colleague, Mrs. Edith Mallory, I opened shop, so to speak. In recognition of my added responsibilities I was given a small salary increase and a new title, assistant in psychology and director of remedial reading. My first publication, "If Only I Could Read Faster," was based on the remedial program I was still in the process of developing. The article appeared in *The Wellesley Magazine* in the late thirties. Soon thereafter the California Test Bureau offered to publish and market the spelling scale. For several years, before the copyrights ran out, the royalties were substantial.

Though the work at Wellesley was now going well, I decided to move on into a more demanding program than what I had found in the School of Education. In short, if the department of psychology in Harvard's College of Liberal Arts would have me, I felt ready to start on a Ph.D. program. It was not without trepidation, however, that I asked for an appointment with the chairman of the psychology department, Dr. Edwin G. Boring. Set up for thirty minutes, the interview lasted almost three hours. Dr. Boring was polite but not very encouraging. He told me that the department did not really welcome female graduate students, that they had accepted very few over the years and that only a handful had survived. But at the end he agreed that if I was ready to "throw myself to the lions," the department would accept me on my terms as a part-time student, beginning in the fall of 1939.

Dr. Boring was right. Women *were* given a hard time at Harvard. Three of us started out in the proseminar, along with about ten men. Most of the men made it at least through the first year. One of the women dropped out before the first hour exam, a second, after the exam. I somehow survived, passed the Qualifying Preliminary Examinations in 1941 and in 1943 became the *eleventh* woman to be granted a Ph.D. in psychology from that institution.

In 1942, I resigned my position at Wellesley and took up my first appointment at Radcliffe. This carried the title of "Tutor in Psychology." In 1943, with the degree in hand, I was promoted to instructor of psychology at Harvard and until 1946 I remained the only woman in the department. My appointment, I'm sure, was not tokenism. It was rather that during these war years fewer men than women were available for non-war-related posts. How did I fare?

The following incidents highlight the lowly status of women at Harvard at this time. In those days, before Harvard and Radcliffe "merged," classes for the two groups were held in different buildings. Students were also segregated by sex for their final examinations. This was the plan: At Harvard, the instructor was responsible for handing over the printed examination questions to the male graduate student who was assigned to proctor the examination. After so doing, the instructor's next task was to go over to Radcliffe to tend to the females who had been enrolled in that same course. Here a female proctor would already have started the examination. Having been carefully informed of this procedure by Dr. Boring the first time I was scheduled to give a Final, I dutifully appeared in Emerson D prepared to hand my experimental psychology questions over to the male proctor. But he would not permit me to enter the room. He kept saying "You must go to Radcliffe." And I kept saying, "I know. I'll go there next." Finally, sensing that the real problem must be my sex, I gave up and telephoned my course assistant, Leo Postman, to come down from the third floor of Emerson Hall and take over. He was admitted. No matter that the students were deprived of ten minutes of working time—the segregation of the sexes had been preserved.

When second semester rolled around, I was determined not to be shut out. My final examination in child psychology was scheduled for the auditorium in the Fogg Art Museum. I arrived there, questions in hand, a good fifteen minutes before the proctor was likely to appear, and sat down in a front row seat. When the proctor came in he approached me menacingly.

But I was ready for him. Pointing to the printed examination papers on my lap, I said, "Giving, not taking." He seemed puzzled, but he let me stay.

The reaction of the faculty as a whole to having a female teaching courses at Harvard comes through in this next incident. President Jordon caught up with me one day as I was crossing Harvard Square. "Dr. Alper," he said, "I've been wanting to apologize to you for some time. When it was announced to the faculty that a woman would be teaching child psychology in the following year, there was quite an uproar. Several professors predicted that while the Radcliffe enrollment might not change, the Harvard enrollment in this course would certainly show a sharp drop. But as you know, it did not." The male undergraduates, it seems, were more seemingly prepared than the male professors to accept women on what had for centuries been an all male faculty!

The anomaly of a female member of the faculty at Harvard in the early forties comes through again in the next two incidents. First, how does one address the invitation to the president's annual reception to new faculty members when the new faculty member is a married woman? The decision reached by one of the secretaries in the president's office resulted in "Mr. and Dr. Thelma G. Alper."

The second incident involves the Harvard Dames, a group of faculty wives who met regularly for tea and sociability. In my second (or was it my third year at Harvard?) someone discovered me. The formal invitation to join the group urged me to come and bring my mending. I did not accept but was tempted to write back asking if, in addition to my mending (of which there were many piles), I might also bring my bluebooks. It was not difficult to resist this temptation.

Finally in 1946, another woman, Dr. Eugenia Hanfmann, accepted an appointment in the newly created social relations department. Now there were two of us and we could be, and were, mutually supportive. But Harvard was not prepared to offer tenure to women and eventually Genia and I both left Harvard for other posts.

In the thirties, forties, and fifties, discrimination against women on college faculties was not limited to Harvard. Both Tufts and Boston University offered me appointments while I was still teaching at Harvard. But both made it clear that since I was a woman, the appointment could not carry tenure. I turned them both down. Basically, the discrimination against women in academia must have troubled me more than I let myself know. But my feelings finally did come out, clear and loud. On the day I wrote Dean Buck that I was resigning my Harvard appointment, I left the Faculty Club, not through the ladies entrance, but through the main door, a GANZ

VERBOTEN bit of behavior. In 1948, when Clark University asked me to join their psychology department, I accepted. But it turned out that now I was the only woman on the entire faculty. Nevertheless, I quickly felt accepted at Clark by both the administration and the teaching staff. However, Worcester was too far away from Boston, my home base. By 1951, my husband was very ill and I needed to get closer to Boston. The offer in 1952 from Wellesley of an associate professorship, the guarantee of tenure, and full professorship by 1954, as well as a promise that the college-operated Nursery School would not be discontinued as long as it was a useful adjunct to my work in child psychology, all won me over.

The Wellesley years, from 1952 until my retirement in 1973, were interesting and productive. But before turning to my last stint in academia, I must acknowledge my debt to Dr. Boring. In my first year as an instructor at Harvard I had the rare opportunity to work closely with him. Our warm and enduring friendship dated from this period. So does my long-distance admiration of Alice Bryan. Dr. Boring often spoke of her work, in effect holding her up to me as a model worthy of emulation.

Serving as a section person for one semester in Dr. Boring's psychology was, in itself, a liberal education. Next came our joint work on two books, *Psychology for the Fighting Man* and *Psychology for the Returning Veteran*. As his co-editor, my major task was to rewrite the separate chapters submitted by various experts for each book in order to achieve at least a semblance of uniformity of style. Dr. Boring's own style was delightfully smooth and clear but he often had trouble with mine. Certain of my recurring grammatical errors were particularly puzzling to him. In the end, the instruction in English grammar I had missed in grade school, by skipping the sixth and eighth grades, was given a much-needed assist under his patient tutelage.

One of the many valuable things I learned from Dr. Boring is that smooth writing does not necessarily come easily, even to a Boring. His advice was that one must write, rewrite, revise and revise. He assured me that it was not unusual in his own case to rework the draft of a manuscript five or six times, more if time permitted. As I look back, I'm not quite sure how either I or my husband survived the eighty-hour work week pace Dr. Boring took for granted for himself and his assistant. But survive we did. Working with, and for him, was often exhausting to be sure, but it was never dull.

In 1959 I was due for a sabbatical semester and I spent this at the Judge Baker Guidance Center. Miss Clapp, president of Wellesley at this time, agreed to my continuing on at the center upon my return to the college. In addition to my regular teaching I now devoted one day a week to my ongoing clinical research while furthering my training in therapy. At the center I worked primarily with Dr. Bessie Sperry. For a number of years we cooperated on several projects, including a five year stint serving as consultants to a Head Start set-up in Charleston, Massachusetts. Finally, in June of 1979 I retired from my part-time post at the Judge Baker, six years after my retirement from Wellesley and fifty-one years after my encounter with my first testee. Since retirement I have maintained a small private practice working mainly with adult patients.

Looking over the titles of my published research, I now recognize some common themes. First and foremost, I was attracted by controversy. A few relevant studies are cited below.

A statement by Professor Kurt Lewin in a Harvard class one day stimulated my interest in memory for completed vs. incompleted tasks: Rosenzweig's finding that completed tasks were *better* remembered than uncompleted, said Dr. Lewin, must be incorrect, since it was contrary both to Bluma Zeigarnik's experimental results and to the demands of Lewin's own tension theory. How account for the contradiction? Two years later I came up with an answer that completed my work for the Ph.D. (Alper 1943). But were they really contradictory? It finally became clear to me that Zeigarnik and Rosenzweig were studying dynamically different phenomena. Zeigarnik was dealing with what I labeled the recall of non-self-esteem threatening material, Rosenzweig with what he termed "repression." Differences in tasks (Alper and Black 1949), in experimental instructions, and even in age of subjects could account for the seemingly contrary findings. Differences in toleration for incompletion, as a function of ego strength, moreover, had to be considered (Alper 1957, 1952). It also turned out that the distinctions between task-orientation and ego-orientation, as manipulated by the experimenter's instructions, and between task involvement and ego involvement could also be shown to be critical. The latter terms, concerned with the subject's individual reaction to the experimental conditions, moreover, turned out to be crucial personality-related determinants of what was actually recalled. The self-rating Psychological Insight Test (Alper 1948a and b), validated by a clinical interview, were byproducts of this initial study. Later, applying some of these same concepts to a different area of controversy, reminiscence, helped to bring lawfulness into what Buxton had once termed a "now-you-see-it, now-you-don't phenomenon" (Buxton 1948).

Moving on to the controversy in the area of achievement motivation in women, it has been possible to account for at least some of the difficulties researchers have had in replicating Matina Horner's early results (Alper 1977; Tresemer 1973). One of the more useful by-products of this research has been the development of a role-orientation measure, the Wellesley Role-

Orientation Scale, or WROS for short (Alper 1974). Women who score high on this scale are likely to favor for themselves the nonachievement-oriented role our culture typically assigns to women. These are the traditionalists among us. Success in an area the culture regards as appropriate only for men, medicine, for example, arouses in these women the fear that others will not like them. Thus, Horner's finding that women more often than men are afraid of success fits very well the traditionally role-oriented woman. It does not equally well fit the non-traditionalists. Women who score low on the WROS are likely either to feel unconflicted about functioning in traditionally male roles, or else are extremely angry that the culture frowns on women who strive to achieve in such areas. Fear of success is unlikely to appear in either pattern of lows. Finally, there are also two patterns within the highs—the Unambivalent High, for example, who happily confines her achievement strivings to culturally female-appropriate areas, wife, mother, nurse, secretary, etc. The Ambivalent High also elects to stay within these areas but is likely to *resent* having to do so. In stories told, for example, to "The Kitchen Scene," a picture showing a young woman in a kitchen setting, doing a portrait of a small child, the Unambivalent High typically tells us that the lady is the child's mother, an amateur painter who paints as a hobby. The finished portrait will be hung in a place of honor either by a loving father or by doting grandparents. The Ambivalent High also assigns the amateur artist role to the mother figure, but now either the cake in the oven burns or some other household disaster occurs. She cannot do two things at once, tend house and be a successful artist. The Unambivalent Low, on the other hand, can permit the woman to be successful at her task, sometimes both as mother and artist, sometimes as a professional who is called in to do the portrait. And finally, the Ambivalent Low tells us that no one appreciates her efforts regardless of whether she is an amateur or a professional. Since any random sample of college women could very well include all four role-orientation patterns, it should not surprise us to find that fear of success is not necessarily characteristic of most females, regardless of whether the area of success in the stimulus is ambiguous, as in "The Kitchen Scene," or is clearly culturally more male- than female-appropriate, as in Horner's original stimulus, "After first term finals Anne finds herself at the top of her medical school class."

Recently, mostly out of sheer curiosity, I sought information about the current make-up of the staff of the Harvard Department of Psychology and Social Relations. This is what I learned: There are now 32 members in this combined department, 28 men and 4 women; 15 of the men are tenured, but none of the women is tenured. According to Harvard's 1979–80 catalogue, 15 of the men hold the rank of full professor, 4 are associate professors, 6 are assistant professors and 3 are listed as senior lecturers. Of the 4 women, 2 hold the rank of associate professor and the other 2 are listed as assistant professors. In 1979 there were no female full professors. In brief, women in the College of Liberal Arts at Harvard have clearly not yet obtained academic equality with their male peers, at least not in the combined department of psychology and social relations. Since then, one woman has been granted a full professorship in this department.

How are women psychologists at other nearby coeducational institutions now faring? Dr. Judy Rosenblith gave me the figures for the Massachusetts Institute of Technology (MIT). Currently there are 16 full-time members of the teaching staff in MIT's psychology department, 13 men and 3 women. All of the women are tenured, as are also all but two of the men. At Clark University, according to Dr. Seymour Wapner, there are 17 full-time staff in psychology, 13 men and 4 women. All of the women and all but one of the men are tenured. If these figures are truly representative, then clearly the situation for women in academic psychology has greatly improved over the past four decades. Yes, Virginia, women psychologists in academia *have* come a long way, and one day they may even lose their minority status, numerically speaking, in relation to their male peers.

REFERENCES

Alper, T. G. *See* Representative Publications by.

Buxton, C. E. 1948. Status of research in reminiscence. *Psychological Bulletin*, 40:313–340.

Tresemer, D. 1973. Fear of success: Popular but unproven. In C. Tavris, ed., *The Female Experience*. Del Mar, Calf.: CRM.

Representative Publications by Thema G. Alper

1943. Memory for completed and incomplete tasks. Dissertation, Radcliffe College.

1948a. Memory for completed and incomplete tasks as function of personality: Correlation between experimental and personality data. *Journal of Personality*, 17:104–137.

1948b. Task-orientation vs. ego-orientation in learning and retention. *Journal of Experimental Psychology*, 38:224–238.

1949. With A. Black. The effect of instruction, task and population sample on mental set. *American Journal of Psychology*, 62:295–299.

1952. The interrupted task method in studies of selective recall. *Psychological Review*, 59:71–87.

1957. Predicting the direction of selective recall: Its relation to ego-strength and n achievement. *Journal of Abnormal and Social Psychology*, 55:149–165.

1974. Achievement motivation in college women: A now-you-see-it, now-you-don't phenomenon. *American Psychologist*, 29:194–203.

1977. Where are we now? Discussion of papers presented in the 1975 AERA symposium on sex differences in achievement motivation and achievement behavior. *Psychology of Women Quarterly*, 1:294–303.

MARY D. SALTER AINSWORTH

If this were a clinical history rather than a brief sketch of a career, it would begin with my family, and continue to discuss in detail my relationships with my parents and two younger sisters as they changed in the course of my development. Except for stating that we were a close-knit family with a not unusual mixture of warmth and tensions and deficiencies, I shall confine myself to a few bare facts.

My parents were Pennsylvanians, both graduates of Dickinson College, where my father earned a Master's degree in history before he went to work for a large manufacturing firm in its Cincinnati office. My mother groped for a vocation after her graduation, tried teaching, began nursing training, then was called home because of her mother's illness. Five years after her graduation she married my father, and henceforward had no thought of a career other than homemaking. I was born late in 1913, and my sisters two and seven years later, respectively. In 1918 the family moved to Toronto, my father having been transferred to a Canadian branch of his company. Later the foreign branches split from the parent company, and in due course he became president of his branch. Realizing that he was committed to a career in Canada, he became a naturalized citizen, as did I as a minor.

From the beginning it was assumed that we girls would go to college, for both of our parents placed high value on a good liberal arts education. My parents' expectations of outstanding academic achievement were reinforced by my eagerness to learn to read when I was three years old. It was my mother who located appropriate materials and got me off to a good start. With this early beginning, both grade school and high school were easy. I thoroughly enjoyed learning, which posed no problems until high school when I pretended to be indifferent to learning in order to ingratiate myself with peers.

A regular event in our family life was the weekly trip to the library. We returned home with the maximum number of books that our five cards would allow. When I was fifteen and in my final year in high school, one of the books brought home was William McDougall's *Character and the*

Conduct of Life (1927), which I read with great excitement. It had not previously occurred to me that one might look within oneself for some explanation of how one felt and behaved, rather than feeling entirely at the mercy of external forces. What a vista that opened up! I decided thereupon to become a psychologist.

This decision was half forgotten when I first enrolled at the University of Toronto in the fall of 1929. Because I was underage I had to enroll in the first year of the "Pass Course," and could not take psychology until my second year, but after an introductory course then my enthusiasm was renewed, and I transferred to the honor psychology course for my final three years. The honor course had a very intensive, comprehensive, structured curriculum, which I was privileged to explore with only four classmates.

I gobbled everything up with great enjoyment and shared in the messianic spirit that permeated the department—a belief that the science of psychology was the touchstone for great improvements in the quality of life. Although now this belief seems naive, we all firmly held it then, even in the midst of the Great Depression—and it has never entirely deserted me. Nothing that I studied seemed irrelevant, and no one who taught me failed to engage my interest in his or her field of expertise.

Before I graduated in 1935, I had already decided that I wanted to continue in graduate work in psychology, and it did not occur to me to apply elsewhere than Toronto. My parents went along with my wishes, although my father had previously thought that it would be nice for me to be a stenographer for a while before marrying. Although my undergraduate record had been excellent, I did not assume that I would be accepted, and was delighted when I was not only accepted but also offered a stipend of $200 for the year as a teaching assistant to the head of the department, Professor Edward A. Bott, in his introductory course for medical students. If the stipend was low, so were other costs in the thirties. Moreover, I lived at home and my parents refused to let me pay board, which I could have done because from my second year of graduate work on I had quite adequate financial support through scholarships, teaching evening courses, and higher teaching assistant stipends.

I cannot recall how many graduate students there were in the department of psychology. My retrospective impression is that the sexes were evenly balanced, although more of the women than men were headed toward a terminal master's degree. Let me mention a few with whom I overlapped: Mary Northway, who studied for her doctorate at Cambridge with Bartlett, and returned to a position in the university's Institute of Child Study; Donald Snygg who was enthusiastic about phenomenology and subsequently became well-known in American psychology; Louis McQuitty, who went to Illinois after his Ph.D, and subsequently Michigan State, then Miami; Carl Williams, who after faculty appointments at the Universities of Manitoba and Toronto, became president of the University of Western Ontario; Gordon Turner, who had been a classmate in the undergraduate honor course, later went to the University of Western Ontario where he was chairman of psychology for some time; Mary Wright, who also wound up at the University of Western Ontario and also served as chairman there; Herbert Pottle, who eventually became Minister of Education for Newfoundland; and Nora Weckler, who is a member of the faculty of California State University at Northridge.

To me it seemed to be a tightly integrated group of graduate students. We had tea together in the late afternoon in the graduate lounge, and planned numerous social events, including an annual picnic with faculty that featured a softball game, and an annual Christmas party with skits and songs prepared for the occasion. I remember our morale as being high.

During the seven years of undergraduate and graduate studies in the department of psychology, three professors emerged as major influences: Sperrin N. F. Chant, William E. Blatz, and Edward A. Bott. Chant spent a year with our fourth-year undergraduate class in an experimental project involving the galvanic skin response. I owe to him chiefly the discovery that research can be fun. When I decided to enter graduate work, he immediately offered to supervise my master's research, and we proceeded to investigate the relationship between attitudes and emotional response, using the GSR as the measure of emotion (with Chant 1937). Whatever skills I now have in supervising the theses and dissertations of graduate students owe much to the supervision he offered.

Blatz's influence also began while I was an undergraduate. I was impressed by his courses in genetic (developmental) and abnormal psychology, in which he talked of his own theory of development—security theory. This was a programatic theory that owed much to Freud—although Blatz was careful not to acknowledge this because of the very strong anti-psychoanalytic bias in Toronto at that time. It was a theory of personality development, and that was what I had been waiting for! I was honored when, having completed my master's thesis, Blatz proposed that I undertake my dissertation research within the framework of his security theory.

In briefest summary, his position was that in infancy and early childhood the individual needed to develop a secure dependence on parents in order to gain the courage necessary to brave the insecurity implicit in exploring the unfamiliar world and learning to cope with it. A child needs to feel confidence in the secure base provided by parents to learn the skills and to develop the knowledge that will gradually enable him or her to depend confidently on self and eventually to gain a secure emancipation from parents. However, since it is impossible in this social world to be totally independent of others, the immature dependent security of the relationship with parents should be gradually supplanted by a mature secure dependence on peers from the individual's own age group and eventually on a heterosexual partner, implying a relationship in which each partner finds security in the skills, knowledge, and emotional support contributed by the other. Of course, some persons are characterized by more insecurity than security from all three sources combined, and some rely on defensive maneuvers (which Blatz termed "deputy agents") to hold their insecure feelings at bay.

Blatz's proposition was to develop instruments to assess the balance between security (from all three sources) and insecurity/defensive maneuvers in all major aspects of a person's life. My dissertation research was to be devoted to the construction of two self-report pencil-paper scales to assess young adults regarding their relations with parents and with age peers (1940). There was at that time no approved quantitative technique for selection and weighing of items on such scales, but with Chant I settled on a roughly satisfactory method. Validation of the scales also presented a problem. This was handled by using the same college student subjects who had written autobiographies for a course of Professor J. Davidson Ketchum's. I found no way of quantifying the autobiographical material, but it "blew my mind" to find out how similar this material was for persons yielding the same pattern of scores on the two scales. I emphasize *patterns*. I have been searching for—and finding—patterns in my research ever since.

The third person who exerted a profound influence on my career development was Professor Bott, the head of the department. I continued for four years as his teaching assistant, not just in his introductory course, but soon in two experimental/statistical courses that he taught. As a graduate student, I attended his seminar in systematic psychology, which he conducted in a Socratic manner. Like many other Toronto Ph.D. students, I failed to appreciate at the time the significance of Bott's thinking, for his manner was dry. But in later years I came to realize what an important influence he had been in the way I viewed the scientific approach. I believe that science is a "state of mind"—not that he ever said just that. Science is implicit in the way one thinks about problems and approaches data, rather than being irretrievably vested in the hypothetico-deductive method, experiment, or specific quantitative techniques.

Since I later became a clinical psychologist I should mention that I did indeed think of becoming one during my first year as a graduate student. Through the help of one of the faculty, C. Roger Myers, I was appointed as a psychological intern at the Ontario Hospital in Orillia in the summer of 1936. Discouraged by the seeming impossibility of helping effectively the mental patients served by this hospital, I abandoned thoughts of a clinical career in favor of research relevant to personality development.

In the spring of 1939, Professor Bott did what he could to find jobs for all of the new Ph.D.'s, arranging job interviews with potential employers. I did not want to leave Toronto. I was in the full flush of excitement about my Ph.D. research based on Blatz's theory of security. Blatz himself wanted me to stay to become co-director of an expanded program of security research. In blissful ignorance of the academic facts of life, including such matters as vacancies, and tenure-line slots, I told Professor Bott that I wanted a faculty appointment in his department and did not want to go elsewhere.

Nevertheless he arranged an interview for me with Professor George Humphrey, then head of the psychology department at Queens University in Kingston, Ontario, who was searching for a young experimental psychologist to establish a new laboratory. Because I did not want the position I downplayed my skills and abilities and was honest in my admissions of weakness. Perhaps because of this openness, Humphrey decided that I was precisely the person he wanted for the job. Two weeks later he visited again to tell me sorrowfully that the Senate of Queens University refused to appoint a woman. This is the only instance of discrimination in regard to employment that I encountered in my career. As for Humphrey and Queens, everything turned out well, for they hired Donald Hebb. Even then I believed that they made the better bargain. As for me, my naive faith was rewarded by an appointment as lecturer at the University of Toronto, beginning in the fall of 1939.

Great Britain (and Canada) declared war on Germany in September 1939, and everyone's career plans were changed. Professor Bott immediately threw himself into plans for maximum contribution by Canadian psychologists to the war effort, and turned over all of his undergraduate classes to me with scarcely two weeks' warning. Within a year Professors Bott and Myers had left to become advisors to the RAF in regard to pilot selection, Line to head personnel selection in the Canadian Army, Chant to do likewise in the RCAF, and Blatz to set up model wartime day nurseries in Great Britain. Male graduate students and recent Ph.D.s joined the armed services in personnel selection, and several members of the staff of the Institute of Child Study joined Blatz in England. Several recent female Ph.D.s, including Magda Arnold (who subsequently became well-known for her work in the field of emotion), were appointed to help carry on the work of the department. I remained for three years, and then no longer content to be away from where the action was—and belatedly wanting to get away from home—joined the Canadian Women's Army Corps in July 1942.

I spent that summer in basic and officer's training and then was tapped by Bill Line—then Colonel William Line, Director of Personnel Selection—to become an Army Examiner, as the personnel selection officers were called. In this capacity I was posted to the Canadian Women's Army Corps Training Center at Kitchener, Ontario. The work had a distinctly clinical flavor, including administering tests, interviewing, history-taking, and counseling, as well as recommending placement. I was impressed with how much could be learned from such an approach and entertained the idea of becoming a clinical psychologist at war's end in order to pursue more effectively my interest in personality development. A few months later, however, I was posted to headquarters in Ottawa, as the CWAC advisor to the director of Personnel Selection. There I encountered the reverse of sex discrimination, despite the fact that CWAC pay was four-fifths of men's pay. After arriving at Headquarters as a second lieutenant, I was promoted to major within a year.

The directorate of Personnel Selection was under the director general of Medical Services—a psychiatrist, General Brock Chisholm, who subsequently became director of the World Health Organization. He and Line shared the idealistic perspective that personnel selection should be a thoroughgoing clinical service to army personnel with the Army Examiners working closely with company officers on the one hand and with the various professionals of the Medical Corps on the other—physicians, psychiatrists, and social workers. So acute was the manpower shortage, however, that the need for infantrymen frustrated the male Army Examiners in their efforts to place men in the work to which they were best suited. But Line's goal was feasible for the women in the service, and it was my job to work with CWAC Army Examiners all over Canada to see that the goal was approximated. My work was entirely administrative, entailing much traveling back and forth across Canada. In the winter of 1943–44 I was assigned to a four-month tour in England, where I especially enjoyed visiting the Personnel Selection service of the British Army. My opposite number there, Senior Commander Edith Mercer, not only made me welcome at that time, but also later played an important role in my career.

After V-E Day, I was invited to retire from the Army to become the superintendent of Women's Rehabilitation in the Department of Veterans' Affairs. The director general of Rehabilitation Services was my previous mentor, Sperrin Chant, although he was about to leave to become head of psychology at the University of British Columbia. Doubtless he thought that I was set up for a continuing administrative career in government service. The work was significant and demanding, but much like what I had done in the Army. Within a year I felt that I had done all that I could to set up the women's rehabilitation program and was tired of administrative work. When Professor Bott, back at the University of Toronto, invited me to return as an assistant professor, I accepted with pleasure and anticipation. Nonetheless I valued highly my four years in army and government service. I came to value a clinical perspective. I learned a great deal about administration. I learned to value and to work within a multidisciplinary perspective.

Upon returning to Toronto, I taught introductory psychology to medical students and experimental psychology as before—a twelve-hour teaching load, made light because of it being my first year. The problem was what to teach, especially to graduate students, the following year. The courses I especially wanted to teach were being dealt with very competently by Magda Arnold, whom I admired. Knowing that it was uncertain whether her war-time appointment was to continue, I wanted to propose nothing to Professor Bott that might encroach on her territory. I asked her how we might share teaching in the personality area. Since she was teaching the theoretical courses, she suggested that I teach personality assessment. I protested that I knew nothing about this specialty, but she replied "You can learn, can't you!" Therefore, at her suggestion, I attended a summer workshop in the Rorschach technique directed by Bruno Klopfer, and contacted William Henry of the University of Chicago for references to his work on the Thematic Apperception Test. I read all that I could lay my hands on relevant to both projective and paper-pencil tests, practiced administering these various appraisal techniques to volunteers. I offered my volunteer services to a Department of Veterans' Affairs hospital, where at least I received neuropsychiatric supervision from the clinical director. And that is how I began as a clinical psychologist.

Next autumn, 1947, I offered a graduate course in personality appraisal, and it captured the interest of my students as well as engrossing me. The following summer I attended another Klopfer workshop, this time at the advanced level. I prepared a mimeographed booklet for the use of my students—to fill in the gaps that I observed in *The Rorschach Technique* by Klopfer and Kelly (1942), which was distributed by the university bookstore.

Magda Arnold departed for an appointment at Loyola University in Chicago, and I fell heir to the courses of hers that I had coveted—emotion and motivation and theories of personality. And throughout the years 1946–50 I was co-director, with Bill Blatz, of a research team focused on developing scales to assess security in various aspects of life—a clear sequel to my dissertation research.

I became engaged to marry one of that team—a veteran student, Leonard Ainsworth, who was just completing his master's degree. The prospect of his continuing for a Ph.D. in the same department in which I had a faculty appointment seemed uncomfortable, so when he was accepted by University College, London, as a doctoral student it was there that we went after our marriage in the summer of 1950. Len had DVA educational benefits and expected to be able to pick up the same kind of teaching and research assistantships there had been available to him in Toronto, although that proved not to be the case. My efforts to line up a position for myself in advance proved to be unavailing. But I thought that I might write a book. Since my mimeographed manual on the Rorschach technique had unexpectedly sold hundreds of copies, a book-length version of it seemed worth considering. I wrote to Bruno Klopfer seeking his approval, since it was his version of the technique that I proposed to write about. He replied with an invitation to be a co-author in a book he was planning. So we set off for London in September 1950, with high hopes but inadequate financial resources. As it turned out, I did collaborate with Bruno and Walter Klopfer and Robert Holt in *Developments in the Rorschach Technique*, volume 1, conducting all our exchanges by correspondence. The book was not finally published until 1954, so it did not help at all with our immediate financial needs, but royalties have been steady ever since.

Upon arrival in London, I immediately cast about for a job. I also looked up relatives and friends, including Edith Mercer from my army days. One day she drew my attention to an advertisement in the London *Times* Educational Supplement for a job that seemed precisely suited to my qualifications. It was for a research position at the Tavistock Clinic in an investigation, directed by Dr. John Bowlby, into the effect on personality development of separation from the mother in early childhood. I applied, was interviewed, was enthusiastic about the project, and was hired. So Edith Mercer and a newspaper advertisement reset the whole direction of my research career.

Psychologists do not ordinarily expect crucial research to stem from a psychoanalytic setting, so it may seem paradoxical that it was at the Tavistock Clinic that I finally realized what kind of research strategy would best serve me in exploring the problems of personality development in which I had been interested from the beginning. First, the clinical perspective tends to emphasize patterns of personality or behavior (syndromes) as they relate to patterns of antecedents, rather than searching for a one-to-one cause-effect relationship between a single antecedent and a single outcome variable. Second, James Robertson, one of my new colleagues, had been observing at first hand the responses of young children to separation from and reunion with their families in the course of visits to the home before and after the separation and to the separation environment to observe the child's responses. Although he himself was very modest about his data—transcriptions of his observational notes—I was deeply impressed with their value. I was entranced with the prospect of a future study of my own in which I would employ simple, direct, naturalistic observation, and use simple descriptive statistics to deal with its findings.

Third, both the problems in which John Bowlby was interested and his nondoctrinaire approach to theory were very congenial to me. To be sure, Blatz had been theory-oriented, but the experience with Bowlby was my first with a theory in the making. John became increasingly interested in the implications of evolutionary theory and the ethological approach in accounting for the findings of separation research—findings that could not be accounted for adequately by either psychoanalytic theory or psychological learning theory. Although I was intrigued with Lorenz's imprinting studies, I myself was so brainwashed by psychological theories of the day that I felt uneasy. To me at that time it seemed self-evident that a baby becomes attached to his mother because she fulfills his basic needs or drives. Indeed, after I left London, John and I had an exchange of correspondence in which I urged him to reconsider his new theoretical position. He may have reconsidered, but fortunately he was not deterred by my reaction.

My husband, who was completing his Ph.D. in the autumn of 1953, had been talking about how much he would like to go to Africa. Again it was our friend Edith Mercer who drew his attention to an advertisement in the London *Times* for a research psychologist in the East African Institute of Social Research in Kampala, Uganda. I was not enthusiastic about this prospect, fearing that it would be even more difficult to break into the academic stream in Canada or the United States after such a venture than before it. Nevertheless, Len's application and interview resulted in an appointment. We had scarcely arrived home in Canada when the news of the appointment reached us, and on New Year's Day, 1954, we sailed from Halifax, bound for London, and then Mombasa and Kampala.

Although I had it in mind to undertake a short-term longitudinal and naturalistic study of mother-infant interaction at the first opportunity—and now the opportunity was in Uganda—I was unsuccessful in obtaining funding from such a distance and at such short notice. I was happy that Dr. Audrey Richards, director of the institute, scraped together enough salary for me and for an interpreter to make such a study feasible. The study of Ganda mother-infant dyads turned out to be every bit as rewarding as I had hoped a short-term longitudinal, naturalistic study could be. I welcomed Dr. Richards' directive that there be an anthropological component to the study, for this ensured that I would view current mother-infant interaction and maternal care practices in their cultural context, and I valued the opportunities presented by the institute again to interact with a multidisciplinary team.

It is a pity that one cannot require field work in another society of every aspiring investigator of child development. Despite all the language and other difficulties, I am convinced that it is easier to be objective when viewing another society, and then, as I discovered later, it is easier to take a fresh, unbiased view when later undertaking research in one's own society. Despite many cultural differences, it was a profoundly moving experience for me to perceive the basic common core of parental concern for their children's welfare. Furthermore, I had not spent many weeks in observation before I was convinced that the previous "self-evident view" of the basis of an infant's attachment to its parents squared not at all with what my eyes saw, and that Bowlby's new ethological approach did indeed provide a much more useful framework. I am sorry that I did not immediately inform him of my volte-face.

For complex reasons, the analysis and publication of the Ganda data was substantially delayed (1963, 1967), but perhaps a few reflections are pertinent here. The hypothetico-deductive method that has guided so much psychological research is inapplicable to the kind of exploratory, naturalistic study that I undertook in Uganda. To be sure, one needs to have some notion of what one is looking for, and hence some selectivity of observations—and indeed I did have some such notions. But I left myself open to observe and descriptively record as much as possible beyond these initial notions, rather than boxing myself in with check lists conceived *a priori*. I learned so much *new* that was not covered by my initial notions (hypotheses) that ever since I have tried to avoid deciding in advance what the relevant variables must be and how I am going to analyze my data. I let the raw observational data suggest to me what the relevant variables are. In exploratory studies post hoc variables may well be the most valuable. Whereas I acknowledge that later replicatory studies of a more rigid kind are needed, for hypothesis-*discovering* studies, too rigid an adherence to the hypothetico-deductive approach is clearly counterproductive.

At the end of our two-year tour in Uganda, it was not easy to find jobs in Canada or the United States from our Kampala base. Acting on the assumption that it would be more difficult for Len, with his relatively new Ph.D., to get placed than for me to do so, we put the emphasis on the position for him. With the initial aid of the APA Employment Bulletin, he found a position as a forensic psychologist in Baltimore. It was not until late 1955 that our visa arrangements were completed and we were settled. I then began my explorations for a job by visiting the chairman of the department of psychology at Johns Hopkins University, Wendell Garner. Extrapolating from Professor Bott's intimate knowledge of opportunities in Ontario, I expected Garner to be knowledgeable about opportunities in the Baltimore area. He did offer me an evening course (which I snapped up), and made several suggestions about possibilities for full-time jobs in the area. I began to follow up his suggestions, but within two weeks Dean Wilson Shaffer of Johns Hopkins called me in to offer me a position. It emerged that he and Garner had been hoping to find someone to offer some clinical-type instruction in an otherwise highly experimental department, and to provide supervised clinical experience to a few students who wished it. There was no ready-made slot for such a person, but they patched up a position for me, supported in part by the department, in part by the evening college, and in part by Sheppard and Enoch Pratt Hospital, where I was to work two days a week providing psychological service with the aid of one graduate student assistant. I jumped at the opportunity to join the Hopkins faculty, even though I was disappointed to be appointed as a mere lecturer.

Paradoxically, it was this academic appointment that gave me my first extended opportunity to gain clinical experience. The work at Sheppard-Pratt was essentially diagnostic evaluation, and I had no difficulty with this. I have never been able to understand why American clinical psychologists have so chafed at the diagnostic role, feeling that this limited them to being mere psychometricians, subordinate to all medical personnel. On the contrary, I found that diagnostic skills gave me very substantial status and respect. In addition to a quite heavy hospital load, I gradually set up a part-time private practice, on referral from psychiatrists, psychoanalysts, social agencies, and schools in the Baltimore area, being mostly concerned with children. In the beginning, my research experience at the Tavistock Clinic was especially useful. At that time there was almost no literature pertaining to diagnostic evaluation of children. It was necessary to extrapolate principles from adult evaluation to work with children, and of course research experience with disturbed children was very helpful.

Our marriage came to an end in the summer of 1960. Although I do not wish to write about this personal disaster, I can say that I do not believe career conflicts to have been a factor. A depressive reaction to divorce led me to seek professional help, which culminated in an eight-year psychoanalytic experience. Sometimes I believe that this was the most important positive influence on my career, despite the fact that I had already been very fortunate in both mentors and turns of fortune. Certainly analysis helped me to become very much more at peace with myself and very much more productive.

I felt a great urge to immerse myself in the psychoanalytic literature, especially Freud. I emerged with a profound respect for psychoanalytic therapy, and with a firsthand understanding of the psychoanalytic process—unconscious processes, repression, transference, resistance, and the like—experience that has made me a better psychologist, even though there remains much in classical psychoanalytic theory that I believe to be obsolete, especially instinct theory and metapsychology. All of this both enriched my teaching of courses focusing on personality and various approaches to assessment and my understanding of research data.

The Sheppard-Pratt responsibility left very little opportunity for research. All that I could do was to work on the data analysis and publication of research from previous years and settings. I proposed to Garner, my chairman and good friend, that I withdraw from the hospital commitment, shift my teaching to developmental psychology, and begin the naturalistic, longitudinal research into mother-infant interaction that I had been longing to do ever since leaving Uganda. He readily agreed, and indeed both then and since could not have been more encouragingly supportive of what I wanted to accomplish. So in 1961 the shift was implemented.

Let me interrupt this narrative to mention the degree to which I experienced discrimination. It must be clear that I had experienced none in regard to appointments since 1939, and that for a position that I did not want. It was otherwise in regard to salary at Johns Hopkins. My low initial salary was understandable because the appointment was not to a "tenure-track" slot; I had to wait only two years before being appointed associate professor, but it took a very long time to overcome the initial salary handicap. Three chairmen in a row recommended me for annual increments designed to bring my salary to the level appropriate to my age, experience, and contribution; year after year these were cut back, and it was clear that the difficulty was sex-linked. It was not until Hopkins faced the pressures of affirmative action that the situation was rectified, and then only after I wrote a strong letter to the Dean.

It rankled also that at noon the Johns Hopkins Club relegated women to a separate dining room for lunch, so that female faculty could not meet members of other departments in the normal way. The House Committee felt that it would be offensive to the sensitivities of the gentler sex to encounter male faculty in informal garb at lunchtime, not seeming to recognize that they encountered their male colleagues in the same garb in their departmental interactions. It was not until late in 1968 that this ridiculous restriction was lifted.

Soon reverse discrimination set in! Suddenly the few women faculty members were in great demand. Every university committee had to include a woman. We were very overworked, and this situation still continues in many universities. At Hopkins I was eventually elected by the faculty to the Academic Council—the body responsible for advising the administration on matters of academic policy, appointment, promotion, and tenure. I could detect no signs of discrimination against women in these matters in this council, nor could I do so later when I moved to the University of Virginia, neither in the department of psychology nor during the year when I was a member of the dean's Promotion and Tenure Committee.

I find it difficult to write about my major project—the short-term longitudinal research into the development of infant-mother attachment that I launched at Johns Hopkins in 1962. There is too much to be said, and much of it has already been said in piecemeal publications. This research has turned out to be everything that I had hoped it would be, and it has drawn together all the threads of my professional career. I opted for direct observation in the natural environment of the home supported by a specifically designed laboratory situation—the strange situation. The combination of the two highlighted the importance of observing in various contexts if we are to understand infant behavior and development—a lesson that was also implicit in the cross-cultural comparisons I made with the findings of the Ganda study. Indeed there are many other areas of science in which the mutual feedback between observations in the natural environment and observations in the laboratory yield more understanding than observations in either context alone.

At the Tavistock Clinic I heard the dictum "no research without therapy." In no position to give therapy and not wishing to deliberately intervene, I adapted this dictum in both Ganda and Baltimore studies to a principle of not attempting to take data away from participants without giving something appropriate in return, and I took some pains to find what would be most appropriate in each instance.

Visits were made to the home at three week intervals from three to fifty-four weeks after the baby's birth, each visit lasting about four hours, which resulted in about seventy-two hours of observation for each infant. These long, frequent visits had several clear advantages. The mother could be more easily induced to behave as usual and to follow her normal routine. We attempted to span all aspects of a baby's day, although we could not cover nighttime hours. Frequent visits made up for the inevitable variability of behavior from day to day, so that measures could be used that combined the findings from four visits together, thus making for more stable measures without unduly sacrificing the picture of developmental changes. Seventy-two hours provided a broad data base. Finally, we got to know our families very well, which helped enormously in the identification of possible variables that might be involved in individual differences, and that could then be put to a systematic test.

The evolutionary-ethological orientation provided by even the earliest formulations of Bowlby's theory of attachment (e.g., Bowlby 1958) proved indeed to be helpful. It, as well as my experience in Uganda, suggested behaviors and possible "activating and terminating" situations that we wanted to be especially alert to when they occurred. On the other hand, I tried to keep our observations as open and comprehensive as possible to maximize the chances of finding new hypotheses about how behaviors become organized together and linked to situations. Thus, although benefiting from theory-based expectations, we felt free to undertake post hoc analyses of data. From the beginning emphasis was on understanding the variables involved in individual differences as well as on learning about the normative course of development—as might be expected of a clinician. Finally, although I had for a long time deliberately put my Blatzian orientation and research aside in the interests of making a fresh start with a new approach, I was eventually delighted to realize that there was a striking congruence between the old and the new, and especially in the phenomenon of an infant using his attachment figures as a secure base from which to explore the world. Furthermore, the pattern approach that I had found so useful in my Ph.D. dissertation emerged as the obvious way in which our new data could be ordered to describe qualitative differences in infant-mother attachment.

Soon after I shifted my academic field from clinical to developmental psychology increased numbers of graduate students began to seek me for a supervisor. The ongoing longitudinal research project provided a convenient focus for an aspect of their research training. I have been very fortunate in the associates and students who collaborated with me, and indeed the success of the project owes very much to their time, efforts, and ideas. Of those who remain primarily in academic teaching and research, I want to thank: Mary Main, who is now an associate professor at the University of California, Berkeley; Everett Waters, who is now at the State University of New York at Stony Brook; Mark Greenberg, now at the University of Washington; Inge Bretherton, at Colorado State University at Fort Collins; Rob Woodson, at the University of Texas at Austin; Sally Wall, who teaches at Towson State University in Maryland; and Michael Lamb, professor at the University of Utah, who was with me at Hopkins for only one year. It is perhaps not surprising that even more of my ex-students and ex-associates have moved from research into clinical applications, although they are still known chiefly for their research publications: Silvia Bell, Donelda Stayton, Robert Marvin, George Allyn, Alicia Lieberman, Russel Tracy, and others. Mary Blehar, with whom I have co-authored several publications, has been at NIMH for some years. Barbara Wittig, whose sensitive observations were crucial to my Baltimore project, was a clinical psychologist before working in the project, but has moved into other fields of endeavor. Including also the undergraduates in my project who contributed through laborious coding and the undergraduates in my courses who have gone on to careers in psychology, psychiatry, or pediatrics, I although childless find myself to have a large academic family—dear to me and very gratifying.

As a developmental psychologist at Johns Hopkins, and a relative newcomer to the American scene of development research, I suffered the disadvantages of isolation, as the only one of my kind in the department. Nevertheless, "support systems" soon became available. The friendship and encouragement of my colleagues Wendell Garner and James Deese were significantly helpful; although in the experimental tradition they valued the kind of research I was doing. The Society for Research in Child Development was important to me, both because of its meetings and because of the between-meeting contacts with friends I made through the society. My long-distance interaction with John Bowlby had never lapsed, but from 1960 on it picked up impetus when we realized that our thinking had developed along extraordinarily similar lines. Ever since, we have functioned as partners in attachment research and theory. The renewal of contact with John led to my inclusion in the Tavistock Mother-Infant Interaction Study Group which established a basis of communication with leading developmental scientists of various nationalities and disciplines. For a long time this combination of resources functioned very well for me.

But Garner left Hopkins for Yale, and later Deese left for the University of Virginia. With their departure I felt that I had lost effective intra-departmental encouragement for my approach, and began to feel restive. In due course I accepted a position at the University of Virginia, beginning in the fall of 1975. The Virginia department included a number of other developmental psychologists; communication with them has been a significant feature in my enjoyment of this new and congenial milieu.

Finally, I would like to consider the relation of my research contribution to the women's movement. By some it has been viewed as a stroke against women's liberation, since it has highlighted the importance of sensitive responsiveness to infant behavioral cues on the part of the mother figure and the desirability of continuity of the infant's relationship with that figure, unbroken by separations that are unduly long or frequent. It has been assumed that I believe in full-time mothering during the child's earliest years, and indeed this does seem to be the most usual way of ensuring adequate responsiveness and continuity. I acknowledge that satisfactory supplementary mothering arrangements can and have been made by a not inconsiderable few. Had I myself had the children for whom I vainly longed, I like to believe that I could have arrived at some satisfactory combination of mothering and a career, but I do not believe that there is any universal, easy, ready-made solution to the problem.

I have sometimes been accused of being out of touch with current changes in life-styles, but I believe that the problem is that infants are perhaps a million or so years out of touch with them. Their inbuilt evolutionary adaptations tend not to match new life-styles, much as we would like to believe infants to be infinitely adaptable. In a sense the traditional role of women is also tied to evolutionary considerations. The child-bearing and -rearing role is so essential to the survival of the species—and has for so long absorbed women's energies—that it is small wonder that women have been constrained to that role over many millennia.

Now, however, it is clear that the human species has been too successful in that the world is overpopulated; at least some women have been relieved of their age-old responsibilities for at least some period of their lives. There seems little reason to doubt that the intelligence and dedication that women have devoted to their traditional role can now, when not required by that role, be channeled elsewhere without undue hindrance.

REFERENCES

Ainsworth, M. D. S. *See* Representative Publications.

Bowlby, J. 1958. The nature of a child's tie to his mother. *International Journal of Psychoanalysis*, 39:350–73.

Klopfer, B. and D. M. Kelly. 1948. *The Rorschach Technique.* Yonkers-on-Hudson: World Book.

McDougall, W. 1927. *Character and the conduct of life.* London: Methuen.

Representative Publications by Mary D. S. Ainsworth

1937. [Salter] With S. N. F. Chant. The measurement of attitude toward war and the galvanic skin response. *Journal of Educational Psychology*, 28:281–89.

1940. [Salter] *An Evaluation of Adjustment Based upon the Concept of Security*. University of Toronto Studies, Child Development Series, no. 9. Toronto: University of Toronto Press.

1953. With J. Bowlby. *Research Strategy in the Study of Mother-Child Separation*. Paris: Courrier de la Centre International de l'Enfance.

1954. With B. Klopfer, W. F. Klopfer, and R. R. Holt. *Developments in the Rorschach Technique*, vol. 1. Yonkers-on-Hudson: World Book.

1962. The effects of maternal deprivation: A review of findings and controversy in the context of research strategy. In *Deprivation of Maternal Care: A Reassessment of Its Effects*. Public Health Papers, no. 14. Geneva: World Health Organization.

1963. Development of infant-mother interaction among the Ganda. In B. M. Foss, ed., *Determinants of Infant Behavior II*. New York: Wiley.

1967. *Infancy in Uganda: Infant Care and the Growth of Love*. Baltimore: Johns Hopkins University Press.

1969a. Object relations, dependency, and attachment: A theoretical review of the infant-mother relationship. *Child Development*, 40:969–1025.

1969b. With S. M. Bell. Some contemporary patterns of mother-infant interaction in the feeding situation. In A. Ambrose, ed., *Stimulation in Early Infancy*. London: Academic Press.

1971. With D. J. Stayton and R. Hogan. Infant obedience and maternal behavior: The origins of socialization reconsidered. *Child Development*, 42:1057–69.

1972a. Attachment and dependency: A comparison. In J. L. Gewirtz, ed.,

Attachment and Dependency. Washington, D.C.: V.H. Winston.

1972b. With S. M. Bell. Infant crying and maternal responsiveness. *Child Development,* 43:1171–90.

1973a. With D. J. Stayton and M. B. Main. The development of separation behavior in the first year of life: Protest, following, and greeting. *Developmental Psychology,* 9:213–25.

1973b. With D. J. Stayton. Individual differences in infant responses to brief, everyday separations as related to other infant and maternal behaviors. *Developmental Psychology,* 9:226–35.

1973c. The development of infant-mother attachment. In B. M. Caldwell and H. N. Ricciuti, eds., *Review of Child Development Research,* vol. 3. Chicago: University of Chicago Press.

1974a. With S. M. Bell and D. J. Stayton. Infant mother attachment and social development: "Socialisation" as a product of reciprocal responsiveness to signals. In M. P. M. Richards, ed., *The Integration of a Child into a Social World.* London: Cambridge University Press.

1974b. With S. M. Bell. Mother-infant interaction and the development of competence. In K. J. Connolly and J. Bruner, eds., *The Growth of Competence.* London: Academic Press.

1974c. With I. Bretherton. Responses of one-year-olds to a stranger in a strange situation. In M. Lewis and L. A. Rosenblum, eds., *The Origin of Fear.* New York: Wiley.

1976. With R. L. Tracy and M. E. Lamb. Infant approach behavior as related to attachment. *Child Development,* 47:571–548.

1977a. With M. C. Blehar and A. F. Lieberman. Early face-to-face interaction and its relation to later infant-mother attachment. *Child Development,* 48:182–94.

1977b. Infant development and mother-infant interaction among Ganda and American families. In P. H. Leiderman, S. R. Tulkin, and A. Rosenfeld, eds., *Culture and Infancy: Variations in the Human Experience.* New York: Academic Press.

1977c. Social development in the first year of life: Maternal influences on infant-mother attachment. In J. M. Tanner, ed., *Developments in Psychiatric Research: Essays Based on the Sir Geoffrey Vickers Lectures of the Mental Health Foundation.* London: Hodder & Stoughton.

1978. With M. C. Blehar, E. Waters, and S. Wall. *Patterns of Attachment: A Psychological Study of the Strange Situation.* Hillsdale, N.J.: Lawrence Erlbaum Associates.

1979a. Attachment as related to mother infant interaction. In J. S. Rosenblatt, R. A. Hinde, C. Beer, and M. Busnel, eds., *Advances in the Study of Behavior*, vol. 9. New York: Academic Press.

1979b. Infant-mother attachment. *American Psychologist*, 34:932–37.

1980. Attachment and child abuse. In G. Gerbner, C. J. Ross, and E. Zigler, eds., *Child Abuse Reconsidered: An Analysis and Agenda for Action*. New York: Oxford University Press.

1982. Attachment: Retrospect and prospect. In C. M. Parkes and J. Stevenson-Hinde, eds., *The Place of Attachment in Human Behavior*. New York: Basic Books.

1981. With R. L. Tracy. Maternal affectionate behavior and infant-mother attachment patterns. *Child Development*. 52, 1341–43.

MARY HENLE

Where does one begin the story of an academic career? In my case the story begins with my grandfather, who was a strange combination of liberalism and old-fashioned authoritarianism. One day he came home and announced to my mother, his eldest daughter: "There are not enough women in medicine. I have enrolled you in medical college." Mother had had no thought of going into medicine, and no interest in it; but my grandfather must have been something like Clarence Day's father. It will be recalled that the horse would not go until Father spoke to him. And in the same way, when Grandfather enrolled one in medical college, one went. Mother graduated at the head of her class and, around 1902 or 1903, became the first woman doctor to go out on ambulance calls.

When she applied for a position on the staff of the old Lying In Hospital in New York, she wrote to the director that she hoped her application would not be dismissed

simply because there have not been women on the staff before. Should I be so fortunate as to obtain a position on the staff, I would never ask or expect quarter even in the most inclement weather or under the greatest strain of work; and . . . upon receiving the first intimation of the impracticality of my being on the staff, I would deem it my duty to resign.

I quote this letter because it makes the point I will want to make: Mother understood, as perhaps my grandfather did not, that the issue was to be a good physician, not to be a woman physician.

To come to my own story: One would think that, in my family, the struggle over careers would have ended with the arbitrary incident of my mother's being enrolled in medical school. But there was one more battle to fight, and my brother fought it. The family wanted him to study law, with a view to entering the law firm founded by that same grandfather. My brother stuck out one semester at the Harvard Law School, then turned to graduate work in philosophy. He became a professor of philosophy, and my sister and I were free to pursue any career we chose.

An academic career was inevitable. There was the very powerful influence of my brother's choice. Mother's story has already been related. My father, in 1880, at the age of fifteen, emigrated to this country from Germany when he had completed the gymnasium there (equivalent at the time to the sophomore year of an American college). When he came to the United States, he had to go to work; he had always wanted to be a scientist. He continued his education all his life, by reading, by attending adult education courses, by taking advantage of the not inconsiderable cultural opportunities that Cleveland offered. The stories he told us were the Greek myths; and, through him, we early made the acquaintance of telescopes, microscopes, stereoscopes, and other instruments.

I went into psychology, and my twin sister became a better scholar than I in a field which unfortunately offered fewer opportunities than psychology: classical and preclassical archeology.

I am profoundly grateful that I went to Smith College. I did not get the subtle advice that has steered many women out of the professions. Nobody told us that we could not do professional work or that there was no point in training us for a profession in which we would not remain. In any case, there were outstanding women on the faculty who would have given the lie to any such advice: Marjorie Hope Nicolson, Dorothy Douglas, Charlotte Wilder, Gladys Bryson, Mary Ellen Chase, Eleanor Duckett, Esther Cloudman Dunn, Katherine Gee Hornbeak, Helen Muchnic, among other distinguished women. Nobody suggested that I should stay away from experimental or from theoretical psychology—on the contrary, these fields represented what psychologists were doing at the time and were encouraged. Thus I was never subtly guided into areas of psychology deemed by some to be suitable for women. I entered psychology because the department at Smith was exciting and psychology was therefore exciting. Those were the days when Kurt Koffka was at Smith, an influence on faculty as well as on students. The faculty included James and Eleanor Gibson, Harold Israel, an experimentalist and a gifted systematic psychologist whose influence on me has remained, Elsa Siipola and Hanna Faterson, both academic psychologists who subsequently turned their talents to the clinical field.

I had been a member of the undergraduate class to whom Koffka read his manuscript as he was writing the *Principles of Gestalt Psychology* (1935). At the end of the term, we went to his laboratory to read the final chapters. Exciting times for an undergraduate! From Harold Israel, I had learned enough about systems of psychology to know that something great was happening, that we students had been privileged to read a classic before it was available to the psychological profession.

I stayed on at Smith for the master's degree and an additional year as an assistant in the department. They continued to be stimulating, mind-opening years. The psychology department members were young and sociable and liked one another. As the only graduate student in the department, I was included in the group, as was my brother, when he came to Smith the next year to teach philosophy.

The influence of Koffka continued. I assisted him in some perceptual experiments. One evening a week the department went to Koffka's laboratory, a small frame house a little removed from the main buildings on campus, for his seminar, and the graduate students came too. The contact with Koffka—and with a department influenced by him—was of decisive importance for my subsequent development. By the time I arrived at Bryn Mawr, I was already committed to Gestalt psychology; how clear I then was about this commitment, I cannot say. I remember that Harry Helson once said to me: Whoever influenced you in psychology, it was nobody here. This was not exactly accurate, because I learned a lot from Harry about experimental method; and Donald W. MacKinnon, my dissertation adviser, introduced me to the psychology of Kurt Lewin and took me along to the annual meetings of the Lewin group, the Topological Psychologists, as they called themselves. I continued to attend sporadically until the group dissolved a number of years ago.

It had been almost by chance that I went to Bryn Mawr. Harry Helson was looking for an assistant and visited a number of the women's colleges to find one. We liked each other immediately, he respected my department, and I got the job. There followed three very good years at Bryn Mawr which, like Smith, had a deep and nondiscriminatory respect for scholarship. I recall that, when he hired me, Helson asked if I would mind if he treated me like a man. I suppose he meant that he would ask me to work hard. He didn't have to ask me—I gladly did it.

Bryn Mawr was a good place for a developing Gestalt psychologist, in a way in which few graduate schools in the country would have been. Helson's dissertation had been on Gestalt psychology; it was subsequently published in the *American Journal of Psychology* (Helson 1925, 1926) and, together with Koffka's famous article on perception (1922), constituted a general introduction of Gestalt psychology to American psychologists. Don MacKinnon had studied at the Psychological Institute of the University of Berlin during the time when it was directed by Wolfgang Köhler and was the major seat of Gestalt psychology; he had worked there mainly with Lewin. In addition, Bryn Mawr was close to Swarthmore College, where Köhler had recently come, and there were occasional meetings with the Swarthmore psychologists in a loosely organized group of psychologists in the Philadelphia area. Thus, the psychologists at Bryn Mawr, while not themselves Gestalt psychologists, were friendly to this movement and knowledgeable about it.

My first job after the Ph.D. was as a research associate at Swarthmore (today we would call that position a post-doctoral fellowship). There was no place in the world I would rather have gone. The department was chaired by Robert B. MacLeod, who had also studied at the University of Berlin and whose suggestion to President Aydelotte resulted in the invitation to Köhler to come to Swarthmore; MacLeod is well known for his work in phenomenological psychology. Richard Crutchfield was there, Edwin B. Newman, Karl Duncker, and Hans Wallach, also brought from Germany and appointed through MacLeod's influence. It was another exciting department and, as at Smith, a faculty influenced by its distinguished Gestalt psychologist. I attended Köhler's seminars and did some experimental work with him, and also with Hans Wallach. Before we younger members of the department submitted papers for publication, we would customarily ask Köhler for his criticisms; he was able to improve the English as well as the content—a remarkable achievement for somebody who had emigrated to this country only a few years before (though he had earlier lectured widely in the United States and England). I remember walking back and forth with Köhler in the long corridor of Martin Hall, as did anyone who wanted to discuss a scientific problem with him. I do not know how so productive a scientist was able to be so generous with his time to his younger colleagues and to prepare his classes so carefully. To him I owe my greatest intellectual debt. And my friendship with the Köhlers lasted over the years. I would meet them at the airport with a thermos bottle of Manhattans on their return from a trip abroad; we chopped down trees together; my first ride in a Jeep was with Köhler at the wheel; he named my cat.

During my second year at Swarthmore, Eddie Newman went off to do war work, and I took over his introductory psychology course. It was my first opportunity for more than the occasional lecture on my own, and I loved it. After two valuable years at Swarthmore, my post-doctoral fellowship had ended and jobs were still scarce. I spent a year at the University of Delaware. Psychology there was not much more than a one-man department at the time, and that man, who has remained my friend, was Kermit W. Oberlin, another academic psychologist later lost to the clinical field. By the close of the academic year 1941–42, the year the United States entered World War II, so many psychologists were engaged in war work that the job market suddenly opened up. Harry Helson wrote to invite me to return to Bryn Mawr, and I very happily accepted. First Harry, then Don MacKinnon, went on leave to contribute, as psychologists, to the war effort, and I was left largely in charge of the small department. I found myself for the first time teaching a graduate seminar and directing a master's thesis, in addition to the undergraduate teaching. My schedule of work was very simple: I taught my class, shut myself up in my office to prepare the next one, finished preparation just in time to meet it, and so it continued. At that time I thought there was just enough time—but not a minute more—to do what one had to do. Now I know better: there is never enough time.

In any case, I was obviously in far over my head, but I survived—survived, that is, until one day President Katharine McBride walked into the psychological laboratory and announced that she had "made a deal" with Swarthmore: I was to do some teaching there in exchange for some of Hans Wallach's time at Bryn Mawr. Again, somehow, I survived; I had learned a lot in those two hectic years at Bryn Mawr and Swarthmore.

College teaching, in my youth, was called the migratory profession. The warriors were returning, and it was time for me to move on. This time, I believe on President McBride's recommendation, I joined the psychology faculty at Sarah Lawrence College. I had read up on the educational philosophy of the college, and again I was enthusiastic. During two years there, I once more learned a lot, this time mostly about teaching. The college was dedicated to individual education, so, in addition to class preparation, there was preparation for the weekly conference with each of the two dozen students in one's classes. I profoundly approve of that goal, but I found that I had no time at all for research. Thus I was glad when Solomon E. Asch invited me to join him at the Graduate Faculty of the New School for Social Research; I believe it was on Köhler's recommendation, though Asch and I already had a relation of friendly, mutual respect.

The Graduate Faculty had previously been known as the University in Exile. Originally consisting of ten distinguished scholars in the social sciences, exiles from Nazi Germany, it gradually expanded, as the war did, to include exiles from other countries. This is not the place to recount the dazzling history of that faculty, which was the most distinguished and scholarly faculty I have ever known. Psychology, a part of the philosophy department, was represented by Max Wertheimer, the great Gestalt psychologist. When Wertheimer died in 1943, Köhler took over his courses until Asch was appointed. He was a natural choice for the position: he had worked closely with Wertheimer and shared his point of view in psychology. And it is not surprising that, as the student body was growing and Asch needed help, another Gestalt psychologist was appointed.

This time, with some five years or more of undergraduate teaching behind me, I was ready for the graduate students—that is, ready to work always at the edge of my knowledge and thus to expand it, to stretch my resources to meet students' interests, to value good questions more, perhaps, than answers. We had a most interesting group of students, mature, lively, thoughtful, attracted by the special character of the New School and its Graduate Faculty. I had the inevitable heckler during my first term at the New School, but I learned how to handle him, and it never happened again. In the end, I was no longer intimidated even by very large classes, though that has taken a period of years to achieve. After more than forty years of it, I still enjoy teaching, still learn from it and find that it nourishes my thinking, still enjoy watching students develop into independent psychologists.

Asch and I worked closely together during that first year at the Graduate Faculty. I was sad to see him leave to accept an invitation to Swarthmore. Fortunately, his influence remained; for years he returned once a week as a visiting professor. Our visiting professors also included Rudolf Arnheim, Hans Wallach (who took my place one year when I was away on a Guggenheim Fellowship), Kurt Goldstein; and one year Köhler came to give a course on mind and body. From a two-person department, the department gradually grew and diversified. I have never again had the close working relation with a faculty colleague that I valued so much with Asch. But there have been ample compensations. More and more, I found that my students became my colleagues—and I have always been fortunate in having excellent colleagues. At present, I meet regularly with a group of New School graduates in the best psychological meetings I have ever attended.

My research has consistently been within the framework of Gestalt psychology. Even when I have worked on something that had nothing to do with Gestalt psychology, my background in this kind of thinking showed me the problem. As one example, at this writing, I am also engaged in uncovering the implicit assumptions Freud made about cognitive processes; I would not have recognized the problems to which he was addressing himself and would have missed many of these assumptions without viewing him from the alternative position of Gestalt psychology.

My empirical work started in perception, then shifted to the experimental study of human motivation in the tradition of Kurt Lewin (although I departed from Lewin in bringing specific hypotheses derived from perception to this new area). In this connection, Don MacKinnon and I developed what I believe was the first laboratory manual in this field (with MacKinnon 1948). Our experimental exercises, the majority of them adaptations of the studies of Lewin and his students, were tested with Bryn Mawr undergraduates. Later I became increasingly interested in the question of human rationality and conducted studies on the relation of thinking to logic.

All this time, I was drifting more and more, but with a kind of necessity, to the analysis of ideas in psychology. I became active in Division 26 of APA, the division of History of Psychology, not because I ever claimed to be a historian—I am not one—but because here were people interested in intellectual history, interested in the development of ideas in our field. Here I found new colleagues, with which my own department, because of its great diversity, was no longer able to provide me.

Much of my work in the last decade has been written with an eye to another generation. At a time when the field of cognitive psychology is virtually synonymous with information processing, it would be wildly unrealistic to suppose that one could change anybody's mind. But I can still try to correct some of the current misunderstandings of Gestalt psychology so that later psychologists will have an opportunity to weigh the alternatives. I am honestly convinced that the data themselves will someday lead psychologists away from their obsession with computers and computer models, back to the kind of thinking represented by Gestalt psychology.

As I have already implied, when I received the Ph.D. in 1939, we were living in a period in some respects like the present one: the country had not yet fully emerged from the depression of 1929, and there were practically no academic jobs—in psychology as elsewhere. It is hard to say whether, as a woman, I had special difficulty in finding employment, though I suppose I did. In addition to the scarcity of positions, anti-Semitism was prevalent and often explicit. Thus, if I did not get a job for which I applied, I could not know for sure whether I lacked the qualifications, or whether it was because I was a woman or Jewish. Once I applied to medical school— a phenomenon not uncommon in my generation of graduate students in psychology—and was told by the school of my choice that four women were admitted to each class; no more than 25 percent of them were to be Jewish, and the Jewish woman had already been admitted for the coming year. I was invited to reapply but, fortunately, I came to my senses in the meantime. In another instance, a women's college, I applied for a position and was rejected because I was Jewish and, so I was told, mightn't feel comfortable there. In still another case, I recall hearing later that there had been discussion at the time of my application of "the problem of women in psychology" but I got the job. If I were to summarize my experience, I would say that—with the exception of a single year—if I had been given my choice of all the positions in the country, I would have chosen the job I had. For example, I cannot imagine a better intellectual home for me than the New School for Social Research, where I have happily remained for many years.

Indeed, this experience tempts me to speculate that being a woman and being Jewish were assets when I was looking for a job. These conditions may, at that time, have excluded me from all except those colleges and universities that were good enough, and sure enough of their own worth, to try to select candidates on their merits.

When I was a student, and a young psychologist, and indeed until fairly recently, there was no women's movement in psychology, not much activity of this kind anywhere. The events that had opened opportunities to us were far behind us, falling in the period between the Seneca Falls Convention of 1848 and the Susan B. Anthony Amendment of 1920. The opening of educational opportunities to women, the property laws, the opening of career opportunities of all kinds, were closely connected with the suffrage movement. This whole woman's movement we owe to the determination of a few women to be persons, free persons in a democracy.

It is not my task to give a capsule history of the women's movement. But I would like to mention that 1979, when APA celebrated the centennial of the launching of Wundt's psychological laboratory at Leipzig, was another centennial year that we neglected to observe. Ibsen's play *A Doll's House* was produced in 1879. At the end of the play, Nora gives up being a doll, the plaything first of her father, then of her husband, and becomes a person. She discovers that her duties to herself are as sacred as those to her husband and children, that "before all else I am a human being . . . —or at least that I should try to become one."

Our predecessors in the women's movement made it possible for us to try to become human beings, to obtain and continue an education, to enter a profession. How different our situation from theirs! Susan B. Anthony soon recognized that a "woman must have a purse of her own," and Virginia Woolf (1929) continued this theme. Speaking of the woman writer, she remarked; "Give her another hundred years, . . . give her a room of her own and five hundred a year, . . . and she will write a better book" (p. 164).

In psychology, we women do not need the additional century which Virginia Woolf saw as necessary to establish a literary tradition for women. Women were there almost from the beginning of scientific psychology. Virginia Woolf's five hundred pounds a year meant, in her day, enough to live on. Unlike the writers of that period, we are paid to do the work we want to do. We have stopped being surprised at the ability of our purses to sprout ten shilling notes. And we have rooms of our own—that is, the protection from the constant interruptions that made writing so difficult for the women of earlier days, women who had to do what writing they could against a background of incessant demands on them, in a common family sitting room.

My generation was one of relative quiet between those early women's struggles and the present-day militancy, which is working for the ERA, and which is represented in psychology by Division 35 of APA and by the whole movement—with its courses, journals, textbooks, specialists—that we call the psychology of women. Has my generation left you any legacy?

I believe that we have. We have done it by quietly doing our jobs, not as women psychologists, but as psychologists. We were not thinking much about being women in psychology. We simply took it for granted that women can function well in psychology in all kinds of settings, and we showed that they could by doing our work. What was our tacit assumption is now, I believe, held almost generally. It was by no means generally held in my youth when "the problem of women in psychology" was being discussed. Women are accepted in psychology as they were not forty years ago. I almost dare to say that the acceptance of women in psychology is the legacy of my generation to yours.

Those great women of the nineteenth and early twentieth centuries opened opportunities for us. They made possible our five hundred pounds a year and a room of our own. Our contribution has been to use that room.

Virginia Woolf approves this procedure. "It is fatal," she says, "for any one who writes to think of their sex" (p. 181). Again: "If you stop to curse you are lost" (p. 163). And once more: "She was thinking of something other than the thing itself. Down comes her book upon our heads" (p. 129).

So please accept our legacy. I wish you well with your five hundred pounds a year in a room of your own.

REFERENCES

Helson, H. 1925. The psychology of Gestalt. *American Journal of Psychology*, 36:342–70, 494–526.

—— 1926. The psychology of Gestalt. *American Journal of Psychology*, 37:25–62, 189–216.

Henle, M. *See* Representative Publications.

Koffka, K. 1922. Perception, an introduction to the Gestalt-Theorie. *Psychological Bulletin*, 19:531–85.

—— 1935. *Principles of Gestalt Psychology*. New York: Harcourt Brace.

Woolf, V. 1929. *A Room of One's Own*. New York: Harcourt Brace.

Representative Publications by Mary Henle

1941. With Hans Wallach. An experimental analysis of the law of effect. *Journal of Experimental Psychology*, 28:340–49.

1942a. An experimental investigation of past experience as a determinant of visual form perception. *Journal of Experimental Psychology*, 30:1–22.

1942b. An experimental investigation of dynamic and structural determinants of substitution. *Contributions to Psychological Theory*, 2(3):Durham: Duke University Press.

1944. An examination of some concepts of topological and vector psychology. *Character and Personality*, 12:244–55.

1948. With Donald W. MacKinnon. *Experimental Studies in Psychodynamics: A Laboratory Manual*. Cambridge: Harvard University Press.

1955. Some effects of motivational processes on cognition. *Psychological Review*, 62:423–32.

1956. With Miriam Michael. The influence of attitudes on syllogistic reasoning. *Journal of Social Psychology*, 44:115–27.

1957. Some problems of eclecticism. *Psychological Review*, 64:296–305.

1960. A psychological concept of freedom: Footnotes to Spinoza. *Social Research*, 27:359–74.

1961. Editor. *Documents of Gestalt Psychology*. Berkeley: University of California Press.

1962a. On the relation between logic and thinking. *Psychological Review*, 69:366–78.

1962b. The birth and death of ideas. In H. E. Gruber, G. Terrell, M. Wertheimer, eds., *Contemporary Approaches to Creative Thinking*. New York: Atherton Press.

1965. On Gestalt psychology. In B. B. Wolman, ed., *Scientific Psychology*. New York: Basic Books.

1966. Cognitive skills. In J. S. Bruner, ed., *Learning about Learning*: A

         Conference Report. Washington, D.C.: U.S. Government Printing Office.

1968.   Wolfgang Köhler. *Year Book of the American Philosophical Society*, 139–45.

1971a. Editor. *The Selected Papers of Wolfgang Köhler.* New York: Liveright.

1971b. The snail beneath the shell. *Abraxas*, 1:119–33.

1971c. Did Titchener commit the stimulus error? The problem of meaning in structural psychology. *Journal of the History of the Behavioral Sciences*, 7:279–82.

1971d. Of the Scholler of Nature. *Social Research*, 38:93–107.

1973a. E. B. Titchener and the case of the missing element. In D. Krech, ed. *The MacLeod Symposium.* Ithaca, N.Y.: Department of Psychology, Cornell University.

1973b. Co-editor, with Julian Jaynes and John J. Sullivan. *Historical Conceptions of Psychology.* New York: Springer.

1973c. On controversy and its resolution. In M. Henle, J. Jaynes, and J. J. Sullivan, eds., *Historical Conceptions of Psychology.* New York: Springer.

1974a. With John Sullivan. *Seven Psychologies* revisited. *Journal of the History of the Behavioral Sciences*, 10:40–46.

1974b. On naive realism. In R. B. MacLeod and H. L. Pick, Jr., eds., *Perception: Essays in Honor of James J. Gibson.* Ithaca, N.Y.: Cornell University Press.

1975.   Fishing for ideas. *American Psychologist*, 30:795–99.

1976.   Editor. *Vision and Artifact.* New York: Springer.

1977a. The influence of Gestalt psychology in America. *Annals of the New York Academy of Sciences*, 291:3–12.

1977b. Gestalt psychology. *International Encyclopedia of Psychiatry, Psychology, Psychoanalysis, and Neurology*, 5:209–13.

1977c. United States: A historical review of theoretical trends in psychology. *International Encyclopedia of Psychiatry, Psychology, Psychoanalysis, and Neurology*, 9:331–41.

1978a. Gestalt psychology and gestalt therapy. *Journal of the History of the Behavioral Sciences*, 14:23–32.

1978b. Foreword. In R. Revlin and R. E. Mayer, eds. *Human Reasoning.* New York: Wiley.

1978c. Kurt Lewin as metatheorist. *Journal of the History of the Behavioral Sciences*, 14:233–37.

1978d. One man against the Nazis—Wolfgang Köhler. *American Psychol-*

ogist, 33:939–44. Translated into German in *Psychologie Heute* and into Italian in *Psicologia Contemporanea*.

1979. Phenomenology in Gestalt psychology. *Journal of Phenomenological Psychology*, 10:1–17.

1980. A tribute to Max Wertheimer: Three stories of three days. *Psychological Research*, 42:295–304.

MARGARET HUBBARD JONES

Looking back over a long and very chequered career is difficult for one who is strongly future-oriented. The situation is not improved by a conflicting multitude of interests, as well as the turbulence of the era. From my perspective, a great deal that has occurred is attributable to fortuitous events (and this in spite of being a strongly internal attributor), although of course, the persistent motivation for intellectual activity ("brain itch") accounts for the general direction. The "brain itch" has had to compete with an equally strong "muscle itch" and a "sensory-aesthetic itch" and it all has had to be fitted into a very active family life. Social activities are relegated to last place, although I am fond of a modest number of close friends and enjoy an occasional small gathering. Fitting this all together has not been easy but it has been fun—and still is.

My childhood was closely directed by my mother, with a dozen different kinds of lessons designed to make me a social star (failed). My father, who had wanted a boy, was more supportive and, since he was verbally very bright and a splendid all-around athlete, provided a more acceptable role model. Any psychologist could predict that I would be a tomboy, with athletic interests and ambition for some sort of profession. Needless to say, there were some sparks during adolescence, resulting in a determination on my part to become independent as quickly as possible, and one brush with typing in a short-lived summer job during high school made it clear that I could not tolerate routine jobs even temporarily. At this point, there were no specific career goals, but college, and an academically good one, became a general goal. This was reinforced by my high-school Latin teacher, who challenged me by saying she did not think I could meet the Vassar entrance requirements.

I had no trouble being admitted to Vassar, but I had some trouble staying there for two reasons, one financial and one poor preparation. My college career spanned the depression years 1933–37. In our part of the country, suburban Connecticut, the depression hit hard, so it was very difficult for my father, a lawyer, to pay college bills. We had, by that time, lost through foreclosure a wonderful house and woods. I received some scholarship aid, lived in a cooperative dormatory, and worked at WPA and other jobs which helped a little. Undoubtedly this experience influenced later choices of paying jobs rather than continuing unpaid research. The poor preparation in the public high schools of that era did me no favor at Vassar where many students came from academically excellent private schools. In my freshman year, I had to work hard to catch up and might not have made it without the insistence of the dormitory counselor upon scheduling study time.

Choice of a major was a problem since I knew very little of the world. Within a few months I had run through geology and Spanish. My hopes of being the great American novelist were dashed by the instructor in creative writing who thought my first semester offerings were worth a D. I was tempted by an invitation to major in zoology, but looking back, I believe I was too verbal. Finally, both my roommate and I decided on philosophy, I think for want of anything more interesting. I found it intellectually very stimulating. The professor, Moritz Geiger, a German refugee, was world class and it was obvious. My other philosophy instructor, Margaret Rawlings, was a quiet, profound thinker who was kind and supportive of late adolescents, a model of what I would have liked to be, without the slightest chance of success. But she was a professor and that then became a possible occupational goal, though partly because it seemed to afford the opportunity to sit by a fire of an afternoon, drink cider and eat doughnuts, and think! I also chose psychology as my minor, at the time because I thought it would give me the insights necessary to become the great novelist! However, it was moderately interesting and the department members, all women, were friendly and helpful. The professor was the eminent Margaret Floy Washburn, Titchener's first Ph.D. at Cornell and the author of the first American text in what was then called animal psychology. She was an impressive old lady and gave beautifully organized lectures. For reasons I have never understood and to my complete surprise, she offered me support to go to graduate school. By this time it had become clear, even to me, that there was no market for philosophers of any sex. I had also specialized in epistemology and had progressed to the point of realizing that if one wants to know how real people process information and think, one had better get into the laboratory and find out. Graduate work in experimental psychology seemed the logical step. Margaret Washburn had done it many years before, so it did not seem to be unusual. About this time, in my senior year, Washburn had a serious stroke and all her funds were needed for her care. A fellowship opportunity at Hobart College was brought to my attention. It was a generous one, providing tuition, room, and board. I applied for it and for one at Stanford. Both were offered, but the differences in both amount of aid and travel costs made it Hobson's choice, since I could not ask my father to support me in graduate school. I would have preferred Stanford.

The department at Hobart consisted largely of another Titchener Ph.D., Forrest Dimmick. He had an adequate laboratory for the era, and access to any journals we needed. I spent a great deal of time in the laboratory, running sensory experiments or observing in them with three senior majors. I became very skilled at introspection in its Titchnerian meaning—the observing of the results of psychophysical processes. I also discovered the joys of visual after-images, a blessing at long-winded banquets. More importantly, I learned to become a precise and painstaking experimenter. The results of my master's thesis, published in two articles with Dimmick (1939a and 1939b), have stood the test of time in spite of very crude equipment and calibration methods by today's standards. I also learned that experimental work can be incredibly boring, but that, if properly done, it can also be rewarding.

By this time, I had been exposed to much Cornell tradition at both Vassar and Hobart. Cornell itself was close by and also near enough to home to minimize travel expenses, so I applied there for graduate school and a scholarship. I was accepted and awarded the Susan Linn Sage Scholarship. With some help from home, it was enough, although I (and all my fellow graduate students) lived in miserable rooming houses, ate a substandard diet, and could afford virtually nothing for entertainment.

Late in the spring of my year at Hobart, I and several other students made a trip to Cornell to see the famous laboratory. We were all most impressed by the tall, sophisticated graduate student who showed us around. However, in the course of showing us the apparatus museum, he made a disparaging remark about the spectrometer, the instrument dear to my heart and master's thesis, and I exploded. For some reason that has always baffled me, that was the beginning of a lifelong romance, which has interfered with both my education and my career, less because of gender than because of being tied to a particular geographical area.

I was at Cornell a year, 1938–39. During that time, I completed all the requirements for the Ph.D. except a thesis and a second year's residence. The requirements included a course in physics and two language examinations. The language examinations were very different from today's psychometric niceties, consisting then merely of an appointment with an approved professor in the sciences, who casually reached for some book on his shelf, opened it anywhere, and asked one to read aloud. When he was satisfied that you could read it at approximately normal English pace, he passed you on the spot. My French examination concerned renal function, which was a mystery to me even in English, but maybe the professor didn't understand it either.

The psychological training was in the Titchnerian tradition, with much emphasis on proper introspective experimental techniques, largely in sensory areas, and upon Titchnerian, behavioristic, and Gestalt theories. My later choice of research field was governed by this experience for many years. The area was then called sensation. We were impressed with the importance of the history of psychology and taught to do rigorous bibliographic searches. A requirement for every seminar paper was a complete bibliography, complete meaning all references in any language back to the beginning of time. It was excellent training for that era, but later hampered my research and, particularly, publication because I am not comfortable without that kind of search and it is neither possible nor reasonable with the recent explosion of information and the inferior quality of much of it. All the graduate students took largely the same curriculum; there wasn't much choice. We all took a course in neurology from an outstanding neuroanatomist, James W. Papez, whose theoretical work on brain circuits was at least twenty years ahead of its time. This background was important in my early work in physiological psychology. However, I did find time for one graduate course in Kant, pursuing my interest in epistemology, the last effort for a long time.

We were a small, close-knit group, two of us women. I never discerned any differences in standards, encouragement, or attitudes toward men and women by any of the staff members, nor among the other students. Everyone expected everyone else to become a professional, academic psychologist. There were not many opportunities at that time outside the universities, and none within our ken.

My major professor was Karl M. Dallenbach, editor of the *American Journal of Psychology*, then the most prestigious psychological periodical in this country. His high standards for accuracy and completeness impressed me greatly, but even more unusual was his intellectual generosity. If a student caught him in an error (always minor), he heaped enthusiastic praise upon him, male or female. It built professional confidence and made us eager to work even harder. While encouraging me in my professional ambitions, he engaged in surreptitious matchmaking by telling one of the graduate students that I would make some psychologist an excellent wife. My husband claims he thought of it first.

In June I was married to F. Nowell Jones, on the day he received his Ph.D. We were encouraged by the fact that friends, T. A. Ryan, an instructor at Cornell, and his wife, Mary, a Cornell Ph.D., had managed to combine a happy marriage with continued professional interests. I still had a year to go to complete my degree so we had planned to stay on, Cornell having continued my scholarship and offered my husband an assistantship. However, he received an offer of a real academic job, an instructorship at the University of Alabama. Considering the tight job market, the unlikelihood of our both obtaining jobs in the same place, and the diminishing number of women on university faculties, as well as their lower salary and rank, we made a joint decision to push his career and let mine follow as opportunity presented itself. I attempted to obtain permission to do the thesis *in absentia*, but Cornell would not waive the remaining residence requirement.

The psychology department's quarters for instructors at Alabama consisted of two long, narrow offices which had to serve as research space as well. The normal teaching load of eighteen semester hours meant that research had to be done nights and weekends. We turned out joint research and published (1941a, 1941b, 1942a, 1942b), motivated by both boredom and a strong urge to move to a major university. We were there three years. During the last year, World War II broke out and we became restless, uncertain of what to do. We both worked in war industries in Connecticut and then moved to Los Angeles, where I entered UCLA as a full-time graduate student in psychology, but farther behind than ever because of prerequisites in anthropology and five semesters of mathematics, new language exams, and new qualifying exams. Also, the whole orientation of the department was different. There were a number of women on the faculty and a number of women graduate students. The graduate group was much larger than Cornell's and, since UCLA was even then a metropolitan, commuters' campus, there was less opportunity for discussion or social activities. However, I had plenty of contact with a number of students in very diverse areas, which helped somewhat to broaden my rather narrow perspective. I never discerned any prejudice in treatment of women by the faculty, and graduate students formed friendships based on graduate field rather than gender. The influence of UCLA was more broadening than specific. My committee chairman was Roy Dorcus, whose wife was also a psychology Ph.D., and who was sympathetic to my difficulty in completing one Ph.D. instead of several partial ones. As it turned out, that sympathy would become very important. Kate Gordon (Moore) and Carolyn Fisher were professors in the old experimental tradition and they served to reinforce my determination to become an academician with theoretically-oriented research interest.

After three trimesters at UCLA, we returned to Alabama where I completed the last two calculus courses. I also taught a few courses because the other instructors were on military leave. This was very useful because it helped me to overcome panic at the thought of public speaking and provided some experience necessary for a dossier. I managed a summer trimester at UCLA and did my thesis research. My chairman urged me to select a topic I could complete in the available time and that would be acceptable no matter whether the results were positive or negative. I toyed with several world-shaking topics that would have required half a lifetime, before finally accepting his advice. It was a topic of real interest to women; the effects of menstruation on performance. The FAA had a regulation forbidding women to fly during the menstrual period. I needed the evidence on which this regulation was based to complete my bibliography, so I wrote the Surgeon General of the United States. I received a reply stating that a woman had crashed and in the absence of any obvious cause, it had been attributed to the effects of menstruation; end of letter. This kind of prejudice incensed me and made it somewhat easier to endure causing women in all stages of the menstrual cycle to throw up and then cleaning up, without following in kind. I did complete the work on one summer, wrote it up during the fall and winter back in Alabama, and traveled by train under wartime restrictions to Los Angeles to defend the thesis. It was successful in spite of my moritification about finding zero differences between the major groups, hence having no statistics to display. The survey of previous research, as well as my own experimental findings, convinced me that there was no demonstrable effect on performance. I believe that this conviction is important for women who wish to compete and not ask for special favors. This research was published (Jones 1945).

Shortly thereafter my husband accepted a job at the University of Wisconsin and the war ended. Wisconsin represented a great improvement in intellectual environment: laboratories, colleagues, and library. Although I was not quite one of the group, I was able to keep up, interchange with colleagues, and even helped to start a bit of research. I spent a significant proportion of my time grading papers in a correspondence course in elementary psychology for the armed services. That was all that was available and items for the dossier were needed for future competitiveness. Money was very scarce also. It was the dullest kind of work; I have always detested grading papers and presenting the same material over and over. In some ways, I am fortunate that I have never held a traditional teaching position.

The next year my husband was offered the chairmanship of a new psychology department at Washington State College. We had space, a few bright young colleagues, and a reasonable library. I was part of that group. We also made and maintained contact with the psychologists at the University of Washington who were very cordial to all of us, including me. I helped my husband in his research and taught a course or two when needed, again for dossier material as well as a few extra dollars. But much of my time was spent in the library, searching the world literature for studies of employee selection, a topic on which my major professor, R. M. Dorcus, wanted to publish a definitive work. The book was published (1950a) and was well-received, but the work was deadly and, when asked to do a revision some ten years later, I could not face it. For the next two summers, my husband taught in summer sessions at San Diego State College and at UCLA. We realized the importance of keeping, as well as making, professional contacts, and we both had many old friends in that area. It also gave us access to excellent library facilities, interesting colloquia and discussions, and new developments that had not penetrated as far as the Palouse Hills of eastern Washington. After three years at Washington State, my husband accepted an offer from UCLA in spite of a reduction in rank, because we thought we would both have more opportunities to do research and advance professionally.

My years at UCLA, 1949–1974, were, by and large, happy and productive, although anything but traditional. By the time we arrived, most of the women on the faculty had retired and had been replaced with men. There was a period between the retirement of the first wave of famous women psychologists and the present anti-discrimination drive when there were very few women hired in academic psychology. Some psychologists attained academic appointments at UCLA in education and in physiology. I had a firmly entrenched desire to do basic research, so I set about doing it on my own. My husband's colleagues were always cordial and helpful. I borrowed some space and unused equipment, and turned out several pieces of research in the old Cornell tradition (1952, 1954a, 1954b). I did a factor analysis by hand of visibility data (1950b), working nights for months. We also published a survey of olfactory theories (1953a), for which I taught myself to read Italian. At that time there were not a great many jobs opening up, nepotism rules were stringent, and commuting long distances was not feasible. However, academic salaries were very low and ten years of near poverty had made us long for a house of our own, so I looked around for a paying part-time job, but only at UCLA, for I wanted to do my own research half-time. Basic research grants were few. There were a number of research projects supported by the Armed Forces going on, so I joined a number of them at different times. I also taught an extension course for several years and handled the correspondence course in physiological psychology for the University of California for six tedious years. I was in charge of the psychophysical aspects of a large air-pollution research project, where I was able to do an experimental study of thresholds for smog with odor controlled with a reasonably large sample and many trials, the Cornell tradition enlarged (with Buchberg, Wilson, and Lindh 1963). Beginning in 1950, I was associate research psychologist and then research psychologist in the School of Engineering, at first part-time and later full-time. This Research Series title was parallel to the Academic Series, but without tenure or any support or encouragement for professional activities, research, or updating. This is a real blind spot at the University of California and many other high-ranking universities because it throws away priceless opportunities for closely supervised research experience for graduate students without cost. It became very frustrating, but I was not treated differently from the men in the same position. My job was psychometric, constructing and validating engineering entrance examinations. In many of my subsequent tasks and in much research I would still like to do, a good background in that area is essential for measurement of effects, and I am now grateful that I had that exposure. My colleagues and my superior, Harry W. Case, were friendly and helpful.

During this period, I contributed most of the chapters on sensory processes to a physiological psychology text (with Wenger and F. N. Jones, 1956), occasionally stopping to do an experiment to fill in a gap. This again illustrates moral support by my husband and his colleagues. I began drifting into research on more complex perceptual processes and did some research on perception of complex figures which I never published. This began a tendency to do research, almost finish preparation for publication, and then jump to a new field. I attribute this to much greater time pressure, with a full-time job, a husband addicted to racing sailboats with me as the foredeck crew, and a small child, but also to broadening interests stimulated by weekly psychology colloquia and a growing influx of new faculty members fresh from diverse major institutions. All this time I held an unpaid appointment in the psychology department as a research psychologist, which gave me a number of important privileges. My husband's colleagues were very encouraging, as was my husband. Perhaps if they had not been quite so helpful, I would have broken out and sought one of the non-academic jobs that were by then popping up in the area, though I believe it would still have been difficult for a woman to compete with even a minimally qualified male applicant.

From the mid-fifties to the mid-seventies there was a great deal of time pressure because I wanted to spend as much time with my daughter as she needed, which was a lot. For this, flexible working hours were essential and that is one reason that I stuck with the kind of job I had. I am interested in the development of flexitime in industry partly because I think it is essential to comfortable coping with both job and family, especially for women. Women psychologists could help the cause of women by supporting this concept, especially since the research shows that it increases productivity and job satisfaction, and is the only known strategy to do so across cultures.

I became interested in psycholinguistics in the early sixties, as did several members of the department. With the assistance of a grant from the U.S. Office of Education, Professor Edward C. Carterette and I produced a mammoth statistical study of English (1974). Through the years Carterette has provided more active encouragement of women to do basic research than anyone I know. I became enthralled with developmental psycholinguistics and when I moved to the School of Education in the mid-sixties that extended to cognitive development in general. I taught regular courses for the first time and did research on short-term memory and verbal screens in achievement tests for children. My lack of patience with the naive theoretical approach of education professors made me unsuited to continue, so when an offer arrived (1969) out of the blue to manage a million dollar, four-year study for the State, I took it. It was offered because the Institute of Transportation and Traffic Engineering was given the job, and my colleagues in the School of Engineering had too much else to do. It was basically a large-scale research evaluation of an educational program, in this case driver training, and it was a political hot potato. I knew little of either evaluation techniques or traffic safety. I learned those but not how to be politic. I learned two more fields to add to my collection, while the good research of the past few years remained unpublished. I think that my greatest influence has been on the graduate students who worked so long and hard on that project. Planning, managing, and completing an experimental research involving 15,000 subjects, sites all over the state, dozens of administrators to deal with, and a standard computer program that turned out to contain an error undetected in smaller samples cannot be other than educational. Several of these students have gone on to manage large-scale projects on their own. During this project, I had frequent contact with the relevant people in both the California Department of Motor Vehicles and the State Department of Education. I found no prejudice but willing assistance. I lost here my standard academic bias that no one outside a university is very competent.

By this time many more opportunities for women were opening up, partly because there were more jobs and partly because it had become necessary that institutions demonstrate lack of prejudice. Just as the driver-training project was ending, I received, again out of the blue, an offer from the Institute of Safety and Systems Management at the University of Southern California, across town. To what extent it was due to their need to have a woman on the faculty or to their need for a researcher in traffic safety I do not know, but probably both. I am sure that being a woman helped to gain me an associate professorship and to advance quickly to a professorship with tenure. I detected some slight prejudice in a few colleagues, not surprising among retired military men and men who had been teaching all-male classes at military bases for years, but they did not stand in my way. In my own department, Human Factors, my colleagues were very supportive, particularly Arnold Small, David Smith, and Mark Van Slyke. I was now teaching graduate courses in environmental interactions, organizational behavior, and man-machine systems to Air Force officers. Although a few acquaintances snickered at the thought, I was not aware of a credibility gap, although I expected one. This teaching was at night at distant bases and involved much travel at unpleasant hours, so I depended on contract research to buy off as much of my time as possible. Competitive contract research is a very poor way to generate publishable research because there is typically too little time and money to do even what is required, but it can be done. This research was in the area of human factors in traffic safety, in which I have developed somewhat of a reputation. There is an effort, in this largely masculine area, to get more women involved, so I have been appointed to a number of committees, national and international in scope, which has been interesting. This is an area of great importance both for health and for containment of medical costs and it attracts very few qualified psychological researchers. My early role model was reactivated and I worked hard to excel in teaching, research, university service, and national service. I have given papers at annual association meetings frequently, starting in 1947, which I think is important to a career, but in the last few years it has amounted to four a year, which shows no restraint. I have competed successfully with male colleagues on their own turf and been generously rewarded. I may even have overdone it, partly, of course, to prove that women can do it better and still manage a rather complex household, have warm family relationships, many hobbies, time for athletics and other interests.

I could not have done all this as intensively when my child was young, especially with the amount of travel necessary, but then I probably would not have needed to cram so much into my seven years as a real professor. I could not have had a career at all without my husband's encouragement and assistance with household chores. My daughter, in later years, was also a tremendous help, though demanding of time to swim and chat, a delightful diversion which helped to shake off tension. When too many tasks demanded attention, I learned to establish priorities and to work faster and longer. I never learned to say "no." Careful attention to organization and scheduling was very important after the birth of my daughter. The biggest problem for any executive is efficient management of time. For career women it must be learned early. The energy demanded by my schedule is available to me only with regular vigorous exercise.

I have now retired, having asked and been granted an additional year beyond "normal" retirement. At this point I am more concerned with age discrimination, which is rampant, than with sex discrimination, which has deterrent forces already in motion, but of course the sex discrimination against older women is still extreme, so it is largely the same game. I now face yet another career change and am considering a field that has few women and needs some: human factors consulting in the safety area. But with some colleagues I have been planning a major research on the effects of age on managerial performance, if we can find funding. My husband and I have some ideas for some gerontological research in perception. I would like to pick up an old theoretical interest in the problems in communication between individuals of different backgrounds, and I really want to get into tomorrow's problems of human beings communicating with computers. I still don't know what I'm going to be when I grow up.

It is obvious that women have far greater opportunities in psychology now than they had in the recent past. Not only have academic barriers been eased, but many applied fields have opened up. I think that, because of political pressure, these gains will not be lost with the current and future budget cuts. However, I do think that complete acceptance by colleagues depends upon meeting performance standards and not asking for special favors.

With the academic job market becoming very tight, it may be that there is a useful lesson for women psychologists in the non-traditional aspects of my career. There are large numbers of projects, mostly funded by some federal or state agency, that really need psychological, statistical, psychometric, and evaluation expertise. Although they may seem dull, and usually are, they can be made interesting by someone with good training and some theoretical insight. Applied problems are complex and very challenging; there are jobs in industry requiring psychological expertise that can provide samples of real live people, not college sophomores, for research on complex interactions occurring "out there" that can be much more meaningful than some laboratory work. Two aspects of graduate training are important, however: (1) breadth; (2) training in group research, very different from what is taught in graduate school, with very little transfer. Any woman in today's job market would be well advised to manage her own education in these directions.

REFERENCES

Jones, M. H. *See* Representative Publications.

Representative Publications by
Margaret Hubbard Jones

1939a.   [Hubbard.] With F. L. Dimmick. The spectral location of psychologically unique yellow, green, and blue. *American Journal of Psychology*, 52:242–54.

1939b.   [Hubbard.] With F. L. Dimmick. The spectral components of psychologically unique red. *American Journal of Psychology*, 52:348–53.

1941a.   With F. N. Jones. The chronaxy of pressure in hairy and hairless regions. *American Journal of Psychology*, 54:237–39.

1941b.   With F. N. Jones. The chronaxy of pain. *American Journal of Psychology*, 54:240–42.

1942a.   With F. N. Jones. Vividness as a factor in learning lists of nonsense syllables. *American Journal of Psychology*, 55:96–101.

1942b.   With F. N. Jones. The qualities of pressure and pain. *American Journal of Psychology*, 55:275–76.

1945.   The influence of menstruation upon nausea induced from the vestibule. *American Journal of Psychology*, 58:496–509.

1950a.   With R. M. Dorcus. *Handbook of Employee Selection*. New York: McGraw-Hill.

1950b.   With F. N. Jones. A second factor analysis of visibility data. *American Journal of Psychology*, 63:206–13.

1950c.   A survey of the adequacy of employee selection reports. *Journal of Applied Psychology*, 34:219–44. Rpt. in M. L. Blum, ed., *Readings in Experimental Industrial Psychology*. New York: Prentice-Hall, 1952.

1952.   With F. N. Jones. The critical frequency of taste. *Science*, 115:355–56.

1953a.   With F. N. Jones. Modern theories of olfaction. *Journal of Psychology*, 36.207–11.

1953b.   With S. F. Hulbert and R. H. Haase. A survey of the literature on job analysis of technical positions. *Personnel Psychology*, 6:173–94.

1954a. A study of the common chemical sense. *American Journal of Psychology*, 67:696–98.

1954b. Second pain: Fact or artifact? *Science*, 124(3219):442–44.

1955. With H. W. Case. The validation of a new aptitude examination for engineering students. *Educational and Psychological Measurement*, 15:502–8.

1956. With M. A. Wenger and F. N. Jones. *Physiological Psychology*. New York: Holt.

1963. With H. Buchberg, K. W. Wilson, and K. G. Lindh. Studies of interacting atmospheric variables and eye irritation thresholds. *International Journal of Air and Water Pollution*, 7:257–80.

1967. With E. C. Carterette. Visual and auditory information processing in children and adults. *Science*, 156:986–88.

1968. Some thoughts on perceptual units in language processing. In K. S. Goodman, ed., *The Psycholinguistic Nature of the Reading Process*. Detroit: Wayne State University Press.

1970a. Reliability of coding of the system for the analysis of classroom communication (SACC). In A. Simon and E. G. Boyer, eds., *Mirrors for Behavior: An Anthology of Classroom Observation Instruments*. Supplement, vol. A. Philadelphia: Research for Better Schools.

1970b. *The Unintentional Memory Load in Tests for Young Children*. Center Report no. 56. Los Angeles: University of California, Graduate School of Education, Center for the Study of Evaluation.

1972. Pain thresholds for smog components. In J. F. Wohlwill and D. H. Carson, eds., *Environment and the Social Sciences: Perspectives and Applications*. Washington, D. C.: American Psychological Association.

1973. *California Driver Training Evaluation Study: Final Report*. Los Angeles: University of California, School of Engineering and Applied Science.

1974. With E. C. Carterette. *Informal Speech: Alphabetic and Phonemic Texts with Statistical Analyses and Tables*. Los Angeles: University of California press.

1977. Measuring the outcomes of driver training: The University of Southern California on-road performance test. *Transportation Research Record*, no. 629, pp. 63–67.

1978a. *Children's Understanding of Pedestrian Safety Concepts*. Technical

Report 78–14. Los Angeles: University of Southern California, Traffic Safety Center.

1978b. *Traffic Safety Program Evaluation: A Course Manual.* Prepared for the National Highway Traffic Safety Administration under Contract DOT-HS-5-01243.

1978c. *The Reliability of Driver Performance: Test Reliability or Driver Stability?* Technical Report 78-13. Los Angeles: University of Southern California, Traffic Safety Center.

1980.   Measuring pedestrian behavior. *Transportation Research Record,* no. 743.

MARY J. WRIGHT

Elsewhere in this volume Mary Henle reminded us of the importance of the role of the family in determining one's career. Her story, like mine, starts with a maternal grandfather. However, unlike Mary's grandfather who insisted that her mother become a doctor, my grandfather refused to allow my mother to become a pharmacist. How lucky this was for me!—for right then and there my mother resolved that if ever she had a daughter nothing would be allowed to stand in her way of obtaining any kind of education, or of pursuing any type of career, she desired. The strength of her resolution was probably doubly important in my case, for I was her last born of five children and the *only* girl. Raised, as I was, in a family dominated by men, for my four brothers, who were five to ten years older than I, always seemed to me to be men, I did indeed need my mother's support, and I got it. Although my brothers delighted in telling me to "go help your mother," Mother constantly shoved me away from domestic chores, often over my own protests. Thus I was given all of the freedoms and just as few responsibilities as my brothers, perhaps fewer responsibilities, because my father believed in the value of chores for boys. I automatically followed my brothers to university (the University of Western Ontario, in London, usually referred to in Canada simply as Western) and was supported in my plans to go on to graduate school in Toronto, even though on one occasion, in private, my father, who thought I was destined for marriage, cautiously informed me that he would be happy to hand over the equivalent of what my M.A. would cost for sheets or whatever else girls put in their "hope chests."

I grew up in Strathroy, a small town, then of just under 3,000 inhabitants, in southwestern Ontario. It was a proud little town in which a great many prominent Canadians had been born or educated, including Sir Arthur Currie, who was the Commander-in-Chief of the Canadian Army in World War I and later the principal of McGill University. During my early childhood, which was in the pre-talking pictures, pre-radio, and pre-television era, it was also basking in considerable fame which it had acquired in the arts, especially in theater, and in the latter my father, and his sister Edith, had played a prominent part. However, as in most small towns everyone knew everyone else and, like the members of a large extended family, dispensed praise and blame, freely and liberally, wherever it seemed to be deserved.

I was fortunate in that I belonged to a family which had earned a fair amount of respect. My Dad often laughingly described himself as a "big toad in a little puddle," which he said he preferred to being a "little toad in a big puddle." He was the son of James Wright, an Englishman who had established the first successful "Wright" Company in Strathroy in 1865, and he himself had established the Wright Piano Company,[1] which produced high quality instruments of which my father was extremely proud. More important for his children was, however, that he also operated a musical instruments retail store which became the locus of many of their most enjoyable and educational experiences. Thus, as a family we were never poor, but neither were we affluent. We went through many "hard times" when there were family debates about whether or not I could have a new dress, and I often wore made-over "hand-me-downs" from one of my more affluent cousins in the United States.[2] Born as I was during World War I, I was raised during the economically unstable period which followed it, including the great depression of the early 1930s.

Our family life was highly stimulating. Everyone was exceedingly active and there was never a dull moment. To a large extent we were brought up on music and amateur "show business." Both of my parents were musical. Mother played the piano and sang contralto and Dad had considerable talent as an actor, singer, and entertainer. At one stage, to promote the sale of his pianos locally, Father formed his family into a small entertainment troupe which performed at church garden parties and the like. My four young brothers (aged about eight to thirteen at the time), who were highly versatile in what they could do, were a great hit. I was considered too young to be a performer, but more often than not was taken along with them "for the ride." My father founded the first Boy Scout troop in Strathroy and took the scouts to camp each summer for many years. He helped the boys earn the money needed for the camp by having them put on minstrel shows and Humpty Dumpty circuses, and by obtaining engagements for their "snappy" bugle band. At home, what today would be called our family room, was

---

1. A brief history of the Wright Piano Company is on deposit in the music section of the Public Archives of Canada in Ottawa.
2. The cousin was Pauline Wright, the daughter of my father's brother, Albert George Wright, who practiced medicine in Fenton, Michigan. Pauline was ten years my senior and one of my models. She was for many years the principal of an inner-city school in Detroit.

always cluttered up with instruments which were played from morning to night. The 1930s were the era of the "big" bands and inevitably my brothers formed their own "big" band, the Wright Brothers Orchestra, which ultimately earned considerable acclaim. At one time they contemplated making their band a career, as had Guy Lombardo and his brothers. The Lombardo boys were from nearby London and were well-known to us. They were models for my brothers. But even my father advised them against such an uncertain future. Only one of us made music and entertaining a career and he, my brother Donald,[3] did so only after he had completed his university studies in honors classics, for there *was* a serious side to our life. My mother saw to that. She was Scottish, even though a third-generation Canadian, and valued education highly. She saw that our house was full of books, that we were read to until we became bookworms ourselves, and she made sure that her first-born, who was reluctant to enter university, did so. She was an intelligent and determined woman, but also an exceedingly warm and loving one. When we were young, she was reluctant to send us out into the great wide world and, to our later chagrin, delayed our entry into school until we were seven. She was also the type who often provided six desserts so that everyone could have his or her favourite.

Being the "odd" one in the family—so much younger than my siblings and a girl rather than a boy—I was inevitably left out of many of the most exciting activities which went on at home. I coped by becoming independent and developing a highly active life of my own outside the family. I liked to be liked and I took responsibility whenever I had the opportunity. I was, for example, captain of the softball team in primary school, president of the student body in high school, and president of the Anglican Young Peoples Association (AYPA) at church. My interest in extracurricular activities continued into university and at graduation I was elected to the university's Honour Society, a society which recognized non-academic as well as academic achievements and was listed in *Who's Who of Canadian and American Students*. That year I did well academically too and was awarded the Gold Medal for receiving the highest standing in the honours philosophy and psychology program.

My brothers, but not my parents, had an influence on my choice of a career. I was considering medicine, and all but one of them "ganged up" on me. They argued that medicine would "turn me into a man"; that I would learn about the sordid side of life and that this was a side about which

3. The story of my brother Donald's career and a summary of his work in music is contained in a twelve-volume thesaurus on deposit in the music section of the Public Archives of Canada in Ottawa.

females should be kept ignorant. I think I was a little uncertain about medicine anyway, because I was swayed by them on this occasion and began my university studies in English and history. However, during the summer preceding my entry into university, my eldest brother accidently heard something about psychology—particularly about the testing movement. He told me as much as he knew about it and it made me curious enough to take, as an extra subject, introductory psychology. The course was taught at 9:00 a.m. Tuesdays, Thursdays, and Saturdays. I was not fond of early risings or Saturday classes, but I never missed a single session. The instructor was R. B. Liddy,[4] the head of the department, who was an excellent teacher, and I found the subject matter fascinating. Thus my fate was sealed. I asked permission to transfer to the honors program in philosophy and psychology; permission was granted and I elected the major in psychology. I did not realize, at the time, how new the program in psychology at Western was. It had been started in 1931 only four years before I discovered it. That was the year when the first real department of philosophy and psychology was established at Western and the year that Dr. Liddy was appointed to be its head.

My undergraduate work was done in the second half of the 1930s when psychology had temporarily vacated its laboratories, had ceased to be primarily experimental, and, for many reasons, had gone applied (O'Donnell 1979). Thus, when I graduated, I was strongly oriented in an applied direction. Because I had surprised myself by winning, without even trying, a scholarship in my third year, I was persuaded that I should undertake graduate studies, at least to the master's level, which would equip me for a clinical job or for psychological work in the schools. I had heard about school psychology at Columbia and I applied for admission there. I had also heard a great deal about the University of California at Berkeley from a cousin of my mother's who lived in California, so I decided to apply there. Finally, I applied to Toronto, for it seemed the natural thing for an Ontario student to do. My father wrote to his old friend James T. Shotwell, who was a professor of history at Columbia, to ask if he would provide some support for my application. Shotwell was one of Strathroy's most distinguished sons. He was an architect of the old League of Nations, the forerunner of the United Nations. Shotwell replied "I shall be delighted to say a word about your daughter's application to the Department of Psychology although, as you perhaps know, in a great university like this the depart-

4. Additional information about R. B. Liddy may be obtained in "Psychology at Western" by Leola E. Neal and Mary J. Wright in M. J. Wright and C. R. Myers, eds., *History of Academic Psychology in Canada.*

ments work almost as if they were in different institutions".[5] If Shotwell interceded on my behalf it was to no avail, for I was not accepted there. I *was* accepted at Berkeley. However, Edward C. Tolman's kind and gracious letter informing me of this and saying that "we would be glad indeed to welcome you" also advised me, with the usual regrets, that no financial assistance could be provided.[6] So money finally determined my choice of a graduate school. E. A. Bott, the head at Toronto, offered me an assistant-ship of $200, not a bad offer in those days, so to Toronto I went.

My graduating year, 1939, was also the year in which Great Britain (and Canada) declared war on Germany. I completed my M.A. in 1940 and would have gone to work at that point, but no suitable jobs could be found. The war had curtailed luxuries, such as mental health services. I, therefore, re-enrolled in the university, to begin doctoral studies, only to find that the faculty had been depleted by the war and those with whom I had hoped to study were no longer there. At first I did not know how to cope with this disappointing situation, but what I finally decided to do, which seemed at the time to be anything but purposeful or important, turned out to be highly significant, for it set in train a series of events which, in the end, entirely changed my focus in psychology for the rest of my career.

While a master's student I had taken a most unconventional, but delight-ful graduate seminar with the great W. E. (Bill) Blatz, the director of To-ronto's Institute of Child Study. I had also had some exposure to the insti-tute's preschool, while borrowing some of its pupils to be subjects in my thesis research. What was going on at the institute had intrigued me greatly. The institute staff, apart from Blatz, had as yet not been drawn into the war effort, so I decided to use this year to learn as much as I could from this group. I took all of the courses they offered in child development, early childhood education, and parent education, and I even took a job in the preschool as a part-time pianist. Thus, as student and pianist I came to know the institute people well and formed some warm and lasting friend-ships with them, especially with Margaret I. Fletcher, the principal of the nursery school, who liked my piano playing.

In 1941 I gave up trying to obtain a Ph.D. under wartime conditions and took a job at a place called the Protestant Children's Village in Ottawa, which at that time provided temporary residence for children who suddenly

---

5. The quotation is from J. T. Shotwell's letter to my father dated April 18, 1939, which I have in my personal files.
6. The quotation is from Edward C. Tolman's letter to me dated May 15, 1939, which I have in my personal files.

became dependent because of family crises. I was there, however, for only a few months, for in the early spring of 1942 I got *my* call to go overseas. The call came from the Institute of Child Study. Blatz had been asked by the British government to recruit a team, which would go to England to help with the emergency training of teachers for wartime day nurseries (Blatz 1943).

Six of us went to Birmingham late that spring. They were Blatz, three of his senior staff, Dorothy Millichamp, the assistant director of the institute, Margaret Fletcher, and Anne Harris (later Blatz), and two juniors. Mary McFarlane (later Smith) and I were the juniors. We immediately set about establishing a demonstration day nursery and a teacher-training center (the Garrison Lane Nursery Training School) in an ancient bombed-out primary school with incredibly few resources and opened it on July 1st (Dominion Day, Canada's birthday). Although at the time I did not know it, I was destined to work there for over two years. Blatz and his senior colleagues returned to Canada at the end of the first summer, leaving me in charge of all student instruction and with the added burden of making several speeches here and there that Blatz was supposed to have delivered. It was all quite a challenge, but by the end of my time there, during which I taught wave upon wave of students courses in both nursery school theory and nursery practice and monitored the program so that it truly demonstrated what I was teaching, my identity as a child psychologist and an early childhood educator was firmly established. In addition, I had developed an abiding faith in the potential of preschool education for producing miracles in disadvantaged children, which were the kind of children that we served.

At this time the early results of Beth Wellman's work with underprivileged preschool-aged children at Iowa had been reported (Wellman and Pegram 1944) and her claim that I.Q. was environmentally, rather than genetically, determined was being hotly debated. We therefore decided to assess the effects of our day nursery on the I.Q.'s of our young charges and I was assigned the task of testing them, using the Stanford Binet, every six months. We obtained results similar to those of Wellman. The I.Q.s of almost all of the children tested increased, in some cases as many as twenty I.Q. points (Blatz 1944:254). Unlike Wellman, our group assumed that the children had always had the genetic potential reflected in their higher scores, but suggested that their nursery school experience had been necessary to instill in them the motivation and to help them acquire the learning styles necessary to realize that potential. For me, although the causes of the changes in the children, in both their intellectual and social skills were debatable, I was deeply impressed by them.

In the fall of 1944 when I returned to Canada, it was too late to go back to school. I therefore obtained a job as psychologist at the mental health clinic in Hamilton for a year. However, in the academic year 1945–46 I returned to Toronto, accepted a part-time job as lecturer at the institute and completed all of the requirements I still had to meet for the doctorate, except, of course, the thesis.

By the spring of 1946 the war in Europe had drawn to a close and life in Canada was returning to normal. Jobs for psychologists were now plentiful and qualified psychologists were few. As a result I was seduced back to my alma mater, Western, to a faculty appointment, at the assistant professor level, even though I did not, as yet, have the Ph.D. There I have remained ever since, having produced a thesis and obtained my Ph.D.—finally—in 1949.

To produce the thesis while carrying the responsibilities of a full-time teacher was not easy, especially because I was forced to abandon my earlier plans to study the development of musical abilities in preschool-aged children. It took me three years to do it: the first to draft a new proposal, have it accepted at Toronto, and obtain permission to gather data in the London secondary schools; the second to collect the data; and the third to write the thesis, have it evaluated, and take the required examinations. During both the summers of 1947 and 1948 I taught summer school at the Ontario College of Education at the University of Toronto so that I could afford to live in Toronto and work on my thesis there where I hoped to obtain some help. However, I received only moral support and no real assistance from either my official advisor, William Line, or any of the members of my advisory committee. It was, therefore, with much trepidation that I submitted the thesis and with much relief that I learned that it had been accepted. It was a follow-up study of intellectually gifted children who had attended (or had not attended) advancement classes, the subject of much controversy at the time, in London.

In Canadian universities the late 1940s and early 1950s were hectic years. Returning veterans were encouraged to go back to school to ease their reintegration into society, and enabled to do so by generous Federal grants. As a result, they swarmed into degree programs in huge numbers, greatly taxing the universities' meager pre-War resources, which had not been expanded. All of us on the front line taught four or five courses and supervised sometimes as many as four or five theses each year. We also taught extension and summer-school classes to make ends meet, for our salaries were low. There was, as a result, no time for serious research, but even if such time had been found, funds for psychological research in Canada were extremely limited. Soon after the war, the Canadian Psychological Association had been successful in persuading the National Research Council and the Defense Research Board to allocate funds for experimental research, and the Department of Health and Welfare to provide funds for mental health research (Wright 1974a), but until the late 1960s there was no Canadian money for research in child and social psychology, the kind of research which was of interest to me. So, during the 1950s I spent my youthful extra energy and time in community service, on boards of agencies like the Family Service Bureau, as a consultant for the Children's Aid Society, in training would-be parent educators, and giving speeches to countless associations, mostly of parents or teachers.

It was not that I had not tried to obtain the kind of research facilities I wanted. In 1947, when my doctorate was in sight, I wrote my first brief recommending the establishment at Western of a child study center. I even got approval of funds from Federal sources to support such a center for a five-year period. Those funds were, however, blocked, at either the provincial or university level (I never found out which), presumably because the risk of being left with funding responsibilities after the five-year period was one which some authority did not want to take.

In the 1960s I turned to administration, and dropped most of my service-oriented activities, when I was made head of the psychology department. The appointment of a woman to the chair of a major academic department was a "first" at Western and, in fact, a "first" in Canada, but this appointment was not made before my ability to do the job had been pretested. In the late 1950s Western's president railroaded through an unpopular scheme which called for the establishment at Western of at least two new arts and social science colleges, in addition to University College, in lieu of expanding the latter. The alleged reason for this was to keep classes small when the products of the postwar baby boom, who were expected to flood the campus in the 1960s, arrived. The first of the new colleges was opened in 1960 and six new departments were established there. Psychology was one of these. Its faculty consisted of half of the staff in psychology in University College, who were simply transferred to new quarters. I started off as the chair of this new department with a three-year appointment. Perhaps I should say that I did have one qualm about taking on this post. I was concerned lest, being a woman, I might have difficulty recruiting high quality male staff. It is noteworthy that the senior administrators of the university with whom I discussed this concern did not share it and I am happy to report that it did turn out, as far as I can tell, to have been unfounded.

In the 1950s psychology at Western had not, for a variety of reasons, prospered. On the eve of the 1960s, which was to be a period of rapid university expansion, it needed everything—laboratory space, equipment, and above all high quality research staff. At this time, Canada was dismayed to discover how miniscule its supply of young people who were qualified for academic posts actually was, and how many had to be recruited from non-Canadian sources. Ontario in particular, therefore, made haste to rectify this situation by mounting several new graduate programs. Since Western was one of Ontario's oldest and largest universities it was expected to play a major role in this endeavour.

In 1959 as chairman-designate of the new department, I immediately wrote the first of many briefs to the university explaining what must be done if Western was to produce a first-rate modern graduate department of psychology. It was an aggressive approach, which I took with some misgivings, for I thought this might be considered "unbecoming" in a woman. However, to my great relief it seemed, in at least most quarters, to be welcome and within two years the new college had at least some new properly designed laboratories, some modern equipment, and authority to hire new senior, as well as junior, staff. Also during this period the decision was made to reunite the old and the new departments of psychology under one roof and one head, and I was made that head. This time my appointment was a permanent one (unheard of in most places these days, but common enough at that time for men). In 1962 I had also been promoted to full professor.

I did not stay chairman forever. I resigned after ten years, but during those ten years we brought the department out of obscurity and made it one of the top four in Canada. It was not, however, an easy task. The biggest problem was a lack of sufficient and adequate space for laboratory research. Because my predecessor was a humanist and had no interest in developing a scientifically-oriented department, he had failed to request such space when asked, in the 1950s, to project the needs of the department into the 1960s. Therefore, when I became the department's head, the university had established its priorities and developed its plans for expansion, and these included nothing for psychology beyond additional office space. Also, psychology as a science was still regarded at Western with skepticism and its need for laboratory space with suspicion.

Even though I myself had applied interests, I was convinced that psychology had been indulging in premature professionalism. I concurred with the post-World War II movement in psychology toward a return from the field to the research enterprise until a more adequate base for the profession had been established. Furthermore, I knew that if a strong graduate program was to be launched it was essential to recruit a research-oriented faculty of high quality. But how could high quality researchers be attracted if we could not provide them with the facilities they needed? I should say here that my thinking at this time was greatly influenced by my friend Donald O. Hebb, the head of the department at McGill, from whom I had sought advice on how to go about developing a strong department. I had come to know Don personally through encounters at meetings of the Canadian Psychological Association and at the Opinican Conference on training for research in psychology which was held in Ontario in 1960 (Bernhardt 1961). Don told me that if the department was to thrive it must first earn the respect of the "hard" scientists in the university and this could be done only by demonstrating that psychology did "hard" science, basic research. He pointed out that once this was accomplished support for all aspects of psychology would be forthcoming. To act on Hebb's advice was, however, my greatest challenge because it required obtaining the kind of expensive laboratory facilities which, until the mid-sixties, the university was unable or unwilling to provide. A beginning in physiological psychology was, however, finally made by forming a liaison with the physiology department which loaned us space. This made possible the appointment of Gordon Mogenson, who joined the staff in 1965. Mogenson was highly regarded by the head of physiology, James Stevenson. Stevenson was an influential person on campus and his admiration for Mogenson and his work did much to gain for psychology the kind of respect that Hebb said it required. By 1967 strenuous efforts were finally made by the university to provide the department, on an emergency basis, with the specialized facilities it needed and shortly thereafter plans for a new building which would adequately house the department were made.

Mogenson was not, however, the only person who played an important role in changing psychology's image at Western. During the early 1960's, in spite of our makeshift facilities, some excellent appointments were made. These included A. U. Paivio, who was beginning to do the kind of research on cognition which has earned him international acclaim, D. N. Jackson, and others who were highly productive scientists. The research funds obtained by them from non-university sources had been tripling annually. The number of publications they were producing was growing rapidly and the number and quality of the graduate students they were attracting was increasing by leaps and bounds.

In building the department, a number of other battles were fought, among them nepotism rules. Ours was one of the first departments in the university to obtain permission to hire husband-and-wife teams, and in the late 1960s we appointed three of them. Notable among the women we were able to attract because of this was Doreen Kimura, a physiological psychologist who has attained a high degree of eminence.

In the 1970s a number of attempts were made to compare the quality of psychology departments in the United States, the United Kingdom, and Canada using, among other criteria, citation counts. One of these was done by Endler, Rushton, and Roediger (1978). Most of the eminent psychologists who account for the high citation counts reported for our department by these investigators were recruited during the 1960s.

Finally, I would like to acknowledge the advice and help I received from C. Roger Myers, the chairman of the department at the University of Toronto, in developing the department. He early became interested in the potential of citation counts for identifying young psychologists of promise (Myers 1970) before they had been noticed by others and snapped up in the fierce competition to acquire high quality staff of that era. He shared his citation counts with me and we often cooperated in our recruiting efforts. He also persuaded me to attend the American Psychological Association's chairmen's meetings at which I learned a great deal about running a department, and he introduced me to many people there. He also looked at some of my many briefs to my university's administration and said they were not brief enough and he advised me in many other ways. The help I got from both Roger Myers and Don Hebb led me to think that young women may have an advantage over young men when they are called upon to do the kind of job I had. There are certainly at least *some* gallant senior men, who have themselves arrived, who seem delighted to give a "gal" a hand up.

In 1967 I was elected president of the Canadian Psychological Association (CPA), the first woman to be elected to that post. The success of the department was no doubt a factor which influenced the vote. However, I had been active in CPA almost from its inception in 1939 and had served on its Board of Directors, as well as on a multitude of its committees. I had also been president of the Ontario Psychological Association in the early fifties. Regarding "firsts" I was also, in the early 1970s, the first woman to chair the Ontario Board of Examiners in Psychology.

Finally, we come full circle to my last ten years, the return to my early interests in compensatory education, and my chance, at last, to do some worthwhile research. Some twenty years after my first try I finally did succeed in getting a laboratory preschool established at Western. When, in the late 1960s, we planned our third and final set of new laboratories for psychology, it was decided that one floor of our new nine-story laboratory tower would be devoted to child development research and provide facilities for a preschool. Thus I got a chance to design my "dream" school and, incidentally, the design worked.

In 1970–71 I used my sabbatical year to brush up on what was new in early childhood education. In 1972 psychology moved into its new quarters, I was made director of the Laboratory Preschool, began to recruit a staff, and in 1973 we opened this facility.

Grants from a private foundation enabled us to enroll children from low-income families, along with children from more affluent families who paid fees. Generous research grants from the Ontario Ministry of Community and Social Services supported my research, which included studies of the long-range effects of the program we developed on the low-income children after they were in the primary grades. These grants also made it possible to conduct some basic research on the development and measurement of social competence, the results of which were published last year (Wright 1980a). I was forced to develop a measure of social competence because no satisfactory one was available and I wanted to assess the effects of our program on the children's social skills. To identify positive indicators of social competence we conducted, over a five-year period, a four-phase study which involved more than one hundred three-and four-year olds and examined correlates of the frequency, quality, and effectiveness of various types of initiated and respondent behavior which they displayed in social interaction situations. We found that the only effective discriminator of competence was the successfulness of child-child social influence attempts and developed a measure of social competence based on these findings. Scores on this measure, which was a measure of social influence effectiveness, were positively related to cognitive competence in a variety of problem-solving situations and, as well, to affective and cognitive perspective-taking ability.

The results of our efforts at compensatory education were very encouraging. On the assumption that children from low-income families do not receive sufficient cognitive stimulation at the three- to five-year-old level, when they are making the transition from a stage in which they can deal only with the concrete to one in which they can deal with the more abstract such as representations and ideas, the program was cognitively oriented. We developed assessment and curriculum guides to determine the cognitive levels of each child and to plan individual mind-stretching experiences for each one. The program was, however, an active discovery one, in which direct instruction was avoided.

Our results indicated that the program had positive immediate effects on both the low- and the high-income children who were enrolled in it. Their I.Q.s, cognitive styles and strategies, and social abilities improved significantly (Wright 1980b). More important, however, were its long-term effects on the low-income children. These children were followed up in the primary grades, all of them until the end of first grade, about three-quarters to the end of second grade, and a quarter to the end of third grade. At these levels there was no decline in their Binet I.Q.s and they continued to make cognitive gains in kindergarten which they also maintained. Their academic achievements were superior to the control group of children, without any preschool experience, with which they were compared. The failure rate was three times greater in the control than in the preschool-graduate group (Wright 1981). Suffice it to say that these results have done nothing to shake my faith, developed during the war years in Birmingham, in the potential of early education to produce miracles in disadvantaged youngsters.[7]

Finally, it has been suggested that I should comment on whether or not I ever considered marriage. The answer is, of course, yes!—on more than one occasion. When I was in high school and university I had lots of boy-friends, loved to dance (I still do), and went out as much and considerably more than many of my girlfriends. As they tell me now, they considered me inevitably destined for matrimony, but I never could bring myself to take that fateful step and it is very difficult for me to say why. I have a number of theories, but all of them may be wrong.

First, I tended to find older men (my brothers' age) more interesting than those my own age. So I liked my contemporaries among the male sex, but tended not to think of them very seriously as mates. Second, I had very high standards for the father of my children. I wanted him to have the kind of values which I had acquired in my own home, such as integrity, respect for others (all others, including minority groups), and social responsibility, and I wanted him to be at least as capable as myself. Unfortunately, the men with whom I fell in love and who sought my hand in marriage just never measured up. I maintained a relationship with one man for six years, hoping that I could finally make up my mind to marry him. What finally ended this was that he informed me in 1940 that *he* was not going to be silly enough to get involved in any war, even the one against Hitler. This I found incomprehensible.

The independence I had acquired as a child may also have been a factor. This certainly helped me to choose against marriage when all my friends were matrimony-bound. I know that I was reluctant to lose my identity. I was also anxious about putting my fate in someone else's hands. In those days women could not, as they can today, count on pursuing a career and

7. Further information about the U.W.O. Preschool Project may be obtained from the Educational Resources Information Center (ERIC) Clearinghouse on Elementary and Early Childhood Education, University of Illinois, Urbana, Illinois 61801. Abstracts of the Research Bulletins on the project available from ERIC were published in *Resources in Education*, ERIC's monthly abstract journal, March 1979 #161555; April 1979 #162736; June 1979 #165871; December 1980 #190235.

retaining their own family name in that career, along with their marriage. A clear choice had to be made. In middle-class society it was a disgrace for a husband to let his wife work, suggesting that he either could not or would not provide for her. During the depression women who worked were considered unethical for holding a job which should be made available to a man, presumably the breadwinner of some family. These were the views with which I was surrounded. Even my mother, who had seen to it that I obtained an education, thought of it as something on which I could "fall back" if my husband died. Thus, had I married I would have felt duty bound to devote myself to my husband and family and I realized that I could not make a success of that unless my husband was the "right" kind of person for me.

I have not missed entirely the pleasures and problems of child rearing, for I have twelve nieces and nephews and eighteen grandnieces and nephews in my large extended family, nor have I been doomed to a life bereft of male companionship. So, as I look back, I have no regrets, knowing that under the same circumstances that surrounded me at each choice point, I would have made the same decisions. In addition, I realize that, although I may have missed some of life's highest peaks of fulfillment, I may also have been spared some of its deepest sorrows.

REFERENCES

Bernhardt, K. S. 1961. *Training for Research in Psychology: The Canadian Opinican Conference 1960*. Toronto: University of Toronto Press.

Blatz, W. E. 1943. Child care in wartime England. *Bulletin of the Canadian Psychological Association*, 3:24–26.

—— 1944. *Understanding the Young Child*. Bickley, Kent: University of London Press.

Endler, N. S., J. P. Rushton, and H. L. Roediger III. 1978. Productivity and scholarly impact (citations) of British, Canadian, and U.S. Departments of Psychology (1975). *American Psychologist*, 33:1064–82.

Myers, C. R. 1970. Journal citations and scientific eminence in contemporary psychology. *American Psychologist*, 25:1041–48.

O'Donnell, J. M. 1979. The crisis of experimentalism in the 1920's: E. G. Boring and his uses of history. *American Psychologist*. 34:289–95.

Wellman, B. L. and E. L. Pegram. 1944. Binet IQ changes of orphanage preschool children: A re-analysis. *Journal of Genetic Psychology*, 65:239–63.

Wright, Mary J. *See* Representative Publications.

Representative Publications by Mary J. Wright

1969. Canadian psychology comes of age. *Canadian Psychologist*, 10:229–53.

1971. The psychological organizations of Canada. *Canadian Psychologist*, 12:420–31.

1973. Recent trends in early childhood education in the U.S.A. and Canada. In L. M. Brockman, J. H. Whiteley, and J. P. Zubek, eds., *Child Development: Selected Readings*. Toronto: McClelland and Stewart.

1974a. CPA: The first ten years. *Canadian Psychologist*, 15:112–31.

1974b. Should we rediscover Blatz? *Canadian Psychologist*, 15:140–44.

1975. Changes in the social competence of Canadian preschool and day nursery children of low and high socio-economic status. *Interchange*, 6:16–26.

1977. Research with the children of the poor. *Ontario Psychologist*, 9:6–10.

1980a. Measuring the social competence of preschool children. *Canadian Journal of Behavioral Science*, 12:17–32.

1980b. Compensatory education for preschoolers. A non-technical report on the U.W.O. Preschool Project. *Canadian Journal of Early Childhood Education*, 1:3–15.

1981. Compensatory education for preschoolers: More on the U.W.O. Preschool Project. *Canadian Journal of Early Childhood Education*, 1:15–21.

1982. Ed. With C. Roger Myers. *History of Academic Psychology in Canada*. Toronto: C. J. Hogrefe.

1983. Compensatory education in the preschool: A Canadian approach. The University of Western Ontario Preschool Project. *Monographs of the High/Scope Educational Research Foundation*, Ypsilanti, Michigan.

MAMIE PHIPPS CLARK

My participation as a black woman in the professional field of psychology has been thirty-six years of a most rewarding and fulfilling career.

Fortunately for me, elementary and secondary education—although taking place in a small segregated southern town and although (as I later realized) deficient in substantive areas—was stimulating and entirely enjoyable. In retrospect this, together with the security of a warm and protective extended family, appears to have been the near ideal background for later career satisfaction.

High school was completed toward the end of the Great Depression, which had almost dimmed hopes of going to college at all. However, my parents were undaunted in their efforts to send their two children to college, and this challenge strengthened family ties even more. It was also helpful that in those years college scholarships were available, based on merit as well as need.

In 1934, a southern Negro aspiring to enter an academic college had relatively few choices, as it was rare indeed to gain admittance to the Ivy League schools in the north and was absolutely prohibited to be accepted in larger southern universities. The "elitist" choices for blacks at that time were Fisk University in Nashville, Tennessee, and Howard University in Washington, D.C. Both schools offered scholarships on merit, but there was more excitement about attending college in the nation's capitol and traveling over one thousand miles to study!

The first year at Howard University was spent taking courses toward a major in mathematics and a minor in physics, in addition to trying to make up some deficiencies in elementary English and foreign languages.

At that time, many of the great teachers—Negroes not yet accepted into the major white educational institutions—were at Howard University: Alain Locke in philosophy; E. Franklin Frazier in sociology; Ralph Bunche in political science, Benjamin Brawley and Sterling Brown in English and literature; Francis C. Sumner in psychology; and many others who served as role models of academic excellence.

The wealth of exciting educational paths to take, juxtaposed against the detached and impersonal approach of the mathematics teachers (and I believe particularly toward female students) caused me to take stock of my educational goals.

My entrance into the professional discipline of psychology came about through a close association with my future husband, Kenneth Clark. Having become disenchanted with becoming a teacher of mathematics, I listened when he said one day "Why don't you take up psychology? . . . I find it extremely stimulating, the field has good job opportunities and fits in with your interest in children." This was prophetic.

He introduced me to Dr. Francis Sumner, head of the psychology department, and to Dr. Max Meenes with whom I would later do research. They were warm, friendly, and eager to have me in their courses. Shortly thereafter it was arranged that my scholarship allotment would go toward part-time work in the psychology department. Kenneth Clark was delighted. At that time neither one of us realized that in entering the field of psychology we would enjoy a lifetime of close, challenging, and professionally satisfying experiences.

In the security of the almost completely segregated student body at Howard University, it did not occur to me to ask such questions as: "How will a Negro woman fare in the nearly all white male field of psychology? How will a female psychologist manage to satisfy an interest in working with children in a northern society mainly offering services to white children"? In 1934 we were twenty years away from the Supreme Court's 1954 decision in the *Brown* case. Washington, D.C., was still a rigidly segregated city. There were no Negro women on the psychology staff at Howard University. Perhaps the almost total absence of Negro females with advanced degrees in psychology at Howard University was in itself a "silent" challenge.

Immediately following graduation from college, there was a summer job experience which remains in my mind as an enormously instructive and revealing one in relation to my own identity as a "Negro." Through Howard University I was placed as a secretary in the law office of William Houston. This office was the veritable "hub" of early planning for the civil rights cases which challenged the laws requiring or permitting racial segregation. This opportunity to learn, not only about the plan for the eventual repeal of the *Plessy v. Ferguson* case, but also to observe firsthand the "giants" who were preparing these cases, made a deep impression on me. Frequently there would be much excitement in the office when the Washington-based lawyers would be joined by William Hastie, Thurgood Marshall, and others from the original group of legal activists.

While working on the master's degree at Howard University, my interest in developmental psychology became intensified. A visit to an all-black nursery school in Washington, D.C., resulted in an offer to work with the children while preparing the research necessary for the master's degree. I hesitated to accept this offer with only a vague desire to find out how these children "grew."

By this time Kenneth Clark and I were married, and it was my husband who suggested that I go to New York and talk to Ruth and Gene Horowitz (now Ruth and Gene Hartley) as they were doing some fascinating developmental studies with preschool children (Horowitz 1939). The Hartleys were indeed engaged in studying self-identification in nursery school children, using line drawings of white and Negro children. Further discussion with the Hartleys determined that there was a need to expand on their studies and to involve many more Negro children in the sample. These discussions, along with access to Negro children in the Washington, D.C., nursery school, led to research culminating in my master's thesis entitled "The Development of Consciousness of Self in Negro Pre-school Children" (Clark 1939a).

This research experience was particularly challenging because it opened up new avenues of search for knowledge of self-identification in children. It also became clear that the research tools could be varied in order to broaden the findings. My husband, Kenneth Clark, shared my interest and excitement in this research, and together we published articles (1939b, 1939c, 1940) and also prepared a proposal for further and expanded research on racial identification in Negro children. In this proposal we developed the newer methods of a coloring test and the doll's test. The proposal was submitted to the Julius Rosenwald Fellowship program in 1939. We were awarded a Rosenwald Fellowship in 1940 with renewals in the second and third years. This made it possible for me to enter Columbia University to study for my Ph.D. degree and for Kenneth and me to continue our research. While my husband gathered research data in selected northern and southern states, I completed the first year toward the doctoral degree at Columbia University and took care of our first child, Kate, who was born in 1940.

Studying in the psychology department at Columbia University was again a most satisfying experience. At that time, such giants as Robert S. Woodworth, Otto Klineberg, Carl Warden, A. T. Poffenberger, and others were on the faculty and generated a high degree of excitement. Gardner Murphy, the husband of Lois Murphy, was on the faculty of Columbia University but had left the department just before I enrolled. However, my husband had studied with him and enjoyed his friendship, and this led to a long association with them. Professor Gardner Murphy gave helpful suggestions and criticisms for my Ph.D. study and is acknowledged in the report (Clark 1944).

Ph.D. students in the small graduate classes at Columbia University were all most amiable and supportive of one another. Although there were no women on the graduate faculty in psychology at Columbia University at that time, there were two other women in our graduate class. However, for the first time in my life, I was the sole black student in a graduate department where the faculty members and all the other students were white. (My husband, Kenneth, had received his Ph.D. degree that year I was admitted.) This did not pose a problem for me; in retrospect I never anticipated that it would. An interesting fact about the Columbia University experience is that, to the best of our knowledge, my husband was the first black graduate student to earn a Ph.D. in the psychology department there (in 1940) and in 1943 I was the second and last. It is difficult to understand why this is so in the light of the Civil Rights progress which has taken place in educational institutions and the society as a whole during the past four decades.

At Columbia University, Dr. Henry E. Garrett was my sponsoring professor. He guided me through my Ph.D. research on the development of primary mental abilities with age (Clark 1944). This research was conducted with children in the New York City public schools. When I was nearing graduation, Dr. Garrett, not by any means a liberal on racial matters, stated to me "you are, of course, going back home to teach." It always amused me that he saw my advanced training in psychology as preparation for a career of teaching black high school students in the south. Some years later my husband and I were to meet Henry Garrett in a federal courtroom where the school desegregation case regarding Prince Edward County in Virginia was being tried. We were testifying on opposite sides of the issue—Henry Garrett opposed the desegregation of public schools. He testified to the effect that black and white children had different talents and abilities which presumably justified segregated schools. That was the last time we saw him.

In 1943 I obtained the Ph.D. degree, the Rosenwald-sponsored research identity in Negro children was completed, and our second child, Hilton, was born. Kenneth and I were fortunate to have the results of the research published in several articles (1947, 1950). The major findings of this research were that Negro children become aware of their racial identity at about the age of three years; simultaneously, they acquire a negative self-image. Our findings established the fact that self-identification in these children was determined by the larger society's negative and rejecting definition of them. These studies generated a high degree of interest in the academic world and later were repeated and verified, particularly by the psychologist Mary Ellen Goodman (Goodman 1946, 1952).

The results of our studies were cited in expert testimony which Kenneth Clark provided in the South Carolina and Delaware school desegregation trials and which he and I presented in the Virginia trial.

In 1953, under the leadership of Kenneth Clark, a prestigious group of social scientists prepared a social science brief which summarized the expert testimony and the major research findings on the effects of racial segregation. This brief was submitted to the United States Supreme Court by the NAACP lawyers as a supplement to their legal brief (see Clark 1955, pp. 166–184). The studies of negative self-image in Negro children were an important part of the brief and were alluded to in the 1954 Supreme Court decisions as follows:

To separate them from others of similar age and qualifications solely because of their race generates a feeling of inferiority as to their status in the community that may affect their hearts and minds in a way unlikely ever to be undone . . .

Although my husband had earlier secured a teaching position at the City College of New York, following my graduation it soon became apparent to me that a black female with a Ph.D. in psychology was an unwanted anomaly in New York City in the early 1940s. One of several disappointments in obtaining a satisfying professional position occurred at a major broadcasting company where psychologists were being recruited for research purposes. It was heartbreaking to learn that a number of white men and women with far less qualifications were hired at relatively high salaries. When I applied for a similar position, I was rejected without explanation. Much later, as a member of the Board of Trustees of a major broadcasting company, I could look back on this rejecting with wry amusement.

Finally, through a professor at the City College, I secured a position in a small agency which used psychologists to analyze research data being gathered on nurses throughout the country. The only other person on the staff with a Ph.D. in psychology was the female director of the office. Needless to say, I was the only black person there. It was a humiliating and distasteful first employment experience, but I stayed for one year to gain the benefit of experience in this type of psychological research. Recognizing my career unhappiness, my husband gave me much support and encouragement. Two small and delightful children were also a major part of a strong support system.

Within a year of this experience, I resigned from that position. We were then in World War II and I was able, because of research then being done on behalf of the armed forces, to secure a second position as a research psychologist. This position was a fairly satisfying, but I likened it to a "holding pattern."

A career milestone occurred when we learned of an opening for a female psychologist to perform psychological tests at a private agency for the protection of black, homeless girls—the Riverdale Home for Children. This work experience, in association with psychiatrists, psychiatric social workers, and psychologists, was extremely rewarding and enabled me to develop professionally. However, it also afforded new insights into the enormous lack of psychological services for black and minority children in New York City. There were almost no resources for referring these girls for the plethora of services, particularly mental health, which they needed.

In the early 1940s in New York City, psychological and psychiatric services were available to other children mainly through a network of well-established sectarian agencies. Minority children of Harlem generally did not have access to these programs at that time or, at the least, were not encouraged to apply. The need for such services was so great that my husband and I decided to try to persuade some social service in Harlem to include psychological services for minority children. Together we spent nearly a year of exploration with directors of existing social agencies in Harlem in an effort to persuade at least one of them to include a program of psychological services for black children. We offered to provide the psychological testing and consultation services. One of the oldest and most prestigious social agencies in New York City, which had a branch in Central Harlem, insisted that such services were not needed as that agency was already providing them. This was patently not true. Another branch of a national agency serving blacks was not interested in providing psychological services, seeing them as not being relevant to black children. Churches were completely unresponsive. These reactions on the part of the existing agencies were so frustrating that my husband and I finally made the decision to establish the services ourselves.

We then approached and discussed the problem with a group of friends who were psychologists, psychiatrists, and social workers. In spite of the fact that they were all employed full time, their enthusiasm for opening a new agency to offer psychological services to emotionally disturbed children in the Harlem area was great and all offered to volunteer their own time if we decided to go ahead. This encouraged us very much. We were also encouraged by my family, who provided the funds necessary to cover the cost of furnishing the basement space which we had found for the new center.

Thus, in March of 1946 the Northside Center for Child Development (originally named the Northside Testing and Consultation Center) was founded. At that time it was the first full-time child guidance center offering psychiatric, psychological, and casework services to children and families in the Harlem area. Our friends—psychiatrists and social workers—volunteered enough time (together with our own) to maintain daily services.

In the mid 1940s, the climate of acceptance of any psychiatric or psychological program in the Harlem community was very poor. Many families felt that such services would place a stigma on their children; they did not want to have their children called "crazy." This attitude reflected the prevailing tendency of the larger society to reject the concept of emotional disturbance.

At about this time the movie *Snake Pit* began to have enormous impact in attitudes toward the mentally ill throughout the United States. Most important, too, was the impact of the Roosevelt Administration's awareness of needs of people on all levels, and the federal advocacy of social programs resulting in attention to health and mental health needs of families. Actually, a breakthrough in the Harlem community's acceptance of the new psychological services center came shortly after it was founded. This breakthrough came about because of the acute frustrations of parents with children in the public schools. A group of parents of children who were being incorrectly placed in New York City public school classes for the mentally retarded, known then as Classes for Children of Retarded Mental Development (CRDM), came to our Center for help with the problem. These parents were disturbed because their children, often without parental permission, were being shifted to CRMD classes and thereby stigmatized. Following psychological testing we found that most of the children were in fact above the intelligence level for placement in CRMD classes (I.Q. 70) and that these actions on the part of public school personnel were illegal and indefensible. Moreover, this problem was rampant in those schools located in minority and deprived areas.

As a result of word-of-mouth promotion and considerable newspaper publicity, a larger number of parents brought their children to Northside Center for psychological testing, and most of these children were subsequently able to return to normal classes. Following this effective help to many children and their parents, Northside Center's psychological and psychiatric services received greater acceptance by the community and became well-known. The

Center's staff had thus, in its first months of service, taken on an activist and advocacy role on behalf of disadvantaged children. This active advocacy approach persisted and was intensified over the years, up to the present.

This experience with many children who were thought to be mentally retarded also highlighted a high degree of educational retardation which was either not being recognized or corrected in the public schools. Thus, within the first year of Northside Center's existence, there was established a remedial reading and arithmetic program to supplement the psychiatric and psychological services. Many times educational remediation was the treatment of choice. The introduction of an educational component in a child guidance center such as ours was an innovation for mental health clinics in 1946.

Within the first decade of its existence, the staff of Northside Center made a significant contribution in the area of psychiatric and psychological services to children. Northside Center was able to establish and function in terms of a basic set of assumptions which appear to be most relevant. They are as follows:

Most, if not all, of the presenting problems of our children are symptomatic of the overwhelming pressures of ghetto existence and family disorganization.

The common denominator which runs through the depressed social, emotional, and educational functioning of our children is a lack of self-esteem, a feeling of worthlessness, a feeling of alienation, and an impaired self-image.

The problems of our children are neither purely psychiatric, purely social, nor purely environmental; they are psycho-social.

The traditional orthodox psychoanalytically-oriented psychiatric treatment is not necessarily the most effective way of helping families whose massive problems are associated with living in a ghetto.

The traditional clinic team approach, which assumes a coordinated clinical effort to help children, seems of limited effectiveness in helping them and their families.

Today, with the conceptual frame of reference, we envision ourselves a family-oriented child guidance center offering an umbrella of services to emotionally troubled children, their parents, and, in many cases, their siblings as well. A professional staff of psychiatrists, psychologists, social workers, remedial therapists, special education teachers, a pediatrician, a neurologist, a nurse, and a children's librarian offer these therapeutic services. The professional staff is assisted by paraprofessionals, students-in-training, foster grandparents, and many volunteers. Our children come by appointment for psychiatric therapy, psychological diagnosis and counseling, social work treatment, "think" workshops, and therapeutic remedial education. Other children are helped in our therapeutic day school. In addition, recreational and cultural activities are available to the children as indicated. (Clark 1970)

One other development growing out of the Northside Center experience must be included as it has some bearing on the role of a child guidance agency in the community and the role of a black woman in a black and Hispanic community. In the 1960s the Northside Center staff, together with other community-minded individuals, provided leadership in developing new housing in a deteriorated area at the juncture of the black and Hispanic communities in lower Harlem. The philosophy behind this effort was to extend the advocacy role to low- and middle-income minority families by providing decent housing. It was also intended to extend the concept of helping to ameliorate the psycho-social problems which burden families in Harlem and East Harlem by including a social service component in that housing—namely, the Northside Center. Moreover, it was felt that if the outer boundaries of a deteriorating Harlem could be improved with new housing, that would then generate a domino effect, removing the blight progressively into the center of the ghetto.

Although we did not succeed in managing a housing renaissance in Harlem, we did, with help, achieve construction of the Shomburg Plaza, a 600-family housing unit at the Gateway to Harlem (Fifth Avenue and 110th Street). This is also the present home of the Northside Center for Child Development.

I have been asked: "Based on your experience, how do you perceive the status of women in psychology in regard to future projections and needs?" I would like to respond very briefly, based solely on my experience in New York City. In the field of mental health, particularly in relation to children, psychologists—both women and men—have not yet made their maximum contribution. For nearly three decades psychologists with advanced training have been flooding the area of clinical psychology and attempting to be competitive with psychiatrists, both professionally and monetarily. Indeed, the membership of the American Psychological Association is now quite dominated by clinical psychologists (42 percent).

This flight into the field of clinical psychology has been at the expense of urgently needed research into the effective treatment of emotional disturbance in children and, most importantly, the *prevention* of emotional disturbance in children. Unless this trend away from theoretical and research psychology is slowed, I believe that children, and most particularly minority children, will suffer. Indeed, the flow of federal and private foundation funds for research into issues of child mental health will decrease in exact relationship to the lessening of an advocacy role for these children. We will hope that a steady flow of younger psychologists—male and female—into the field will bring more responsiveness to the need for psychological research in general, and research oriented toward prevention of emotional illness in particular. It is also hoped that some future Administration will be more serious about a National Commission on Mental Health and that widespread concern about children will generate effective mechanisms to grant them their inalienable rights to a constructive role in society—the basis of self-esteem.

REFERENCES

Clark, K. B. 1955. *Prejudice and Your Child*. Boston: Beacon Press.

Clark, M. P. *See* Representative Publications.

Goodman, M. E. 1946. Evidence concerning the genesis of interracial attitudes, *American Anthropologist*, 48:624–30.

—— 1952. *Race Awareness in Young Children*. Cambridge: Addison-Wesley.

Horowitz, R. E. 1939. Racial aspects of self-identification in nursery school children. *Journal of Psychology*, 7:91–99.

Representative Publications by Mamie Phipps Clark

1939a. The development of consciousness of self in Negro pre-school children. *Archives of Psychology*. Washington, D. C.: Howard University.

1939b. With K. B. Clark. The development of consciousness of self and the emergence of racial identification in Negro pre-school children. *Journal of Social Psychology*, 10:591–99.

1939c. With K. B. Clark. Segregation as a factor in the racial identification of Negro pre-school children. *Journal of Experimental Education*, 8:161–65.

1940. With K. B. Clark. Skin color as a factor in racial identification of Negro pre-school children. *Journal of Social Psychology*, 11:159–69.

1944. Changes in primary mental abilities with age. *Archives of Psychology*, no. 291. New York: Columbia Universiy.

1947. With K. B. Clark. Racial identification and preference in Negro children. In T. M. Newcomb and E. L. Hartley, eds., *Readings in Social Psychology*. New York: Holt.

1950. With K. B. Clark. Emotional factors in racial identification and preference in Negro children. *Journal of Negro Education*, 19:341–50.

1961. With J. Karp. A report on a summer remedial program. *Elementary School Journal* (January).

1970. Changing conepts in mental health, a thirty-year view. *Conference Proceedings, Thirtieth Anniversary Conference*. May 7. New York: Northside Center for Child Development.

1980. With K. B. Clark. What do blacks think of themselves? *Ebony* (November), p. 170.

CAROLYN WOOD SHERIF

Why would anyone be interested in my autobiographical account? That question immobilized me in a classic "writer's block." Then, I started to think of how few of the women who entered graduate school when I did, during World War II, are active psychologists today and how few wanted to be social psychologists, even then. With the requisite immodesty, I began to view myself as a "survivor" whose life experiences may be of interest in the following two ways:

1. They represent a rather unusual "mixed model" for career and family involvements. I completed a master's degree in psychology at the University of Iowa in 1944 at the age of twenty-two, worked in survey research for a year, then headed toward a Ph.D. and directly into marriage, which we viewed as both a love and working partnership in social psychology from the beginning. Muzafer Sherif hired me as a research assistant at Princeton, which did not accept women, even in graduate school. After marrying, I enrolled in Columbia for one semester. For the next sixteen years, I was involved in research and writing with Muzafer at Princeton, Yale, and Oklahoma universities. We had three daughters. I accumulated a crazy-quilt vita of research assistant- and associateships, co-authorship of several articles, and two books (Sherif and Sherif 1953, 1956). At age thirty-nine, I earned the Ph.D. at the University of Texas, after which my vita began to show regular academic appointments and senior authorships. At any one time, I was involved in many varied role relationships with different other people. Longitudinally, the ways the mixtures were defined and my status in different role relationships changed markedly over the years. At times, the mixture mixed up me.

2. My life experiences, cross-sectionally and longitudinally, make little sense apart from the larger events in which they transpired. I entered Purdue University in 1940 in the last gasps of the Great Depression and dawn of the United States entry into World War II. My return to graduate work and my marriage was in the year marking the war's end, and which was followed by veterans' return to graduate school and a limited academic marketplace,

then the baby boom (in which we participated within one standard error of the mean number of babies per couple). My Ph.D. in 1961 came as the tremendous growth in American universities and research funding was approaching its peak. Thus academia found room for me, at first on a temporary basis, but on tenure track by 1966 at Pennsylvania State University. I might have been tied to that track as associate professor indefinitely had not the resurgent women's movement changed the atmosphere. I was invited as visiting professor of psychology and sociology at Cornell (1969–70), the year our text *Social Psychology* (1969c) appeared. Pennsylvania State University promoted me to professor in 1970, and I began receiving salary equalization "adjustments" after 1972, when the U.S. Department of Health, Education and Welfare worried my university by investigating charges of discrimination against women faculty. To me, the atmosphere created by the women's movement was like breathing fresh air after years of gasping for breath. If anyone believes that I credit it too much for changes in my own life, I have only this reply: I know I did not become a significantly better social psychologist between 1969 and 1972, but I surely was treated as a better social psychologist.

The historical events and the mixtures in my life bear on opportunities and problems related to my being a woman. I never lacked opportunities for study and work within our marriage partnership, but opportunities external to it and related to being a woman are divided into the wartime period before I was twenty-four and the last decade, with two decades between when it seemed to me the world was saying "not interested." The earlier opportunities came from the aftereffects of earlier feminism in higher education, and from the undeniable irony that women are more chosen when men are involved in all-out war.

I grew up in Indiana with parents who expected that my older brother, sister, and I would excel academically from grade school on and graduate from college, which we did. I later learned that my father's salary was cut during the Depression years, when I was ten to eighteen years old, three times. My mother's dress and coat-making skills fitted my sister and me in the latest fashions, despite the Depression. As a supervisor for teacher training in agricultural education for Purdue University, as well as a high-school teacher of science, my father was located so that all three of us could attend Purdue, but could not have chosen to go elsewhere. Each of us got tuition refunds for making the "distinguished" academic list at the end of each semester, and worked part-time. At Purdue, I had part-time jobs at a bookstore, at the university radio station (scheduling recorded music), and at the Methodist Episcopal Church (contralto in a paid quartet).

My brother graduated in chemical engineering, and my sister in mathematics (while being homecoming and yearbook "beauty queens"), while I was attending West Lafayette Junior and Senior High Schools. During the last two high-school years, I had a weekly fifteen-minute radio show on WBAA, the university radio station, where I sang. Encouraged by Miss Ruth Sinks, a remarkable English teacher, I won three essay contests: One was sponsored by the Chamber of Commerce, the prize money securing my first, very own suitcase; the second by the Daughters of the American Revolution, which took me to Washington, D.C. for a week as Indiana's "first citizen"; the third by the *Chicago Tribune*, which took me to Chicago for a heady week as Indiana's "Citizen of Tomorrow." None carried scholarship money, so it was Purdue for me, too. At that time, that was "all right," as I was literally interested in almost everything, including science, which Purdue offered.

In my family, any ambitions that I might have were encouraged. I specifically recall being encouraged and instructed by my father and by my brother when I expressed some frustration in mathematics and chemistry courses, perhaps because those courses had seemed to come easily to my older brother and sister. The fruits of their efforts were A's in the courses. During the war, Purdue gave mathematics aptitude tests to its undergraduates, in the attempt to identify potential engineers to serve the war effort. To my astonishment, my score fell above the 99th percentile on the distribution of women's scores and above the 90th for men's. Since then, I have believed that women's generally lower achievement in mathematics must be related to the lack of encouragement of the kind I received at home and in the program at Purdue in which I enrolled.

My father once told me that he hoped I would become like Dr. Mary Ellen Mathews, then dean of Purdue's Home Economics School. I must confess that I was somewhat scornful of home economics and its nursery school education at that time. My mother devoted herself completely to her family and her home in considerable contrast to her mother who, despite a physician husband, had taught in high school until her death when I was seven, was state president of the Methodist Home Mission Society, and a feminist, as I later learned. I do not recall either parent discussing my eventual marriage, but it was doubtless expected, as college graduation, then marriage, was the pattern for both my brother and sister and most graduates before the war.

In 1940, I was accepted in the second class of an experimental program for women science majors at Purdue, which had earlier recruited as distinguished visiting faculty Amelia Earhart and Lillian Gilbreth (an industrial psychologist and mother in the book and movie *Cheaper by the Dozen*). Together, about one hundred highly selected women had eight semesters of science and mathematics courses designed by excellent faculty to encourage scientific careers, but also to study science within historical and humanist perspectives. A historian, Dr. Dorothy Babcock, directed the program, closely advising those of us who availed ourselves of her counsel. The program and Dr. Babcock had a great influence on me.

My other courses were chiefly history and literature. The world beyond Indiana began to open for me in a freshman composition course, when my instructor (Herbert Mueller, later a distinguished member of the faculty at Indiana University), encouraged my essays, but wrote marginal queries that simply had never occurred to me (e.g., "closely reasoned, but did it ever occur to you that some people do not believe in God?"). The writers whose works stimulated me as an undergraduate included G. B. Shaw, Isben, Chekhov, Tolstoy, Steinbeck, and Theodore Dreiser, a Hoosier. I had an extravagantly active extracurricular life in music, theater, and radio, regarding these activities as my natural bent. Introductory psychology seemed boring and unimportant to me. I would not have dreamed of taking a course with Harriet O'Shea (who unbeknown to me participated in women psychologists' activities during the war) because she was in nursery school education. The only other psychology course I remember was one on aesthetics, taught by Betty Lark-Horovitz, of whom I have fond memories with no content. How on earth did I ever become a social psychologist?

There is no question in my mind that I might have gone in any number of directions, including directly into marriage on graduation, had not the United States entered the war in my sophomore year. The rapid changes in attitudes from isolationism to war support, in life plans and actions amazed me. Coupled with my own wish to achieve, the urgent desire to do something toward a better world raised the questions that led me to social psychology. In my junior year, one of several one-act plays I had written was published by the U.S. Treasury Department for community use in War Bond drives. My science background led me to wonder what effects such plays might have on audiences. I took a statistics course with H. H. Remmers and spoke of that interest. He said that the question was researchable, in social psychology. My decision to study social psychology in graduate school was made that year, though I never had a course.

My applications to graduate school at Chicago, Iowa, and Wisconsin were accepted. It was wartime, and women were welcome. The University of Iowa offered an assistantship to Wendell Johnson, then director of the clinic, but the stipend was not enough. On a bet with a friend who belonged to

Kappa Kappa Gamma (a social sorority) I applied for their national graduate fellowship fully confident that it would not be given to a non-member. I lost the bet but won the fellowship. So I did not have to borrow money to go to Iowa, which I did in 1943, the month after receiving the B.S. with highest distinction, as a self-declared social psychology student.

My year at Iowa was enormously stimulating. Carl Seashore returned from retirement to the graduate school and registered me in person. I lived in a house for graduate women. Wendell Johnson had me assist in his courses, do library research for his book *People in Quandaries* (1944), and behaved as a benevolent father, leaving me free to choose courses and develop my own research. I was never interested in clinical psychology. The courses I remember were taught by Gustav Bergmann, Kenneth Spence, Claude Buxton, Robert Sears, a social psychologist named Norman Meyers who had been Gallup's teacher, and Marian Radke—a postdoctoral fellow with Kurt Lewin who was given major responsibility for his group dynamics course, since Lewin was away a lot that year. She later married my lab partner in that course, Leon Yarrow, and both have distinguished careers in developmental psychology. Leon and I did a field study for the course in the living room of the graduate house. We used what later came to be called "unobtrusive" observational methods to record the reactions of the women residents to deviant opinions expressed by a visitor on the Morgenthau plan for postwar settlement with Germany, which the women vehemently opposed.

Somewhere, I read F. C. Bartlett's *Remembering* (1932), and began master's thesis research on the effects of attitudinal schema prejudicial to blacks in serial recall. In the library I picked up Sherif's *The Psychology of Social Norms* (1936), which provided the clues on how to design the materials to be recalled, namely without clear organizational structure. After reading Sherif's book, I went around telling anyone who listened "that's the kind of social psychologist I want to be." With benefit of Johnson's fine editorial hand, my thesis was published, with him as senior author, as beneficent father figures expected (with Johnson 1944).

I came out of Iowa conversant with the Clark Hull-Spence brand of behaviorism and the logical positivism that provided its theoretical rationale, influenced by it, but distrustful. I had been exposed to Lewin's social psychology and had learned from it. I was most fascinated by the possibilities for a social psychology that could integrate the study of human cognition, motivation, and social behavior with that of the cultures and social structures of human societies, which I found most nearly realized in the works of Bartlett and Sherif.

I had planned to work after getting the master's, and I do not recall anyone counseling otherwise. The pressure was toward taking a job that would help the war effort, and I was offered one in the RCA plant at Lancaster, Pennsylvania, which made radio tubes. I refused it because the problem I was to work on was how to reduce absenteeism and job turnover among the rural women who worked in the factory, which appeared to me to be related to family issues that RCA had no intention of ameliorating. The women appeared to need child care and family support facilities, not propaganda or improved placement practices.

Through Dr. Meyers' recommendation, I had no difficulty getting a job in 1944 in survey research as assistant to the research director of Audience Research, Inc., a Gallup organization in Princeton. To my disappointment, the research director and I did not do research as I understood that term, but simply collected data to answer commercial questions, mostly about planned Hollywood movies. When I felt it necessary to request a transfer, owing to his Monday morning declaration of love in his office, I decided that I wanted to spend no more time being one of the "girls" in survey research. I wrote to Hadley Cantril at Princeton, whom I knew only through reading his books on collective behavior and social movements. I requested counsel on where to apply for graduate school. The reply was a phone call about a week later, asking whether I'd like to apply for a research assistant-ship with Sherif at Princeton. I said that I would, but that Princeton would not accept me as a graduate student. He replied that he and Sherif had discussed that matter, and would arrange the work so that I could commute to Columbia in New York City.

By this time, I had decided that I wanted to marry an intellectual, as well as sexual and emotional partner, who would encourage my being a social psychologist. The idea was based on literature I had read, not realities I saw, and it was romantic in the extreme. The impact of meeting Muzafer Sherif, already a well-known contributor who espoused social psychology and male-female equality with equal fervor, and whose work had already inspired me, cannot be overdrawn. He asked me how far I wanted to go in social psychology, and I replied "all the way."

Our commitment to one another was strengthened by keen awareness that a marriage between a midwest American and a Turk was not supposed to work at all. Despite the inevitable stresses of two such different people living and working together, our quite different stage of career development, and a great many external pressures experienced by those who choose not to conform to the "usual," that commitment has been complete and continues to this day. I believe that it has endured, despite a road strewn with as many rocks as rose petals, because of a great deal of effort by two individuals who believe that their relationship has meaning beyond day-to-day living, through contributing to social psychology and to values deeply shared. Our decision to have children was part of that relationship. Of course, children spell complications in busy lives, but they also spell fun, love, and, for us, life-long friendships. Since I never built nests, regarding them as for the birds, I never experienced an empty one as our daughters developed and left home.

In the sixteen years that followed marriage before my Ph.D., my being a woman, a faculty wife, and mother labeled me as someone to whom social psychologists were polite, but not collegial. In the atmosphere of the 1950s and early 1960s, I was seen as a wife helping her husband. Other wives did not help their husbands in the ways I helped mine, certainly not by co-authoring books. Their husbands did not want them to. Still I was a wife, not a social psychologist, to most people. Except for a few good friends, who understood and helped us in numerous personal ways, I spent most of that period feeling that I belonged nowhere except in my family and in my work activities. Our children knew babysitters, housekeepers, and nursery school from an early age. On the other hand, we were with them more than most mothers active in golf and bridge, and almost all fathers, in those years. Arrangements were constantly being made, for regular ones were available only for short periods of time. As inspiration, I knew a few somewhat older women psychologists, including Ruth Hartley, Helen Hall Jennings, Anne Anastasi, and Lois Murphy; but none was close by and each was more in-dependent in career than I at that time. Through Muzafer's professional contacts, I had the opportunity to hear and to meet many of the leading contributors to social psychology.

In work, those years were surely among the most exciting. With Muzafer as mentor, I was learning things not then taught in graduate schools, which was my rationale for not continuing at Columbia or attempting to enroll in Yale, where we moved in 1947. I am speaking of the period in which we were absorbed in three different experiments in summer camps on inter-group relations (Sherif and Sherif 1953; Sherif et al. 1961), research on attitudes and social judgment, and in writing a joint text (Sherif and Sherif 1956). When a passage from our work that I had written would be quoted and attributed solely to Muzafer Sherif, my feelings were tolerable only be-cause he recognized the injustice as quickly as I. I was the more dependent member in a work partnership which we both knew was also dependent on my contributions. Though that fact was seldom recognized professionally, the knowledge prevented me from feeling worthless. A careful historian will recognize that both of us were involved in everything published under the name of Sherif after 1945. In several instances, when Muzafer asked me to appear as co-author, instead of in footnote or preface, I declined, a tendency that persisted into the 1960s. I would not do so again. I now believe that the world which viewed me as a wife who probably typed her husband's papers (which I did not) defined me to myself more than I realized.

It was still part of our plan that I would complete the Ph.D., which Muzafer called the "union card," perhaps to soothe my dilemmas of status, but also, as it turned out, because the Ph.D. functioned that way. I refused to enter graduate school at the University of Oklahoma, where we moved in 1949, or any place else where he might be on the regular faculty, as I wanted the degree to be viewed as my accomplishment. So he accepted a visiting professorship offered him in 1958 at the University of Texas, which was primarily for research. I have often thought of that decision since, when problems of "reentering" or "part-time" students were discussed in faculty meetings. I believe that I was correct in thinking that faculty wives reentering as students in their husbands' own universities, especially own departments, are severely handicapped, both at the time and thereafter, even though an automatic handicap is absurd. Robert Sears, then graduate dean at Stanford, had indicated that I would be admitted there, but Stanford required two years' residency at the time. The University of Texas required only one year, and certainly the faculty made the entire process as easy as possible. But it was not easy.

At Texas, I was simultaneously a full-time graduate student for three semesters (with other students at first regarding me as unfair competition), co-author of a recent social psychology text (Sherif and Sherif 1956), wife of a Distinguished Visiting Professor, co-investigator in research on natural groups, and mother of three daughters, the youngest then three years old. Issues of who I was and what was expected with different people, my status relative to others in these very different contexts, and simply managing time would have been completely wild, if they were not also amusing at times. I recall emerging from my first examination in advanced statistics, held at 8 A.M. after Muzafer had already gotten the children organized for school and driven me to the university. Like many a student after many a test, I was feeling the lowest of the low, when a student appeared in the hall with a copy of our book, requesting my autograph.

"Managing" was tough, and would have been impossible without total family commitment and Texas faculty encouragement. The advantage of "reentering" when I did was in knowing exactly why I was there and what I needed to learn. I took no courses in social psychology, but I learned a great deal, especially in statistics, on scaling with Wayne Holtzman, psychophysics with Harry Helson, on the brain with Lloyd Jeffries, and in eighteen hours of sociology.

After one year of residency, I flew to Austin from Oklahoma for comprehensive examinations, two foreign language and final oral exams, with Joan Holtzman providing protective care in her home while I was there. The dissertation data were collected in Oklahoma, with Muzafer serving as my research assistant. The scant two years between leaving Texas and receiving the degree now seem very long, as half a year was spent at the University of Washington where Muzafer was Ford Visiting Professor and I rewrote the manuscript of the Sherif-Hovland book *Social Judgment* (1961) at the authors' request and with payment from Carl Hovland's grant funds. Finally, my parents came from Indiana and took charge of the household in Oklahoma while I wrote the dissertation early in 1961.

Now I was research associate on grant moneys at the Institute of Group Relations, which Muzafer had created, working on projects on natural groups and on social judgment and attitudes. From 1961–65, we published four books (Sherif et al. 1961; Sherif and Sherif 1964a; 1965a; Sherif, Sherif, and Nebergall 1965a). My senior authorship of the last is to be found "corrected" in several reference lists by listing Muzafer first. That book (*Attitude and Attitude Change*) brought a distinguished publications award to Roger Nebergall, the third author, from his national association in speech and communications. It is some satisfaction that it was recently featured as a "Citation Classic" in *Current Contents*, as one of the most frequently cited references since publication.

Muzafer's prediction that the Ph.D. would make a difference was clearly correct. First, the Oklahoma Medical School, then the sociology department at the university, asked me to teach. Such teaching was on a temporary basis, after a form had been filed declaring that, despite nepotism rules precluding a spouse's employment in the husband's institution, my service was essential.

In 1962, Pennsylvania State University invited both of us for a visiting week of graduate seminars. In 1965, we were both invited back as visiting faculty, Muzafer in sociology and I in psychology. When tenure track positions were offered in 1966, we accepted. It was the first and only opportunity for both of us. It was a difficult choice for Muzafer, who felt that his most productive work was in Oklahoma, but he did not look back. He became professor emeritus in 1972. Except for my visiting year at Cornell and a distinguished visiting professorship at Smith College (1979), I have been in the psychology department at Penn State since 1966.

Dale Harris was department head in psychology when we came to Pennsylvania. When he retired a few years ago, I acknowledged his strong support during the departmental gathering, and remarked that I had felt in 1966 that I was being stuffed down the psychology department's throat. Amidst tension-reducing laughter, Charles Cofer joined in: "You *were*."

In part, my early experiences as an "outsider" in a large male department with only one other woman in a tenure track position were related to the absence of other social psychologists and of interest in social psychology by other faculty. It is difficult to separate these two aspects of experience: being a woman and being in a de-emphasized field in a department. When I expressed interest in teaching a graduate seminar, I was told that the social psychology seminar, then offered every other year by a colleague whose graduate training had been in comparative psychology, attracted too few students. I offered the seminar, and the situation was remedied. Over the years, the addition of colleagues in social psychology and the growing interest of both students and faculty in other areas have changed the atmosphere considerably. But there are still fewer than 10 percent women faculty in the department.

In fact, I have been a token woman for the department, and it has been a struggle to keep from functioning as one, which one can do by keeping quiet. I had spoken out at a symposium at Rice University in 1963 (Sherif 1964b), where I was invited by Mary Ellen Goodman, whose research on the development of prejudice for her dissertation at Radcliffe provided the basis for her book on that topic. I deplored the status of women and the ignorance of women in the academic disciplines. But I had been explicitly told by an important colleague in Pennsylvania to "keep my powder dry." At Cornell in 1970, I was a consultant on the first women's studies course offered in that university. On my return to Pennsylania, women graduate students asked me to sponsor a seminar on psychology and women. I am deeply grateful to them and faculty participants, as well as the context of the women's movement, for the opportunity to be honest. Our seminar produced one of the first bibliographies for psychology courses on women (with Baer 1974), with departmental support through Merrill Noble, its chairman. The subsequent course offered in the department grew from that experience.

I had long belonged to the American Psychological Association, as well as the American Sociological Association, but had not been active organizationally. I joined the Association for Women in Psychology, and both Muzafer and I joined Division 35 (Psychology of Women), American Psychological Association, at the earliest opportunity when they were formed. The incident that drove me to become active occurred when I spoke of myself to a well-meaning friend as a "woman psychologist." The friend exclaimed "Don't call yourself *that*." When I asked "why," the answer was that the term implied that I was not a *good* psychologist. I knew then that I had to repay some of my debt to the women's movement. That is why the presidents of Division 35, Florence Denmark, then Martha Mednick and Annette Brodsky, found me a willing worker, when each asked for help. I organized the division's first Affirmative Action Committee, then served as chair for its program at the annual convention of the association. In 1979–80, I was the division's president. I am determined that being a woman psychologist shall say nothing about whether one is a *good* psychologist.

Such activities in academia and in a professional organization have been educational for me, accounting in large part for my current experience of being on the way toward being a better social psychologist. The stimulation, the acquaintance with an ever-growing literature, and the mutual support all contribute to my efforts toward building a social psychology in which the problems of being a woman or man, rich or poor, black or white, American or Turk assume the central position of importance that they have in the lives of individuals, in the formation and functioning of their groups and institutions. My book *Orientation in Social Psychology* (1976a) was part of that effort.

Such intersections between human psychological functioning, social actions by individuals (individually and collectively), and the sociocultural organization of the larger society have long been focal in my research interests. Whether the research topic concerned adolescents' relationships with peers (Sherif and Sherif 1969a), social values and attitudes (Sherif 1980b), or group formation, intergroup conflict and cooperation (currently the topic of my National Sigma Xi Lecture (1981–83), the major interest has been in articulating both psychological and social processes whereby the self system of the human individual becomes involved (ego-involvement) in construing events and in social action. One's gender is a developmentally early and enduring category in one's self, hence should interest social psychologists, as it has begun to during the last decade or so. But, whenever those with higher status and power begin to examine those with less, the opportunities for bias are rampant, both in theory and research. That possibility explains why I have, on several occasions, written in the "sociology of knowledge" tradition on "Bias in Psychology" (1979a) and on methodological issues in research on the distinctly female topic of the menstrual cycle (Sherif 1980a). Recognition of "Bias in Psychology" by the Association for Women in Psychology at the annual meeting in 1981, where it received their Distinguished Publication Award, was a memorable event.

I would hope that no one would take my life as a model for their own, any more than I would wish for them a return to the 1940s, 1950s, 1960s or 1970s. There is no single model for life, but many possibilities in a lifetime. Whether or not our futures hold many or few is never our own doing alone, but does depend in part on the possibilities we help to create through joint actions and decisions with others of like mind. For me, such joint efforts have been with others sharing goals for the social, economic, and political equality of all peoples, including their women and men. If such goals fade, the harsh realities of a world which regards such goals as merely "visionary" will restrict the possibilities in individual lives, especially women's.

REFERENCES

Bartlett, F. C. 1932. *Remembering: A Study in Experimental and Social Psychology.* New York: Macmillan.
Johnson, W. 1944. *People in Quandaries.* New York: Harper.
Sherif, C. W. *See* Representative Publications.
Sherif, M. 1936. *The Psychology of Social Norms.* New York: Harper and Row.
Sherif, M. and C. I. Hovland. 1961. *Social Judgment: Assimilation and Contrast Effects in Communication and Attitude Change.* New Haven: Yale University Press.

We mourn the loss of our beloved friend and colleague, Carolyn Wood Sherif, who died in summer 1982 at the age of 60 years.

Representative Publications by Carolyn Wood Sherif

1944.   [Wood.] With Johnson. John told Jim what Joe told him: A study
          of the process of abstracting. *ETC.: A Review of General Seman-
          tics*, 2(1):10–28.
1953.   With M. Sherif. *Groups in Harmony and Tension: An Integration
          of Studies on Intergroup Relations*. New York: Harper & Row.
1956.   With M. Sherif. *An Outline of Social Psychology*. New York: Har-
          per & Row.
1961.   With M. Sherif, O. J. Harvey, B. J. White, and W. R. Hood.
          *Intergroup Conflict and Cooperation: The Robbers Cave Experi-
          ment*. Norman, Okla.: University Book Exchange.
1962.   With M. Sherif. Varieties of social stimulus situations. In S. B.
          Sells, ed., *Stimulus Variables and Behavior Variance*. New York:
          Ronald Press.
1963.   Social categorization as a function of latitude of acceptance and
          series range. *Journal of Abnormal and Social Psychology*, 67(2):148–
          56.
1964a.   With M. Sherif. *Reference Groups: Exploration into Conformity
          and Deviation of Adolescents*. New York: Harper & Row.
1964b.   Woman's roles in the human relations of a changing world. In C.
          M. Class, ed., *The Role of the Educated Woman*. Houston, Tex.:
          Mary Gibbs Jones College, Rice University.
1965a.   With M. Sherif and R. E. Nebergall. *Attitude and Attitude
          Change: The Social Judgment-Involvement Approach*. Philadel-
          phia: W. B. Saunders.
1965b.   With M. Sherif, eds. *Problems of Youth: Transition to Adulthood
          in a Changing World*. Chicago: Aldine.
1965c.   With M. Sherif. Research on intergroup relations. In O. Klineberg
          and R. Christie, eds., *Perspectives in Social Psychology*. New York:
          Holt. Rpt. in W. Austin and S. Worchel, eds., *The Social Psy-

chology of Intergroup Relations. Monterey, Calif.: Brooks/Cole, 1979.

1966.   With N. Jackman. Judgments of truth in collective controversy. *Public Opinion Quarterly,* 30:173–86.

1967a.   With M. Sherif. *Attitude, Ego-Involvement, and Change.* New York: Wiley; Rpt. Westport, Conn.: Greenwood, 1976.

1967b.   With M. Sherif. Group processes and collective interaction in delinquent activities. *Journal of Research in Crime and Delinquency* (January), pp. 43–62.

1967c.   The own categories procedure in attitude research. In M. Fishbein, ed., *Readings in Attitude Theory and Measurement.* New York: Wiley.

1968.   With M. Sherif. Group formation. *International Encyclopedia of Social Sciences,* 6:276–83.

1969a.   With M. Sherif. Adolescent attitudes and behavior in their reference groups within differing sociocultural settings. In J. P. Hill, ed., *Minnesota Symposia on Child Psychology,* vol. 3. Minneapolis: University of Minnesota Press.

1969b.   With M. Sherif. *Interdisciplinary Relationships in the Social Sciences.* Chicago: Aldine.

1969c.   With M. Sherif. *Social Psychology.* New York: Harper & Row.

1970a.   With M. Sherif. Black unrest as a social movement toward an emerging self identity. *Journal of Social and Behavioral Sciences,* 15:41–52.

1970b.   With M. Sherif. Motivation and intergroup aggression: A persistent problem in levels of analysis. In L. A. Aronson, E. Tobach, D. S. Lehrman, and J. S. Rosenblatt, eds., *Development and Evolution of Behavior: Essays in Memory of T. C. Schneirla,* vol. 1. San Francisco: W. H. Freeman.

1973a.   With M. Kelly, L. Rodgers, C. Sarup, and B. Tittler. Personal involvement, social judgment and action. *Journal of Personality and Social Psychology,* 27:311–38.

1973b.   Social distance as categorization of intergroup interactions. *Journal of Personality and Social Psychology,* 25:327–34.

1974.   With H. K. Baer. A topical bibliography (selectively annotated) on psychology of women. *Catalog of Selected Documents in Psychology.* American Psychological Association, 4:42.

1976a.   *Orientation in Social Psychology.* New York: Harper & Row.

1976b.   With G. Rattray. Psychological development and activity in middle childhood (5–12 years). In J. G. Atkinson and G. M. Andrews, eds., *Child in Sport and Physical Activity*. Vol. 3, International Series on Sport Sciences. Baltimore: University Park Press.

1976c. The social context of competition. In D. Landers, ed., *Social Problems in Athletics*. Urbana: University of Illinois Press. Rpt. in R. Martens, ed., *Joy and Sadness in Children's Sports*. Champaign, Ill.: Human Kinetics.

1979a. Bias in psychology. In J. A. Sherman and E. T. Beck, eds., *The Prism of Sex: Essays in the Sociology of Knowledge*. Madison: University of Wisconsin Press.

1979b. What every intelligent woman should know about psychology and women. In E. Snyder, ed., *Women: Study Toward Understanding*. New York: Harper & Row.

1980a. A social-psychological perspective on the menstrual cycle. In J. Parsons, ed., *The Psychobiology of Sex Differences and Sex Roles*. Washington, D.C.: Hemisphere Publishing, McGraw-Hill.

1980b. Social values, attitudes, and involvement of the self. In H. Howe and M. Page, eds., *Beliefs, Attitudes, and Values*. Nebraska Symposium on Motivation. Lincoln: University of Nebraska Press.

Perspectives on Patterns
of Achievement

SYNTHESIS:
PROFILES AND PATTERNS
OF ACHIEVEMENT

AGNES N. O'CONNELL

It is time to meditate on what the season has meant.
But what is the meaningful language for such meditation?
"Fear and Trembling," Robert Penn Warren

To paraphrase Kluckhohn and Murray's dictum, every woman is in certain respects (a) like all other women; (b) like some other women; and (c) like no other woman. The structure of our knowledge about eminent women in psychology can be analyzed on three levels: the universals that apply to all women; the group differences that apply to women in psychology; and the differences that apply to particular individuals (1953:53).

These three levels of analysis are semi-independent (Runyan 1981) and are found in this volume in varying degrees of completeness. The autobiographies speak to the individual level of analysis. They provide representations of eminent women, the influences on their lives, and their indomitable personalities. In contrast, the chapter by Nancy Felipe Russo presents the social and historical context that existed for the cohort or contemporaries of the women in this volume. It speaks to the universals that affected all women during this period of American history. This chapter provides a syn-

Thanks to Nancy Felipe Russo and Ira Sugarman for their comments and suggestions on an earlier version of this chapter. Thanks also to Mary Jane Zaucha for her assistance in the content analyses of the autobiographies.

thesis of the similarities and differences in the lives of these women and represents the group level of analysis.

Study of these autobiographies and of a biographical information form that was completed by each author has identified relationships among a number of factors which brought these women to achievement in their field. Critical aspects of their experiences emerged after several readings of the autobiographies and the biographical information forms. Categories were established and then a content analysis was undertaken.

No claim is made that the women in this volume represent a scientific sample of eminent women in psychology. Nonetheless the material does provide important insights and has hueristic value.

PERSONAL CHARACTERISTICS

Families of Origin

The lives of the women in this volume span the years from the late nineteenth century until the present time. The oldest, Katharine M. Banham, was born in 1897; the youngest, Carolyn Wood Sherif, was born in 1922. These women were born in the east, northeast, south, and midwest United States; in Canada, England, Russia, and South Africa.

Despite the diversity in birthplaces, examination of demographic variables suggest a number of commonalities. Ten of the seventeen women were first borns, two of these were only children. In addition, three women were born after a five year interval, i.e., in family constellations that provided the special treatment usually reserved for first borns. The literature (e.g., Sampson 1962; Altus 1967) has recognized the relationship between birth order and achievement for males and more recently for females (Hennig and Jardim 1977). The present data dramatically underscore the relationship between birth order and achievement for academic women.

Further, the women were as likely to have brothers as sisters. Of the thirty-eight siblings, twenty-one were male. Only four women did not have at least one brother and two of these were only children. This finding suggests that previous research (Hennig and Jardim 1977) which has indicated that achievement for women is related to having all female siblings should be viewed cautiously. Sex of siblings may not be a critical variable for achievement for women. Examination of parental characteristics, child-parent relationships, and childrearing practices may be a more fruitful approach.

Eminent Woman & Date of Birth	Place of Birth	Birth Order	Siblings [a]	Occupation	
				Father	Mother
K. M. Banham May 26, 1897	Sheffield, England	1	WBS	Physician	Housewife
M. B. McGraw August 1, 1899	Birmingham, Ala.	1	W	Farmer	Housewife
R. Howard March 25, 1900	Washington, D.C.	8	SSBSSSSW	Protestant minister	Teacher until marriage
A. T. Bryan Sept. 11, 1902	Kearny, N.J.	2	BWB	Banker	Housewife
L. B. Murphy March 23, 1902	Lisbon, Iowa	1	WBBSS	Methodist pastor/ Executive	Teacher until marriage
M. Ives April 10, 1903	Detroit, Mich.	1	WB	Psychiatrist & professor	Teacher
M. B. Mitchell December 25, 1903	Rockford, Ill.	1	WBBSS	Engineer	Housewife
E. Hanfmann March 3, 1905	St. Petersburg, Russia	1	WBBB	Lawyer/ editor	Teacher
M. Harrower January 25, 1906	Johannesburg, South Africa	1	WB	Banker	Art lecturer
M. J. Rioch January 24, 1907	Paterson, N.J.	1	W	Lawyer	Teacher
T. G. Alper July 24, 1908	Chelsea, Mass.	2	SWB	Realtor	Housewife
M. D. S. Ainsworth December 1, 1913	Glendale, Ohio	1	WSS	President of mfg. co.	Teacher/ nurses tr. until marriage
M. Henle July 14, 1913	Cleveland, Ohio	2	BWS	Wholesaler	Physician
M. H. Jones April 23, 1915	Fairfield, Conn.	1	WS	Lawyer	Housewife
M. J. Wright May 20, 1915	Strathroy, Ontario, Canada	5	BBBBW	Manufacturer	Housewife
M. P. Clark October 18, 1917	Hot Springs, Ariz.	2	BW	Physician	Housewife
C. W. Sherif June 26, 1922	Loogootee, Ind.	3	BSW	Teacher	Housewife

[a] W = Eminent Woman; B = Brother; S = Sister.

It is evident from the data in table 1 that an overwhelming majority of the fathers of these women were either professionals (59 percent) or high level business executives or entrepreneurs (29 percent).[1] What is perhaps more interesting is the fact that over 47 percent of the mothers of these women were trained as professionals during a time when higher education and professional commitment for women were unusual.[2] Many of these women were born into upper-middle-class famiilies who valued education and achievement, families who shared a great enthusiasm for learning and provided a supportive environment for such endeavors. These pioneers in the field of psychology were born into families where being a pioneer was experienced, valued, and accepted. For many, Lois Barclay Murphy's exclamation, "being a pioneer was in my blood," accurately describes their ancestry.

For the most part, the socialization of these women was not sex-typed. Rather, it was supportive of individual potentials. Discouraging attitudes that did exist within a family unit seemed to be dispelled or counteracted by at least one other supportive member and at times derogatory attitudes by others served to strengthen the women in their resolve to achieve.

INTEGRATING ACHIEVEMENT AND AFFILIATION

Marital Status

Although the women carried on in the pioneer spirit, they chose to do so on their own terms. As a group, the mothers of these women had an average of three children. Two mothers had one child each, another two mothers had five children each; one mother had six children; another, eight. Their eminent daughters (71 percent) did not become mothers nor could they be considered housewives under the usual definition of the term. By earning a doctorate, all except one surpassed her own mother's educational level. The one exception was Mary Henle; her mother had earned an M.D.

1. Census data for 1900, 1910, and 1920 indicate that combined professional, technical, and kindred workers, managers, officials, and proprietors comprised between 10 percent and 12 percent of the occupations of the male labor force. In 1970 the comparable percentage was 25 percent (HSUS 1975).
2. The percentages of employed women as compared to all women in 1900, 1910, and 1920 ranged from 14 percent to 17 percent; the comparable percentage was 29 percent in 1970. Of those employed, census data for these years indicate that combined professional, technical, and kindred workers, managers, officials, and proprietors comprised between 9 percent and 14 percent of the female labor force during the early twentieth century. In 1970 the comparable percentage was 18 percent (HSUS 1975).

Table 2
Demographic Variables of Eminent Women in Pyschology: Marital Status*

Eminent Woman	Age at First Marriage	Marital Status	Occupation of Husband	Age at First Child	Children
K. M. Banham	27	Single (marriage annulled after 19 years)	Professor		None
M. B. McGraw	37	Widowed	Engineer	38	Daughter
R. Howard	34	Widowed	Psychologist		None
A. I. Bryan	22	Divorced Divorced Widowed	Engineer Sculptor Hotel owner/ operator		None
L. B. Murphy	24	Widowed	Psychologist	28	Son and daughter
M. Ives		Single			
M. B. Mitchell	44	Married	Accountant		None
E. Hanfmann		Single			
M. Harrower	32	Divorced Widowed	Neurosurgeon Business executive		None
M. J. Rioch	31	Married	Physician/ neuropsychiatrist		None
T. G. Alper	24	Widowed	Lawyer		None
M. D. S. Ainsworth	37	Divorced	Forensic psychologist		None
M. Henle		Single			
M. H. Jones	24	Married	Psychologist	40	Daughter
M. J. Wright		Single			
M. P. Clark	21	Married	Psychologist	23	Daughter and son
C. W. Sherif	23	Married	Psychologist	25	3 daughters

* As of 1982.

In a society where marriage was perceived as the preferred road to fulfillment for women, these women sought alternatives. Four remained single
and chose to focus on their careers. They resolved affiliation needs through
their families of origin and through social and professional friendships. Most,
however, chose to pursue primary affiliation with a marital partner, combin-

ing marriage with a career. Thirteen were married at some time during their lives. One married before graduating from college; six married after earning a baccalaureate or master's degree; seven married after earning a doctorate, one of these for the second time. Timing of marriage before or after the doctorate was not a good predictor of whether or not the marriage would last. Of the marriages before the doctorate, one ended in divorce the same year as the doctorate was earned, another in an annulment nineteen years later. Of the marriages after the doctorate, three ended in divorce. Of the thirteen first time marriages, three ended in divorce, one in an annulment. Despite the high percentage of women who married (76 percent), these women were less likely to marry than women in the general population.[3]

Marriage, when it did occur, generally occurred later in life. It is significant to note that the average age at first marriage was 29.1 years with a range from 21 years (Mamie Phipps Clark) to 44 years (Mildred Mitchell). The median age was 27 years. The median age at first marriage for females in the general population between 1920 and 1947 ranged from 21.2 years to 20.5 years (HSUS 1975).

Husbands

The first husbands of these women were professionals. Six were psychologists; one, a professor; two, physicians; two, engineers; one, a lawyer; and one, an accountant. These were marriages of professional couples who often but not always chose to remain childless. Some of the women wanted children but did not have them (Mary Ainsworth, Ruth Howard, Margaret Rioch). The single or childless status added to flexibility in career choices and contributed to uninterrupted career patterns.

Career patterns were interrupted or advanced by a number of variables. One of them was relocating. Several of the women relocated for their husbands' careers (Mary Ainsworth, Ruth Howard, Margaret Hubbard Jones, Margaret Rioch) and in a reversal of the traditional pattern, one husband relocated for his wife's career (Carolyn Wood Sherif). In some instances, relocating with one's husband served immediate (Lois Barclay Murphy) or long range (Mary Ainsworth) career advancement or goals.

Many husbands were very supportive (Thelma Alper, Mamie Phipps Clark,

3. In the late 1930s, a low of 91 percent of women fifty years of age in the general population were or had been married; in the 1950s the comparable percentage was 96 percent. The current percentage for women who marry sometime during their lives is 94 percent (Glick 1975; Rohrbaugh 1979).

Ruth Howard, Margaret Hubbard Jones, Lois Barclay Murphy, Margaret Rioch, Carolyn Wood Sherif). Although others could be described as less supportive, none was antagonistic to his wife's career.

Marriage partner seems to have a significant impact on life-style in professional as well as personal domains. Being married to a psychologist seems to provide entree into a great many professional networks. Yet such a union is not without its liabilities. Several women wrote of the problems of being taken seriously and of having one's work judged on its own merit when overshadowed by a more prominent spouse. The camaraderie, the professional networks, the shared understandings, and the informal learning do make such partnerships stimulating and rewarding for wives. According to research, however, this arrangement has a differential benefit for the husbands of such couples. Wives of psychologists are more professionally productive (number of articles published, papers presented at conventions, books published, or grants received) than other female psychologists, but husbands of women psychologists are the most productive of any group (Bryson et al. 1976).

Children

Among the married women, 38 percent had children.[4] Two women had one child each, a daughter; two had two children, one son and one daughter; and one had three children, three daughters.[5] The women who had one child were thirty-eight and forty years of age, respectively, at the birth of the first child. The women who had two children were considerably younger at the birth of their first child, twenty-three and twenty-eight years of age, respectively. The woman who had three children was twenty-five years of age. These ages are considerably higher than the ages for the general female population at the birth of the first child.[6]

4. It is approximated that 83 percent of the women in the general population are mothers (Rohrbaugh 1979:175, 194).

5. The fertility rate during the depression years was 2.3 children, the lowest level on record up to that time; the highest fertility rate was 3.8 children recorded in 1957; in 1973 the fertility rate was a low 1.9 children. The birth rate remained around 15 per 1,000 population from 1973 through 1976; in 1977 it increased to approximately 15.4 per 1,000; in 1979 the figure rose and continued to rise to approximately 15.8 per 1,000 in 1980 and 15.9 in 1981; for 1982 it is estimated at 17.1 per 1,000 (Glick 1975; Dolan and Stanley 1982; *Asbury Park Press*, March 20, 1982, A 10).

6. The birth of the first child generally occurs within the first 24 months after marriage. The median age at which the married female population become first time mothers is approximately 23 years (Van Dusen and Sheldon, 1976).

Juggling career and family tested the ingenuity of the women, especially for those who had children. Finding good child care was a serious concern. Husbands often shared child care responsibilities. Families of origin and hired help also were sources of assistance for some women. Children served to shift the major emphasis from career to family for some women at least for a number of childrearing years (Lois Barclay Murphy and Carolyn Wood Sherif). During such periods, career goals continued to be salient with progress continuing on a part-time, if not full-time, basis.

While examining these data it is important to note that achievement and affiliation are aspects of the individual, not the setting, and that these characteristics can exist simultaneously in both occupational and interpersonal domains (Fiske 1980; O'Connell 1981, 1982; Richardson 1981). The autobiographies in this volume attest to the widespread integration of achievement and affiliation in the lives of these distinguished women and support the notion that these characteristics are not dichotomous, but compatible, and further that the individual is best served when they are integrated or balanced.

EDUCATIONAL AND PROFESSIONAL VARIABLES

Earning the Doctorate

As undergraduates, the women represented nine different majors or double majors; psychology (7), philosophy (2), German (2), French (1), sociology (1), science (1), economics (1), liberal arts (1), and mathematics (1). Although seven chose psychology in college and many more after graduation, four continued to search for a career discipline as graduate students. All but one earned her doctorate in psychology. Dr. Rioch earned her doctorate in philology after earning a master's in psychology. The mean number of years from completion of baccalaureate to completion of doctorate was 9.68 years with a range from three (Margaret Rioch) to eighteen years (Carolyn Wood Sherif).[7]

In the early decades of the twentieth century, universities that offered a doctorate in psychology were limited. Columbia University was one of the first schools to offer a doctorate in psychology and to admit women students

7. The mean number of years from completion of baccalaureate to completion of doctorate in the field of psychology for the years from 1920 through 1961 was 8.7 years; the range of the means extended from a low of 8.2 years for the period 1930–39 to a high of 9.4 years for the period 1960–61 (Harmon et al. 1963:40; HEN 1968b:64).

(see chapter by Nancy Felipe Russo). Three of these eminent women earned their doctorates at Columbia University between 1927 and 1935, a fourth in 1943, Bryn Mawr trained two of the women in the 1930s. The remaining doctorates were earned at various universities including Yale, Radcliffe, Smith, the University of Minnesota, and the University of Michigan—Ann Arbor. All of the doctorates except one (Carolyn Wood Sherif, 1961) were earned between 1927 and 1949: two in the 1920s, ten in the 1930s, four in the 1940s.[8]

All received graduate support except Alice Bryan who was an instructor of psychology at the Child Education Foundation in New York from 1929 to 1939. Six received scholarships; six, fellowships. Three of these received both a scholarship and a fellowship. The remaining women received support as research or teaching assistants; many engaged in both research and teaching.

Subdisciplines in psychology varied. Child development was the most often chosen area of study, which may reflect the influence of the progressive education and child development movements of the early 1900s (Russo and O'Connell 1980). Personality and clinical psychology were other frequently chosen specialities. It was not always clear from graduate training what the eventual direction contributions to the field would take. Interests changed over time. As opportunities arose, new directions and goals were pursued. These women were well served by their flexibility and readiness to take on new endeavors.

Innovations

The women were pioneers, groundbreakers, innovators. They contributed handsomely to the field of psychology. Their presence, determination, and scholarship helped gain acceptance for women. Although they were not the only women to contribute to the discipline nor the only women to help lower barriers, their contributions and innovations encompass an impressively broad spectrum. Their influence stretches from academia to industry; from libraries to hospitals; from the courts to the military; from research to training; from therapy and counseling to social action programs.

8. The number of doctorates awarded to women in all fields increased substantially between 1920 and 1978. Sample years and number of doctorates awarded to women follow: 1920—93; 1930—353; 1940—429; 1950—643; 1960—1,028; 1970—4,000; 1978—8,500. The comparable figures for men were: 1920—522; 1930—1,946; 1940—2,861; 1950—5,990; 1960—8,801; 1970—25,900; 1978—23,700 (HEW 1968b; SAUS 1980).

Table 3
Education, Interests, and Innovations of Eminent Women in Psychology

Eminent Woman	BA/BS	MA/MS	Doctorate	Graduate Support	Interests	Innovations
K. M. Banham 1897	1919 Psychology Manchester	1923 Psychology Cambridge & Toronto	1934 Psychology Montreal	Lecturer Toronto	Child development Clinical and research	First woman psychologist at School of Medicine McGill University and at Duke University. First woman to obtain Ph.D. at University of Montreal.
M. B. McGraw 1899	1923 Sociology Wesleyan	Religious Education T.C. Columbia	1927 Psychology T.C. Columbia	Rockefeller fellowship	Child development Research and clinical	Demonstrated swimming reflex. Pioneer in longitudinal research observation and twin study.
R. Howard 1900	1920 Liberal Arts Howard	1922 Social Work Simmons	1934 Psychology Columbia & Minnesota	Scholarship Howard Fellowship Simmons Fellowship Columbia & Minnesota	Child development	Landmark work with triplets and adolescents. First black woman Ph.D. in psychology.
A. I. Bryan 1902	1929 Psychology Columbia	1930 Psychology Columbia 1949 Library Science Chicago	1934 Psychology Columbia		Library science Bibliotherapy	Bibliotherapist. Formed National Council of Women Psychologists.

Name (birth year)						
L. B. Murphy 1902	1923 Economics Vassar	1928 Religions of India Union Theological	1935 Psychology T.C. Columbia	Scholarship Union Theological	Child development Psychoanalysis	First paper on "projective techniques". Research in child development. Research on sympathy. Helped found Head Start.
A. Ives 1903	1924 Psychology Vassar	1929 Psychology Michigan (Ann Arbor)	1938 Psychology Michigan (Ann Arbor)	Fellowship Vassar	Experimental Clinical	Built psychology department Ford Hospital. Helped gain recognition for psychologists as experts in giving court testimony.
M. B. Mitchell 1903	1924 Mathematics Rockford	1927 Philosophy Radcliffe	1931 Psychology Yale	Research scholarship/ fellowship Yale	Learning/Clinical Research Applied bionics	Opened numerous psychology departments in applied settings. First clinical psychology Army Examiner for Astronaut program.
E. Hanfmann 1905			1927 Psychology Jena, Germany	Assistant	Cognition Clinical Personality	Studied cognition in schizophrenics. Developed Student Counseling Service. Military Psychologist. Research on personality assessment.
M. Harrower 1906	1927 Psychology Bedford, London		1934 Psychology Smith	Research associate Smith	Perception Personality Neuropsychology Rorschach	Research on surgical patients. Adaptation of Rorshach for groups. Poetry in therapy.
M. J. Rioch 1907	1927 German Wellesley	Psychology Washington University	1930 Philosophy Bryn Mawr 1943 Certificate Psychology Washington, D.C.	Scholarship Bryn Mawr	Clinical Testing Psychotherapy	Trained mental health paraprofessionals. Tavistock Group Relations Conference in U.S.

Table 3
Education, Interests, and Innovations of Eminent Women in Psychology (continued)

Eminent Woman	BA/BS	MA/MS	Doctorate	Graduate Support	Interests	Innovations
T. G. Alper 1908	1929 German Wellesley		1943 Psychology Radcliffe	Assistant Wellesley	Experimental Memory Ego strength Women	Experimental approaches to ego strength, achievement motivation.
M. D. S. Ainsworth 1913	1935 Psychology Toronto	1936 Psychology Toronto	1939 Psychology Toronto	Teaching assistant Toronto	Child development Personality Attachment Clinical	Longitudinal naturalistic cross-cultural studies of mother-infant attachment.
M. Henle 1913	1934 French Smith	1935 Psychology Smith	1939 Psychology Bryn Mawr	Assistant Smith Bryn Mawr	Gestalt psychology Perception Human Motivation Cognition	First lab manual in psychodynamics. Fifth woman president of EPA. Research on logic and thinking and Gestalt psychology.
M. H. Jones 1915	1937 Philosophy Vassar	1938 Psychology Hobart	1945 Psychology Cornell UCLA	Fellowship Hobart Scholarship Cornell	Physio-sensation Cognitive development Safety research	Application of theoretical approaches and rigorous methodology to social action programs.
M. J. Wright 1915	1939 Psychology Philosophy Western Ontario	1940 Psychology Toronto	1949 Psychology Toronto	Assistant Toronto	Child development Administration	First woman to head a department in Canada. Headed and developed psychology department at University of Western Ontario. First woman president of C.P.A.

M. P. Clark 1•17	1938 Psychology Howard	1939 Psychology Howard	1943 Psychology Columbia	Scholarship Howard Fellowship Columbia	Child development Racial identification	Joint research on development of self-awareness in black children—basis of U.S. Supreme Court decision on desegregation of public schools. Founded Northside Center for Child Development.
C. W. Sherif 1922	1943 Science Purdue	1944 Psychology Iowa	1961 Psychology Columbia Austin, Texas	Assistant Iowa	Social psychology Women	Integration of naturalistic experiment, observational studies, and quantitative methods. Developing and operationalizing concepts on structure of social attitudes and small-group interactions. Synthesis.

Whether their work was theoretical or applied or in traditional or emerging areas, it reached the highest standards of excellence. They were often first: the first woman to obtain a Ph.D. at the University of Montreal, the first woman psychologist on the faculty at the School of Medicine, McGill University, and the first woman in the psychology department at Duke University (Katharine Banham); the first black woman to earn a Ph.D. in psychology (Ruth Howard); the first to build a psychology department at Ford Hospital (Margaret Ives); the first to found a psychology department at the U.S. Naval Hospital in Bethesda and other applied settings (Mildred Mitchell); the first woman to head a college department in Canada, the first woman to head and develop a psychology department at the University of Western Ontario, and the first woman president of the Canadian Psychological Association (Mary Wright). They brought innovations to testing (Katharine Banham) and to projective techniques (Molly Harrower and Lois Barclay Murphy); to the study of infants (Mary Ainsworth, Katharine Banham, Ruth Howard, Myrtle McGraw), cognition and schizophrenia (Eugenia Hanfmann), achievement motivation (Thelma Alper), and Gestalt psychology (Mary Henle); to social psychology (Carolyn Wood Sherif) and to social action programs (Mamie Phipps Clark, Ruth Howard, and Margaret Hubbard Jones); to bibliotherapy (Alice Bryan); to training mental health paraprofessionals (Margaret Rioch); and to selecting astronauts (Mildred Mitchell). The range of their accomplishments is remarkable and their pioneer spirit, inspirational.

MAJOR PROFESSIONAL POSITIONS

Places of Employment

The universities and colleges which employed these distinguished women at some time during their careers were numerous and varied. They included Ivy League and both public and private universities, and women's colleges. As shown in table 4 the places of employment include Harvard (Thelma Alper and Eugenia Hanfmann), McGill (Katharine Banham and Molly Harrower), Sarah Lawrence (Lois Barclay Murphy and Mary Henle), Columbia (Alice Bryan), Wellesley (Thelma Alper and Margaret Rioch), the University of Toronto (Mary Ainsworth and Mary Wright), the University of Southern California (Margaret Hubbard Jones), Duke University (Katharine Banham), George Washington University (Margaret Ives), the University of Oklahoma and Pennsylvania State (Carolyn Wood Sherif), Johns Hopkins and the University of Virginia (Mary Ainsworth). The women also were employed in hospitals, research institutes, government, and the military. It is interesting to note that married and single women, mothers and not mothers were similarly represented among the highest ranks in academe or elsewhere.

For these distinguished women the route to the highest academic rank, full professor, seems to have taken either of two paths: (1) a strong almost continuous commitment to academe (e.g., Mary Ainsworth, Thelma Alper, Alice Bryan, Eugenia Hanfmann, Mary Henle, Margaret Hubbard Jones, Carolyn Wood Sherif, Mary Wright) or (2) an established reputation as a psychologist primarily outside academe (e.g., Mamie Phipps Clark, Molly Harrower, Margaret Rioch). However, distinction outside academe did not always bring the academic rank merited (Mildred Mitchell). Some women established prestigious reputations and remained in other settings (Ruth Howard and Myrtle McGraw). Some women moved from academe into other settings (Lois Barclay Murphy). Movement seems to have been in both directions and overlapping.

These remarkable women often held multiple positions. They moved in and out of various employment sectors, integrating interests with opportunities. Their ability to shift employment settings so readily is an element of their flexibility. The great variety in their employment patterns provides an instructive model for current and future generations of psychologists.

BARRIERS, COPING STRATEGIES, AND HISTORICAL INFLUENCES

Barriers

Examining the contributions of these distinguished women might mislead one to believe that these achievements were made in professionally supportive environments. This was not the case. These women functioned and made their contributions in environments which ranged from benign to hostile. Twelve of the seventeen described encountering some form of discrimination because they were female; others because they were Jewish or black. The most frequent barriers were denial of educational and career opportunities.

So pervasive was the discrimination against women at Cambridge University that although Katharine Banham was allowed to study in the psychology laboratory of Charles S. Myers and to sit for examinations, she was denied the right to a university degree because she was a woman. It was not until

Table 4
Major Professional Positions

Eminent Woman	Institutions	Title	Dates
K. M. Banham	University of Toronto	Lecturer	1921–1924
	Canadian National Committee for Mental Hygiene	Psychologist	1924–1930
	McGill University	Assistant professor	1929–1936
	Leicester (Eng.) Education Committee	Psychologist	1936–1942
	Iowa Board of Control Psychological Services	Acting director	1943–1945
	Duke University	Associate professor	1946–1967
	N.C. Cerebral Palsy Hospital	Consultant psychologist	1967–
M. B. McGraw	Child Development Institute T.C., Columbia University	Research assistant	1925–1927
	Florida State College for Women	Instructor	1927–1928
	Child Guidance Institute Columbia-Presbyterian Medical Center	Psychology intern	1928–1929
	Normal Child Development Study	Associate director	1930–1942
R. Howard	National Youth Administration	Counselor and supervisor	1938–1940
	Provident Hospital School of Nursing	Psychologist	1948–1966
	Chicago Board of Health Mental Health Division	Psychologist	1967–1973
	Abraham Lincoln Centre	Developmental and clinical psychologist	1967–1981
	Private Practice	Developmental and clinical psychologist	1940–1981

Name	Institution	Role	Years
A. I. Bryan	Child Education Foundation, New York	Psychology instructor	1929–1939
	School of Fine & Applied Arts, Pratt Institute	Head, psychology department	1935–1939
	School of Library Service, Columbia University:	Consulting psychologist	1936–1939
		Associate in library service	
		Assistant professor	1939–1952
		Associate professor	1952–1956
		Professor	1956–1971
		Professor emeritus	1971–
L. B. Murphy	Sarah Lawrence College	Member of faculty	1928–1952
	Menninger Foundation	Director of developmental studies—psychotherapist	1952–1969
	Children's Hospital Washington, D.C.	Consultant, infant study	1967–1970
M. Ives	Wayne County Clinic for Child Study, Juvenile Court, Detroit. Michigan	Staff psychologist	1929–1932
	Henry Ford Hospital Detroit, Michigan	Staff psychologist	1935–1943
	Saint Elizabeths Hospital Washington, D.C.:	Staff psychologist	1943–1951
		Director of psychological services	1951–1972
		Associate director for psychology	1972–1973
	George Washington University Washington, D.C.	Lecturer	1946–1955
		Professional lecturer	1955–1970
	American Board of Professional Psychology (ABPP)	Executive officer	1977–1981

Table 4
Major Professional Positions (continued)

Eminent Woman	Institutions	Title	Dates
M. B. Mitchell	Independence and Mt. Pleasant State Hospitals, Iowa	Chief psychologist	1939–1941
	U.S. Naval Hospital Bethesda, Maryland	Chief psychologist	1942–1944
	V.A. Mental Hygiene Clinic Fort Snelling, Minn.	Chief clinical psychologist	1947–1951
	V.A. Center, Dayton, Ohio:	Chief clinical psychologist	1951–1956
		Clinical psychologist	1956–1958
	Wright-Patterson AFB, Ohio Biophysics Laboratory	Clinical psychologist	1958–1960
	WPAFB, Ohio—Bionics Electronic Technology Laboratory	Research psychologist (engineering)	1960–1965
	University of Tampa	Associate professor	1965–1967
E. Hanfmann	Psychology Institute, Jena (Ger.)	Assistant	1928–1930
	Smith College Research Lab	Assistant	1930–1932
	Worcester State Hospital	Research associate	1932–1937
	Masonic Order	Grant for research in schizophrenia	1937–1939
	Mount Holyoke College	Assistant professor (with interruption for war work)	1939–1946
	Harvard University	Lecturer	1946–1952
	Brandeis University	Professor, director of counseling, consultant	1952–

M. Harrower			
	"Psyche"	Associate editor	1927–1928
	Smith College	Research associate	1928–1930
			1931–1932
			1933–1934
	Wells College, N.Y.	Instructor	1930–1931
	Bedford College, University of London	Senior lecturer	1932–1933
	Douglass College, Rutgers University	Director of students	1934–1937
	Montreal Neurological Institute, McGill University	Chief Clinical psychologist Lecturer in psychology	1938–1941
	Josiah Macy Jr. Foundation	Grantee	1941–1944
		Private practice, psychodiagnosis and therapy, consultation, research, and lecturing	1944–1967
	Department of State (part-time)	Psychological consultant	1947–1950
	U.S. Army (part-time)	Psychological consultant	1947–1952
	Air Surgeon's Office (part-time)	Member of technical advisory committee	1948–1951
	Children's Bureau (part-time)	Consultant in psychology	1951–1952
	Johns Hopkins Hospital (part-time)	Consultant psychologist	1957–1962
	Manhattan Children's Court (part-time)	Research director, Court Intake Project	1952–1954
	University of Texas Medical Branch Department of Psychiatry	Visiting lecturer	1953–1957
	Temple University Medical School Department of Psychiatry	Associate Professor	1957–1958
		Professor	1959–1964
	New School for Social Research	Visiting professor of psychology	1964–1967
	University of Florida:	Professor of clinical psychology	1967–1975
		Professor emeritus	1975–

Table 4
Major Professional Positions (continued)

Eminent Woman	Instititions	Title	Dates
M. J. Rioch	Wilson College	Assistant Professor	1931–1933
	Wellesley College	Instructor & ass't professor	1933–1939
	Montgomery County Mental Hygiene Clinic	Psychologist	1944–1947
	Chestnut Lodge Sanitarium	Research psychologist	1947–1957
	Nat'l Inst. of Mental Health	Research psychologist	1959–1963
	Children's Hospital	Director of program	1964–1967
	Washington School of Psychiatry	Executive director of A. K. Rice Institute	1967–1970
	American University	Professor and professor emeritus	1971–
	Private Practice	Clinical psychologist	1950–
T. G. Alper	Radcliffe College	Tutor in psychology	1942–1943
	Harvard College	Instructor in psychology	1943–1946
		Lecturer in psychology	1946–1948
	Clark University	Associate professor	1948–1952
	Wellesley College	Associate professor	1952–1954
		Professor	1954–1973
	Harvard University	Lecturer	1946–1952
	Brandeis University	Professor, director of counseling, consultant	1952–

M. D. S. Ainsworth	University of Toronto	Class assistant to instructor	1935–1942
	Canadian Army	CWAC consultant to director of Personnel Selection (final rank, Major)	1942–1945
	Dept. of Veterans Affairs, Ottawa	Superintendent of Women's Rehabilitation	1945–1946
	University of Toronto	Assistant professor, research fellow, Institute of Child Study	1946–1950
	Tavistock Clinic, London	Senior research psychologist	1950–1953
	East African Inst. of Social Research, Kampala, Uganda	Senior research fellow	1954–1955
	Johns Hopkins University	Psychologist	
		Lecturer, associate professor, Professor	1956–1975
	University of Virginia	Professor	1975–
		Commonwealth professor	
M. Henle	Swarthmore College	Research associate	1939–1941
	University of Delaware	Instructor	1941–1942
	Bryn Mawr College	Instructor	1942–1944
	Sarah Lawrence College	Psychology faculty	1944–1946
	Graduate Faculty, The New School	Assistant professor	1946–1948
		Associate professor	1948–1954
		Professor	1954–
	John Simon Guggenheim Memorial Foundation	Fellow	1951–1952
	Harvard University	Research fellow in cognitive studies and lecturer in social relations	1963–1964
	Educational Services, Inc Cambridge, Mass.	Senior scholar	1964–1965
	Cornell University	Visiting professor	Fall 1981

Table 4
Major Professional Positions (continued)

Eminent Woman	Instititions	Title	Dates
M. H. Jones	University of Alabama	Instructor	1944–1945
	State College of Washington	Instructor	1948–1949
	University of California Correspondence Instruction	Instructor	1951–1957
	University of California Los Angeles	Research psychologist, Engineering	1950–1966 1969–1974
		Education	1966–1970
		Psychology	1963–1975
	Univ. of Southern California, Institute of Safety and Systems Management	Associate professor	1974–1981
		Professor, professor emerita, human factors	
M. J. Wright	Protestant Children's Village Ottawa, Ontario	Child care	1941–1942
	Garrison Lane Nursery Training School, Birmingham, England	Instructor	1942–1944
	Mental Health Clinic Hamilton, Ontario	Psychologist	1944–1945
	Institute of Child Study University of Toronto	Lecturer	1945–1946
	University of Western Ontario	Assistant professor	1946–1955
		Associate professor	1955–1962
		Professor	1962–1980
		Professor emeritus	1980–
	Middlesex College	Chairman, psychology department	1960–1963
		Head, psychology department	1963–1970
		Director, lab preschool	1972–1980

	Institution	Position	Years
M. P. Clark	American Public Health Association	Research psychologist	1944–1945
	U.S. Armed Forces Institute	Research psychologist	1945–1946
	Riverdale Children's Association	Psychologist	1945–1946
	Northside Center for Child Development	Executive director	1946–1979
	Yeshiva University	Visiting professor	1958–1960
C. W. Sherif	University of Iowa	Graduate assistant	1943–1944
	Audience Research, Inc. Princeton, N.J.	Assistant to research director	1944–1945
	Princeton University	Research assistant	1945–1947
	University of Oklahoma	Research and writing	1949–1958
	Institute of Group Relations	Research associate	1959–1965
	University of Oklahoma Medical School	Consulting assistant professor	1963–1965
	Pennsylvania State University	Visiting lecturer	Oct. 1962
	University of Oklahoma	Associate professor of sociology	1963–1965
	Pennsylvania State University	Visiting associate professor of psychology	1965–1966
		Associate professor of psychology	1966–1969
	Smith College	Distinguished visiting professor	Spring 1969
	Cornell University	Visiting professor of psychology and sociology	1969–1970
	Pennsylvania State University	Professor of psychology	1970–1982

Table 5
Barriers and Coping Strategies of Eminent Women in Psychology

Eminent Woman	Barriers	Coping Strategies
K. M. Banham	Denied Cambridge degree because female.	Changed geographical locations for career flexibility.
M. B. McGraw	Work not taken seriously because female.	Flexibility, ingenuity, changed jobs.
R. Howard	Denied position because black.	Changed geographical locations, changed jobs, continued education, flexibility, integration.
A. I. Bryan	Denied just salary and earned promotion because female.	Took initiative when denied access. Earned post Ph.D. degree in Library Science.
L. B. Murphy	None mentioned.	Flexibility, integration, continued education, changed jobs.
M. Ives	Denied just salary because female.	Flexibility, changed jobs.
M. B. Mitchell	Denied position and justified promotion because female.	Spirited—persistence, assertiveness, changed jobs.
E. Hanfmann	Denied access to faculty meetings at Harvard because female.	Flexibility, changed jobs and geographical locations. Analysis.
M. Harrower	Faculty isolation because female.	Established priorities. Changed geographical locations. Analysis.
M. J. Rioch	Anti-nepotism.	Flexibility, continued education.
T. G. Alper	Denied status and tenure track positions because female.	Flexibility, determination, changed jobs.
M. D. S. Ainsworth	Denied position, denied just salary, and endured faculty isolation because female.	Flexibility, adaptability, resourcefulness. Open to new experiences.
M. Henle	Denied admission to medical school and job opportunities because Jewish.	Flexibility, persistence.
M. H. Jones	Anti-nepotism.	Flexibility, determination. Established priorities. Continued education.
M. J. Wright	None mentioned.	Flexibility, assertiveness, adaptability.
M. P. Clark	Denied position because black female. Employed as token.	Flexibility, perserverance, resourcefulness.
C. W. Sherif	Denied status and not taken seriously because seen only as wife of eminent psychologist.	Flexibility, inner-directedness, strong self-esteem.

1948 that women gained full student status at Cambridge (Banham 1978; Russo and O'Connell 1980). Mary Henle describes the discrimination against Jews that she encountered in seeking admission to medical school.

Denial of career opportunities, equitable salaries, tenure, and promotions were described as barriers by several of the women (Mary Ainsworth, Thelma Alper, Alice Bryan, Mamie Phipps Clark, Margaret Ives, Mildred Mitchell.)[9] Isolation and denial of access and status were described as barriers encountered by others (Mary Ainsworth, Eugenia Hanfmann, Molly Harrower, Myrtle McGraw, Carolyn Wood Sherif). Anti-nepotism policies also worked to deny job opportunities to women. The power of such institutional barriers was experienced by Margaret Rioch and Margaret Hubbard Jones and others during their careers. Ironically, data collected by Bryson et al. (1976) indicate that psychology couples who are employed at the same institution are even more productive than those who are employed at different institutions.

The barriers to achievement made confrontation an everpresent alternative. The women chose their battlefields with great discretion and indomitable spirit (Thelma Alper, Alice Bryan, and Mildred Mitchell).

Coping Strategies: Personal Characteristics

Despite obstacles, these women were willing to take risks. If one pathway became blocked, they chose another. They took the initiative in attaining monetary support (Molly Harrower, Ruth Howard, Lois Barclay Murphy). They changed jobs (Thelma Alper, Margaret Ives, Myrtle McGraw, Mildred Mitchell, Lois Barclay Murphy), geographical location (Katharine Banham, Eugenia Hanfmann, Molly Harrower, Ruth Howard), and strategies, turning dead ends into career opportunities (Mary Ainsworth conducted a cross-cultural study on mother-infant interactions when she accompanied her husband to Africa).

One cannot help but be impressed by the resourcefulness, flexibility (see table 4), and persistence of these women. They were open to change and to new experiences; learning was an integral part of their lives. Several continued their educations formally after earning their doctorates (Alice Bryan, Ruth Howard, Margaret Hubbard Jones, Lois Barclay Murphy, and Margaret Rioch) and thereby broadened their options. All continued their educations informally.

9. Denial of career opportunities based on sex continue to exist. In a Gallup poll conducted in June 1982, 68 percent of the college-educated adult women surveyed reported that they did not have equal opportunities in employment. *The New York Times*, August 15, 1982, p. 10.

Coping Strategies: Mentors and Professional and Social Networks

The professional careers of these distinguished women were aided by mentors, most often men of great stature in the field, e.g., Bowlby, Koffka, Köhler, Maslow, Murray, Prince, but sometimes women, e.g., Goodenough, Heidbreder, Shirley, Stolz, Washburn. It is not surprising that men were more often mentors than women in view of their larger numbers.

The mentors provided professional socialization for these women and formed critical links in the professional and social networks so necessary for reaching eminence in psychology or other fields (Clawson 1980; Hennig and Jardim 1977; Kantor 1977; Levinson 1978). The mentors provided support, advice, knowledge, challenge, guidance, and visibility for the aspiring professionals. Recommendations for positions often came from mentors, professors, or members of a woman's professional network (Mary Ainsworth, Eugenia Hanfmann, Molly Harrower, Mary Henle, Mildred Mitchell, Lois Barclay Murphy, Margaret Rioch, Carolyn Wood Sherif). Social networks also served as a means of entree.

In times of crisis the women depended upon their own inner resources, their flexibility, adaptability, persistence, and strength, but they also vigorously employed their social and professional networks. These networks provided effective coping strategies and worked well to accomplish goals— whether to secure a position or to obtain a grant.

Historical Influences

Fifteen of the seventeen women witnessed the Great Depression and two major wars, World Wars I and II. The impact of these significant historical events on career patterns varied with the woman's stage of professional attainment. The Great Depression interrupted education for two (Molly Harrower and Margaret Ives), brought a career opportunity for two (Ruth Howard and Myrtle McGraw), and made household help available for one (Lois Barclay Murphy). Overall, World War II brought career opportunities for eight of the seventeen women (Mary Ainsworth, Katharine Banham, Eugenia Hanfmann, Molly Harrower, Mary Henle, Margaret Ives, Mildred Mitchell, and Carolyn Wood Sherif). Several were significantly involved in the wartime effort (Mary Ainsworth, Eugenia Hanfmann, and Mildred Mitchell). Ruth Howard worked with the Civilian Aeronautics Board during the war. Two others (Alice Bryan and Myrtle McGraw) became officers of the National Council of Women Psychologists "to promote and develop emergency services that women psychologists could render their communities as larger numbers of their male colleagues were drawn into military services" (Finison and Furumoto 1978; Russo and O'Connell 1980). For the most part, however, the work of these distinguished women focused on other sub-disciplines of psychology during the war years.

EMINENT WOMEN AS A GROUP: LIKE SOME OTHER WOMEN

What Have We Learned?

What have we learned about these eminent women as a group from the autobiographies and biographical information forms? How are they like some other women? They predominantly came from privileged, well-educated middle- or upper-middle-class families.[10] They were born to successful fathers and well-educated mothers; raised with warmth and great appreciation for learning and achievement. Nurtured in this environment, several showed early signs of achievement by reading as preschoolers (Mary Ainsworth, Mary Henle, and Ruth Howard) or by skipping grades in elementary school, graduating high school or starting college at sixteen years of age. In order to fulfill their individual potentials, their identities stretched beyond accepted gender role prescriptions. They saw creativity and achievement as purposeful work.

They attended prestigious colleges and universities seeking challenges in education and career. They were risk-takers, self-reliant, energetic, and flexible. They had great curiosity following their interests and inclinations into new subdisciplines and new opportunities. They found that solving one problem uncovered others. They saw the world as it was and as it might be. Their lives were marked by complexity of purpose, by weaving and reweaving of endeavors, by the forward movement of progress. They made wide use of support systems, professional and social, but were not afraid to be pioneers and go it alone. Their lives resound with integration and complexity.

They set priorities in their personal as well as their professional lives and chose to remain single or marry later in life and remain childless. Those

10. In the past, the social context and the limited access to higher education for capable women often made economic and family privilege almost a prerequisite for professional achievement in psychology. At present, the social context and the widespread access to higher education are encouraging factors for professional achievement for women of excellence from less privileged backgrounds.

who did marry married supportive professional husbands and those who had
children limited the sizes of their families. They were clearly in control of
their lives within the limits of the social context.

They were dismayed, but not deterred, by setbacks and discrimination.
Rather than focusing on the discrimination (barriers) that being females
sometimes wrought, they used the discrimination as added incentive for
achievement. They did not think of themselves as inferior in any sense of
the word and did not accept that judgment from others. They persisted and
they succeeded.

The profile of eminence which emerges surely strikes familiar chords in
one aspect or another in aspiring and young professionals whether in socialization, concept of self, experiences, intellectual strivings, goals, approaches
to life, or some other dimension. For some readers, specific aspects of these
women's lives are salient. For all women, and for men, there are more
general lessons to be learned.

As talented and competent as these women were, talent was not enough
for them to have successful careers. Persistence in the face of obstacles; large
amounts of courage and determination tempered with flexibility and adaptability; willingness to take risks and to be open to new experiences and new
directions were critical factors. An additional critical factor was the use of
social and professional networks. Being connected to other professionals,
especially in the same profession, was essential. These women were guardians of their own integrity and truly committed to their skills. There are
lessons here for all of us.

Then and Now

What these distinguished women and others like them have given us are
increased opportunities and decreased overt discrimination. By their example and their very presence, women are less likely to be required to stand
out in the cold waiting for a man with a key to open the door to a laboratory
or to be physically excluded from libraries, faculty meetings, or classrooms.
While there have been gains in job opportunities, tenure, and promotions,
exclusions continue to exist, if in somewhat diminished and covert forms.
Women, in representational numbers, are still excluded from the tenured
faculty at the most prestigious universities. It continues to be true that the
representation of women on faculties of colleges and universities is inversely
related to the prestige of the institution.

These women were pioneers. Other pioneers are needed until the trail is sufficiently well blazed so that pioneers are no longer necessary (Gruber and Wallace 1981).

These women were innovators at the forefront of knowledge. They have shaped the profession of psychology, the history of our times, and the quality of our lives. We owe them a debt of gratitude and a commitment to carry on in the fine tradition they have so handsomely helped establish.

REFERENCES

Altus, W. D. 1967. Birth order and its sequelae. *International Journal of Psychiatry*, 3:23–36.

Banham, K. M. 1978. A brief professional history of a woman psychologist. North Carolina: Duke University. MS.

Bryson, R. B., J. B. Bryson, M. H. Licht, and B. G. Licht. 1976. The professional pair: Husband and wife psychologists. *American Psychologist*, 31:(1)10–16.

Clawson, J. G. 1980. Mentoring in managerial careers. In C. B. Dear, ed., *Work, Family and the Career: New Frontiers in Theory and Research*. New York: Praeger.

Dolan, B. and A. Stanley. 1982. The new baby bloom. *Time*, February 22 pp. 52–58.

Finison, L. and L. Furumoto. 1978. An historical perspective on psychology, social action and women's rights. Presented at the Annual Meeting of the American Psychological Association, Toronto, August.

Fiske, M. 1980. Changing hierarchies of commitment in adulthood. In N. J. Smelser and E. H. Erikson, eds., *Themes of Work and Love in Adulthood*. Cambridge: Harvard University Press.

Glick, P. C. 1975. A demographer looks at American families. *Journal of Marriage and the Family* (February), pp. 15–26.

Gruber, H. E. and D. B. Wallace. 1981. Integrative strategies in creative lives. Presented at the Annual Meeting of the American Psychological Association, Los Angeles, August.

Harmon, L. R. et al. 1963. *Doctorate Production in the United States, 1920–1962*. Washington, D.C.: National Academy of Sciences.

Hennig, M. and A. Jardim. 1977. *The Managerial Woman*. New York: Anchor-Doubleday.

HEW. 1968a. *Digest of Educational Statistics*, 1968. Washington, D.C.: Department of Health, Education, and Welfare.

—— 1968b. *Students and Buildings: An Analysis of Selected Federal Programs for Higher Education*. Washington, D.C.: Department of Health, Education, and Welfare.

HSUS. 1975. *Historical Statistics of the United States: Colonial Times to 1970*, part 1. Washington, D.C.: Bureau of the Census.

Kantor, R. M. 1977. *Men and Women of the Corporation*. New York: Basic Books.

Kluckhohn, C. and H. A. Murray. 1953. Personality formation: The determinants. In C. Kluckhohn, H. A. Murray, and D. Schneider, eds., *Personality in Nature, Society and Culture*. New York: Knopf.

Levinson, D. J. 1978. *The Seasons of a Man's Life*. New York: Knopf.

O'Connell, A. N. 1981. Career and personal identity synthesis in professional men and women. Presented at the Annual Meeting of the American Psychological Association, Los Angeles, August.

—— 1982. Predictors of life style orientation for professional men and women. Presented at the Annual Meeting of the Eastern Psychological Association, Baltimore, April.

Richardson, M. S. 1981. Occupational and family roles: A neglected intersection. *Counseling Psychologist*, 9:(4)13–23.

Rohrbaugh, J. B. 1979. *Women: Psychology's Puzzle*. New York: Basic Books.

Runyan, W. M. 1981. Approaches to the interpretation of lives. Presented at the Annual Meeting of the American Psychological Association, Los Angeles, August.

Russo, N. F. and A. N. O'Connell. 1980. Models from our past. Psychology's foremothers. *Psychology of Women Quarterly*, 5:(1)11–54.

Sampson, E. E. 1962. Birth order, need achievement, and conformity. *Journal of Abnormal and Social Psychology*, 64:155–59.

SAUS. 1980. *Statistical Abstracts of the United States*. 101st ed. Washington, D.C.: Bureau of the Census.

Van Dusen, R. A. and E. B. Sheldon. 1976. The changing status of American women; A life cycle perspective. *American Psychologist*, 31(2):106–15.

Warren, R. P. 1981. Fear and trembling. In R. P. Warren, *Have You Ever Eaten Stars: Poems 1979–80*. New York: Random House.

INDEX